THE ROAD TO KOMATSUBARA

Harvard East Asian Monographs 124

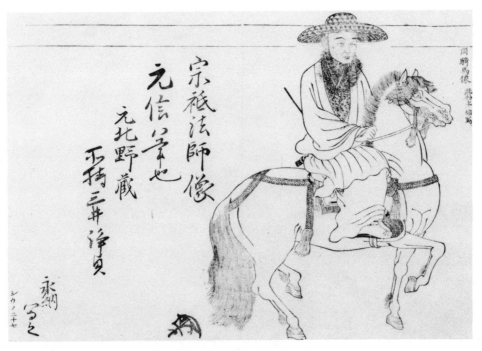

Sōgi on Horseback from the
Kitano Kōsō collection. Photograph courtesy of Kaneko Kinjirō.

THE
ROAD
TO
KOMATSUBARA

A Classical Reading
of the
Renga Hyakuin

STEVEN D. CARTER

Published by the Council on East Asian Studies, Harvard University and distributed by Harvard University Press, Cambridge (Massachusetts) and London   1987

The Council on East Asian Studies at Harvard University publishes
a monograph series and, through the Fairbank Center for East
Asian Research and the Reischauer Institute of Japanese Studies,
administers research projects designed to further scholarly understanding of China, Japan, Korea, Vietnam, Inner Asia, and adjacent
areas.

Library of Congress Cataloging in Publication Data

Carter, Steven D.
    The road to Komatsubara.

    (Harvard East Asian monographs ; 124)
    Bibliography: p.
    Includes index.
    1. Renga—History and criticism—Theory, etc.
2. Japanese poetry—1185–1600—History and criticism—
Theory, etc. 3. Sōgi, 1421–1502—Criticism and interpretation. 4. Shōhaku, 1443–1527—Criticism and interpretation. I. Title. II. Renga hyakuin. III. Series.
PL732.R4C36   1987   895.6'12'09   87-15713
ISBN 0-674-77385-3

To Professor Kaneko Kinjirō

who taught me the meaning of the word

Sensei

CONTENTS

CONTENTS

ACKNOWLEDGMENTS

THIS BOOK began as a dissertation written for the Department of Oriental Languages, University of California, Berkeley, under the guidance of Helen Craig McCullough, Aoki Haruo, and Irwin Scheiner. To Professor McCullough in particular I must acknowledge a great debt for wise counsel, kindly given. My most earnest hope is that my work will measure up to her high standards of scholarship.

For aid and encouragement in various forms I am grateful also to: Professors William H. McCullough and Walter Ben Michaels of the University of California, Berkeley; Professors Ben Befu, Robert Epp, and Herbert Plutschow of the University of California, Los Angeles; Professors George Perkins, Masakazu Watabe, and Gary Williams of Brigham Young University; and to the faculty and staff—especially Professors Murase Fumio and Kaji Mitsuo—of the Japanese Literature Department of Tōkai University, where I was fortunate to spend the 1978-1979 academic year pursuing my research.

Professor Kaneko Kinjirō, to whom this book is dedicated, was my advisor during my year at Tōkai University, and since then has graciously continued to offer me his assistance. Original research on the rules of linked verse and on Sōgi's solo sequence of 1492 was conducted under his care and with the benefit of his knowledge and wisdom. Needless to say, any mistakes that remain are my own.

For financial support that allowed me to undertake my research in Japan I wish to thank the Fulbright Commission of the United States Government. Over the last several years I have also been the beneficiary of grants and other kinds of aid from the College of Humanities, Brigham Young University. The curators and staffs of the Japanese collections at Berkeley, UCLA, and Brigham Young University have been unfailing in their support of my research needs. For assistance in obtaining permission for use of illustrations, my thanks go to Mack Horton.

Assistance in typing and editorial work has been rendered by Judy Jenkins, Kevin Dunn, and Edward Peng, and in final revisions of the manuscript on computer by Melvin Smith of the College of Humanities Resource Center, Brigham Young University. Esperanza Ramirez-

Christensen, who read the final draft and made many useful suggestions for its improvement, is also due a word of special thanks. The writing and writer have benefited from the good taste and care of two editors, Mary Ann Flood and Florence Trefethen.

Most of Chapter 3, including the translation of Shōhaku's rulebook, has appeared in a somewhat different format in the *Harvard Journal of Asiatic Studies* 43.2:581–642.

Throughout my labor I have rejoiced in the patience of my children; and to my wife, Mary, who has read the manuscript in all of its several stages, I am indebted for many stylistic suggestions as well as for the kinds of moral support that only a companion and friend of many years can give.

CHAPTER ONE

Introduction

In a far recess of summer
monks are playing soccer.

John Ashberry
From "The Picture of Little J.A. in a Prospect of Flowers"

FOURTEEN NINETY-TWO was a busy year for Sōgi (1421–1502), the great itinerant poet-scholar of Japan's late medieval age. At seventy-two he was still an energetic man, and one at the height of his power and prestige in the elite society of the imperial capital at Kyoto. This meant a full schedule of activity in his primary genre, linked verse (*renga*), as well as participation in poetry and perfume-blending competitions and frequent requests to give lectures on the court classics that had become so central to his scholastic reputation. His weighty duties in aristocratic circles in fact seem to have kept him near his home in the northeastern corner of the city for the most part of the year, allowing him a rare rest from his usual habit of travel. Yet the colophon of a *renga* sequence preserved by disciples shows that, even during this brief respite from the rigors of life on the road, the old master sallied forth at least once into the provinces. The trip took place in the summer, when travel was easier for a man of advancing years, and his destination was in nearby Kii Province—specifically, the Komatsubara estates of a warrior patron named Yukawa Masaharu.[1]

Masaharu, a sometime official of the Ashikaga government, was one of the many military figures who frequented the literary salons of Japan's late fifteenth century. Only five of his poetic attempts appear in the pages of *Shinsen tsukubashū* (New Tsukuba collection, 1495), the second imperially recognized anthology of linked verse, proving that he was not a truly significant poet even among the *renga* connoisseurs of the warrior class. Records do show, on the other hand, that he was an active participant in shogunal *renga* sessions throughout the 1480s and on into the early 1490s. In particular, he seems to have been a member of the circle surrounding Hino Tomiko (d. 1496), wife of the great Ashikaga Yoshimasa

(1435–1490). Spending much of his time in his home province but coming into the capital as often as possible in order to enjoy the artistic life that thrived there as nowhere else, Masaharu was a typical *renga* patron of the period after the Ōnin War.[2]

It was probably in the capital that Masaharu first met Sōgi. The home of the Yukawa clan, Komatsubara, was neither a major center of provincial culture nor a place often favored by the *renga* master in his travels. Thus it seems most likely that the two men met in one of the many *renga* sessions sponsored by the shogunate. Masaharu was the author of the second verse in the 1488 sequence that celebrated Sōgi's appointment as Kitano Shrine Renga Master—the title of the official Linked-Verse Steward (*bugyō*) of the Ashikaga government.[3] Perhaps it was by way of such formal meetings that the warrior and the poet were first brought together.

A tradition noted in the chronicles of the Yukawa house claims that Sōgi adopted the Yukawa name at the time of his selection as Steward, supposedly in order to avoid embarrassment over his low birth and status. The great master was, after all, of the most common stock. Since this assertion exists only in Yukawa records, however, it is probably best to read it as the ornamentation of a family scribe. A more plausible explanation for Masaharu's prominent role in the celebratory session of 1488 is his well-documented relationship with the Kitano Shrine, the official annals of which list him as a protector of the shrine manors in his province.[4] So far from being a paternalistic supporter of Sōgi—who was by any account the more prominent of the two men in the literary world of the 1480s—Masaharu was no doubt one of many who sought the poet's attentions: a low-ranking bureaucrat with literary pretensions. To Sōgi the Yukawa house was only one among a host of patron families and institutions, and one of little consequence at that. After 1488, Masaharu and Sōgi seem to have seen little of each other. Indeed, one of our few indications that they saw each other at all is the sequence composed when Sōgi visited the Komatsubara domains, evidently at Masaharu's request, in the summer of 1492.

Nor is the 1492 sequence a particularly famous example of *renga* art. As a solo work (a *dokugin,* or sequence composed by one poet) it is in fine company, to be sure: the two works from his own opus that Sōgi commended to his students for special study were both solo efforts.[5] But the 1492 sequence has attracted little of the attention given to those sequences or to others from his long career, such as *Minase sangin hyakuin* (Three poets at Minase, 1488) or *Yuyama sangin hyakuin* (Three poets at Yuyama, 1491). The circumstances of its composition are largely unknown; and it is surrounded by none of the "critical history" one confronts when reading texts of greater reputation. In a word, the sequence of 1492 is one of the more obscure works of the *renga* canon—a work not without its charms, to be sure, but in all an unexceptional record of what appears to have been a quite ordinary literary occasion.

Such obscurity would not generally recommend a text for study. Yet this lack of history and reputation suits the Komatsubara sequence for the project of this book—the reconstruction of the way the *renga* was read in its own time. A work of great notoriety inevitably diverts some attention toward itself and away from the process of reading that has of late become so central a concern in literary study. But there is little danger of such a diversion in the sequence of 1492. It is a work that more easily than most can be read not as an individual text but as an expression of the genre it represents—a genre, one must add, that is itself an ideal object of study for those interested in the dynamics of interpretation.

The idea of reading any work of literature, be it a modern novel or an ancient poetic sequence like the Komatsubara *dokugin*, has never been so problematic as it is today. A number of studies over the last decade or so have shown conclusively that reading is no innocent and uncomplicated activity; rather it is a highly circumscribed operation involving strategies of understanding. "Reading poetry," insists Jonathan Culler in one influential study of the topic, "is a rule-governed process of producing meanings"—an oversimplification, it may be argued, but still a useful description of what it means to make sense of a literary text.[6] Yet the problems produced by such a conception are obvious, for in most cases the "rules" of a genre operate below the level of conscious cognition and are not readily available for examination. Only rarely do the conventions of literary art achieve explicit formulation in the historical record. Such is the case, however, with Sōgi's genre, the *renga hyakuin*, or "poetic sequence in one hundred verses." Even among scholars of Japanese poetry the *renga* is not well known; and systematic study of the genre *as a genre* (rather than as a group of independent texts) is still in its infancy. But one thing about linked verse is clear: no other genre in history has left us so complete and accessible a guide to its own reading. Thus the relative obscurity of the solo sequence of 1492 is no final impediment to its analysis. We know almost nothing of how it was received in its own time as an independent "artifact"; but we know a great deal about how it must have been received as an example of the *renga* form. As Earl Miner has said in a recent survey of the genre's history, "Much of what passes for scholarship and criticism of western literature—or in Japanese monogatari—amounts to mere guesswork by comparison with what can be known about the practice of *renga*."[7]

Linked verse was the chief poetic genre not only of Sōgi's day but of the entire Muromachi period (1336–1568) of Japanese history. And its beginnings can be traced back to a much earlier time still—the Heian period (794–1185), when verse-capping was a game indulged in by court poets of the *uta*, the thirty-one-syllable form that was the dominant genre of Japanese poetry for the entire court era. Indeed, during its early history linked verse was little more than a kind of *uta* composed by two people in "dialogue" fashion. In time, however, the *renga* developed into a recognized genre of poetry quite distinct from its progenitor. By the early thirteenth century it was one of the major genres of the classical tradition, a poetic form composed in one-hundred verses according to elaborate rules and conventions of its own. Under the influence of court poets it came to share the aesthetic ideals of the literary world from which it had sprung. At the time of its florescence, in fact, linked verse functioned as a decidedly neoclassical force: a poetry dedicated by its very nature to the preservation of the aesthetic ideals of the court heritage in what was considered a degenerate age.

The best-known feature of linked verse is that it was usually composed not by one poet but by a number of poets producing verses in alternating sequence. In this sense it fits well into a medieval tradition that stressed community over individuality. But an even more interesting characteristic of the genre for the student of poetics is its rejection of one of the criteria that Western critics often assume to be essential to the very nature of poetry—namely, thematic unity.[8] Treated in the beginning as a kind of elegant game, the *hyakuin* retained throughout its history one of the distinguishing features of play by insisting on values involving structure rather than content. Even the aesthetics of the genre speak more of concern for dynamics than for conventional thematics. Speed, pace, and timing, Muromachi critiques of the genre intimate, are the guiding principles of linked-verse composition. The one inalienable rule of the form is constant change, as embodied in the credo that no verse may show rhetorical, semantic, or grammatical dependence on any other verse in a sequence, nor bear a necessary relationship to any but the verses immediately following or preceding it. So it is not a unified scheme of thematic interpretation but a principle of obligatory change that produces the progression in a *renga* sequence. And this means that in the reading of a *hyakuin* the interpretive act is always provisional: it is always followed by reinterpretation. Any linked-verse sequence presents its reader with a stream of images, ideas, statements, scenes, and speakers, but never a unified "stream of consciousness." The essence of linked verse is discontinuity.

Yet it is equally true that a *renga* sequence is not simply a random progression of verses. To begin with, the genre's historical situation provides it with a definite grounding. Taking the classical *waka* tradition of the court as its foundation, the genre operates always within fairly strict limits of subject matter, decorum, and diction. So the progression of themes, scenes, and images that characterizes any *hyakuin* generally remains within the boundaries of a well-established stock of associations inherited from the imperial *waka* collections. Change in linked verse is patterned and controlled, not haphazard or arbitrary: although an associational leap from "white hydrangea" (*unohana*) to "snow" may seem unusual on the surface, study will show it to turn on a classical metaphor that makes it entirely conventional. And it is this fact that makes the genre such a fine field of study for those interested in the dynamics of reading. Progressing through a *renga* sequence is a complex activity, involving reason and logic, of course; but at the most fundamental level reading the *hyakuin* is largely a process of "linking" words and concepts by reference to conventional associations that are founded on known precedents.

Anyone acquainted with court poetry has taken a large step toward competence in the reading of linked verse. And for those not so well grounded in the tradition of *waka* (a group that includes most modern readers) linked-verse poets have bequeathed handbooks and dictionaries of such customarily "linked" words and ideas in order to show exactly how progression in a sequence should take place. The existence of these written sources cannot promise the modern reader a way to total mastery of the conventions of the genre, needless to say. Yet such sources can allow him something that he will find in few other traditions—an opportunity to reconstruct the major features of an interpretive community in verifiable detail. The most useful of these handbooks of conventional associations, *Renjugappekishū* (Strings of linked jewels, 1476?) by the courtier scholar Ichijō Kanera (1402–1481), contains literally thousands of entries in forty-two different lexical categories, providing an encyclopedic guide to the mindset of fifteenth-century readers.[9] The book was written as an aid to poets, but, since in the classical era poet and reader were usually synonymous, the detail of such a work, when inverted, provides a means of tracing the set of expectations that constitute reading. The *renga* canon, in other words, makes it possible to follow the process of signification itself—to study how the expectations of a reading public determine a text's interpretation, thereby verifying that any literary work, as Culler maintains, "has meaning only with respect to a system of conventions which the reader has assimilated."[10]

The competence of fifteenth-century Japanese readers of course consisted of much more than a knowledge of conventional associations. Specifically, it included, in addition, a knowledge of the rules of composition in the genre. Poetic creation in the *hyakuin* form was governed by strict rules regarding the seriation, intermission, and repetition of specific words and word categories listed in *Renjugappekishū* and other such sourcebooks. These rules differed somewhat from period to period over the genre's seven-hundred-year history. But extant sources can give us a very good idea of the rules current in any particular era. *Oan shinshiki* (New rules of the Ōan era, 1372), for instance, is a guide to practice in the late fourteenth century and on into the early 1400s; and later additions to the rules recorded in that work made by poets in the fifteenth and sixteenth centuries make it possible to obtain a detailed knowledge of linked-verse conventions for the entire "golden age" of the genre. By strict attention to these rules of composition one can acquire a basic competence in the classical reading of the *hyakuin*.

The important thing in this for the student of reading and interpretation is, once again, that the rules show us what makes the *renga* what it is: they give us a guide to the composition of linked verse, which guide in turn serves as a map to the genre's self-definition. For if we always employ a strategy when we read, in the case of the *hyakuin* we have one such strategy available for the reconstruction. Even a cursory look at the rules of 1372, for example, shows some of the biases at work in the *renga* tradition—biases that must have held for readers as well as writers. Restrictions regarding seriation and repetition, for instance, can be seen as an enforcement of the idea of constant change; and proscriptions against the use of any but classical sources in allusion can as easily be interpreted as what might be called an ethic of neoclassicism. On an even more mundane level, the smaller details of the rules also appear to embody a distinctive interpretive approach. Any attempt to place a verse in thematic context, for example, is governed quite strictly by extensive vocabulary lists that limit the possibilities of such an interpretive act. The rules of the genre, in other words, not only tell us how a sequence of verses was produced; they also go far in dictating how those verses may be consumed.

The *hyakuin*, then, is a rarity among the genres of world literature. As a genre of explicit conventions, it can give readers even today a guide to its own classical interpretation. And as such it represents a useful illustration of the conventional nature of reading. The reading dictated by the rulebooks of the art is not absolute in its authority, of course; certainly the critical history of some major works from the *renga* canon shows that other approaches to interpretation are possible. But a rule-based reading has the virtue of at least *approximating* the basic approach of a fifteenth-century reader—of reconstructing a part of the classical poet's literary consciousness. And, despite the limitations such a reading implies, it is of great interest because it is openly verifiable in ways that other so-called reconstructed readings cannot hope to be. Following public sources, it can "recode" a text such as the Komatsubara *dokugin* within the same set of conventions used to "encode" that text classically.

Thus it will be the chief purpose of this book to produce a conventional reading of Sōgi's solo sequence of 1492—a minor text, but one that will serve well to illustrate what the rules and conventions of the *renga* tradition yield as they perform their special work. Subject always to the kinds of limitations noted above, the reading will be strictly generic in emphasis, meaning that it will be less an elucidation of the text for its own sake than an exercise in interpretation.

The reading will be incremental, which is to say that it will follow through the text from verse to verse. This is the most natural way to study any *renga* sequence, because it allows the reader to see the text as it was written. Students of current critical theory, however, will not fail to see in this method a debt to the step-by-step approach to interpretation employed by Roland Barthes in his *S/Z*–a debt that anyone involved in literary hermeneutics would not want to disallow. It should be apparent to readers of Barthes's work, however, that his purposes in *S/Z* contrast sharply with my own in the analysis of Sōgi's solo sequence. As Barthes says in the opening pages of his book, he is "concerned not to manifest a structure, but to produce a structuration."[11] To this end he employs a number of "codes" (the hermeneutic, the semic, the symbolic, the proairetic, and the cultural) of his own creation. His aim is clearly to escape a "traditional" reading, "because the goal of literary work . . . is to make the reader no longer a consumer, but a producer of the text."[12] The aim of a so-called classical or conventional reading is precisely the opposite: to produce a meaning, yes, but always by reference to existing standards of interpretation and not self-construed ones. The rules confine a reading within bounds; they dictate not only the general course of interpretation but its final outcome. So the purposes of a rule-based reading of the *renga* are in contrast with Barthes's at the most fundamental level. It can be argued that either approach involves a final reduction of the text. But the goal of a conventional reading must be to carry out that reduction in terms that allow for a minimum of deception. In other words, such a reading must confine itself to Barthes's cultural code, making more claims to simple verifiability than to absolute artistic validity. The *renga* presents a case in which the cultural code is especially well known; and this fact alone seems reason enough to undertake an *explication* of the text, however, compromising such a choice of terms may appear to be.

It is a matter of significance, moreover, that Barthes should choose a step-by-step method to contravene a classical reading while a rule-based study of the *renga* demands such a method to follow one. What this may well mean is that a classical reading of the *hyakuin* goes far in yielding what Barthes himself calls "the triumphant plural, unimpoverished by any constraint of representation (of imitation)."[13] Barthes's goal is, after all, to account for, or at least draw attention to, the multivalent interpretive possibilities within any text; and the *renga*, read by the conventions of its own tradition, may be said to include a plurality of interpretations within itself from the very beginning. To be sure, this does not mean that linked verse offers any infinite regression of meaning, for the rules of the genre impose limits on interpretive possibilities within the context of any one link in a sequence. But, at the same time, the rules dictate that each link has only temporary status as an interpretive event. Thus the acts of reading and re-reading, interpretation and reinterpretation, are characteristic of the *hyakuin* in its most traditional formulation. Linked verse offers us a case in which to an extraordinary degree classical modes of reading make the reader a self-conscious producer of the text.

I will touch upon the theoretical implications of this paradox in the conclusion of this book. The body of the work must deal with more practical concerns. As a foundation for the reading of Sōgi's sequence, the next chapter will give a brief historical view of the *renga*'s development from roots in the court tradition; succeeding chapters will present the rules and conventions of a reading as they appear in late fifteenth-century sources, leading up to the focus of our study—a step-by-step reading of the Komatsubara *dokugin*.

CHAPTER TWO

The Evolution of Linked Verse as a Poetic Genre

For all the history of grief
An empty doorway and a maple leaf.

Archibald MacLeish
From "Ars Poetica"

The Genre in Historical Context

Every genre arises from a particular historical context. In the case of linked verse, that context was the poetic tradition of the Japanese court. As Nijō Yoshimoto (1320–1388), one of the first great *renga* poets, explains the matter of origins in his *Renri hishō* (Treasured notes on the principles of linked verse, 1349), "Linked verse is one of the miscellaneous styles of *uta.*"[1] Echoed in many other poetic treatises and essays of the Muromachi period, this sentiment defines the historical situation of the *renga* as a genre. Linked verse is part of the heritage of court poetry—a literal extension of the thirty-one-syllable *uta* form.

Linked verse throughout its early history was little more than a variety of *uta* composed by two poets instead of one. The late Heian poet-critic Minamoto no Toshiyori (d. 1129) indeed describes the genre by referring to "the separate halves of an ordinary *uta.*"[2] Thus while linked verse as composed by Heian poets may have been less a literary than a social activity—a kind of parlor game—the identification of linked verse with the serious *waka* establishment was nonetheless clear from the beginning. An early couplet by Emperor Murakami (r. 946–967) and a lady-in-waiting, for instance, shows the usual court concern for proper diction and decorum:

Sayo fukete
ima wa nebutaku
narinikeri

The night has grown late
and yet still here I sit,
more and more sleepy.

The Tenryaku Emperor

9

Yume ni au beki	Perhaps the one you await
hito ya matsuran	will come to you in your dreams.[3]

Shigeno no Naishi

Couplets such as this do little for the artistic reputation of the court tradition; but, if linked verse in Heian days was characterized by wit and virtuosity rather than by more self-consciously literary criteria, the same was true of many *uta* written during the same period and by the same poets. Any differences between *uta* and *renga* in the late classical era were in degree, not in kind. Both genres were products of court society, both shared that society's values, and both were to a great extent bound by that society's biases. And if this seems to labor a point, the labor is justified by the demands of historical precision. In its maturity the *renga* came to be associated with the middle classes of Muromachi society—with monks, warriors, and even tradespeople. In a word, it became almost a *popular* verse form. But the genre's beginnings, it must be emphasized, were at the Heian court; and it is not an overstatement to suggest that this earlier affiliation was the deciding factor in the development of linked verse into a poetic tradition in its own right. In later years the *renga* evolved from a two-verse form (*tsukeku*), to a "chain of verses" (*kusari renga*), and at last into the standard *hyakuin,* or sequence in one hundred verses—but always with the world of *waka* as a backdrop.

Scattered examples of two-verse *renga*, often simply dialogue poems or riddles in verse, appear in imperial *waka* anthologies of the late Heian period. But partly because examples are not numerous and partly because what examples we do have are of little artistic interest, these early attempts at linked verse are rarely given serious attention by scholars. And much the same can be said for the *kusari renga*. It was only after the emergence of the *hyakuin* in the early thirteenth century that linked verse began to gain recognition as more than a literary curiosity, and it is only with the full one-hundred-verse form that traditional scholarship has chosen to concern itself. What this means, however, is not that the earlier forms of *renga* are historically insignificant; rather it means that their significance is always subordinated to the idea of a larger development. Although they may be of some artistic interest taken individually, those same individual *tsukeku*, whether dating from late Heian or mid-Muromachi, attain true integrity and identity only when seen as elements of the *hyakuin* as an independent genre.

The first extant texts of complete *hyakuin* date from the early fourteenth century, fully one hundred years after records indicate that poets had actually begun to compose in what was to become the standard form of the genre. What we know of early sequences is therefore based on fragments—random references in diaries, the headnotes to links recorded in later collections, and so forth. We do know, on the other hand, a great deal about the poets who were composing linked verse in the 1200s, for they were also the major *waka* poets of the famed Shinkokin generation—men such as Emperor Go-Toba (1180–1239), Fujiwara no Teika (1162–1241), Fujiwara no Ietaka (1158–1237), and later their heirs, Fujiwara no Tameuji (1222–1286) and Fujiwara no Tameyo (1250–1338). By common consent some of the most innovative and productive of all Japanese poets, these courtiers contributed much to the development of the genre. Under their influence the *renga* achieved not only its standard length of one hundred verses, but also developed the rudiments of a system of rules and an elaborate system of etiquette.

For all this, however, the *hyakuin* of Teika's age was in one important way different from the genre of the Muromachi period. Shinkokin poets wrote a *unified* sequence, one integrated throughout by means of a complex method of punning reminiscent of the "hidden topic" poems of the *Kokinshū* (Collection of ancient and modern times, 905) and later *waka* anthologies.[4] Commonly referred to as *fushimono renga* (the word *fu* meaning "distribution"), this early variety of *renga* composition involved a technique of weaving hidden words and images from certain prespecified categories into the syntax of each verse in a sequence. There were many different kinds of these *fushimono*; in a "Five Color Sequence," to offer one example, the first verse was designed to include a reference to the color green, the second to yellow, the third to red, the fourth to white, the fifth to black and so on in that order through the entire *hyakuin*. The following verses illustrate the technique:

Kaze zo aki	This is a fall wind—
matsu o ba somuru	but no dew yet enriches
tsuyu mo nashi	the color of the *pines*.
Ominaeshi chiru	The *maidenflowers* scatter
ame no yūgure	on a rainy evening.
Kojika naku	A young deer cries out
sueno no irihi	as the *sun sinks* in the hills
yama koete	at the field's far edge.
Izuru ka tsuki no	Is it about to come out?
kage zo honomeku	*Moonlight* on the horizon.
Sora no iro	The sky's *dark color:*
kuraki wa kumo no	it must be a result
ōran	of the passing clouds.[5]

In other types of early *fushimono* the names of birds and fish, or rivers and fish, or sinking and floating phenomena, and so on, were placed in alternating sequence throughout a *hyakuin*.[6] But no matter what their specific content, all *fushimono* were alike in their total effect: they gave the hundred verses of a *renga* sequence a sense of unity and coherence, although perhaps only in a very artificial way. And since strategies of reading and writing develop not independently but in unison, it is fair to say the *hyakuin* of the thirteenth century was therefore not only written but interpreted in a fundamentally different manner than was its Muromachi descendant. The *fushimono renga* was composed with a unifying principle in mind; hence a kind of thematic unity was the legitimate aim of those who read the finished product. The focus was on the categories themselves and on the ingenuity with which they could be worked into the verses of a sequence. When in later times the *fushimono* was all but eliminated as part of linked-verse composition, the aim of a reading of the genre was also directed along new lines. But, as long as the *fushimono* figured in the creation of links, the genre emphasized above all the idea of wordplay.

Although the historical record gives scant attention to them, certain rules and conventions no doubt governed composition of the *fushimono renga*. The catalog of the Reizei House Library, one of the largest stores of medieval manuscripts, contains nearly twenty Kamakura-period rulebooks for linked verse, one of which seems to have been written by the great Teika himself.[7] And though the titles of most of the works say nothing about the specific nature of their contents, five of them bear the name *fushimonoshū*, "A Collection of *Fushimono*." From this and other evidence it seems clear that the punning and wordplay that were such a part of Heian linked verse also characterized the *renga* of the Shinkokin era.

In the classical revival of the fifteenth century, *fushimono* sequences were once again composed by court poets. By that time, however, the old form was no more than an historical curiosity studied and practiced in conscious imitation of the past. In its place, a new form had developed, the standard *hyakuin*. Exactly when this transition took place is unclear, but the process was definitely gradual. As new rules of seriation and repetition developed, the *fushimono* took less and less part in the *hyakuin* as a whole. In the beginning it had been a component of every verse in a sequence; by the early 1300s, however, its use was restricted to the first section of a *hyakuin*; and by 1349 it was no longer always a part of even the first section of most sequences being composed at court.[8]

The reason for this change in focus is not difficult to determine in retrospect. From early in the evolution of the *renga*, the ideal of constant change asserted itself as a fundamental premise of the art of linking. And it appears that this principle of change eventually led to the abandonment of obligatory punning in each verse. The possibilities for serious expression in the old form were limited to begin with, and it must have been obvious to poets writing as early as the Shinkokin period that, as long as the *fushimono* remained a governing factor of the genre, linked verse would remain a mere amusement. One might almost say that the *renga* was afflicted in its developing period with a contradiction in its terms, and only in the resolution of this contradiction could it finally reach maturity as an art form. Teika and his peers, who were responsible for the sophisticated techniques of integration and progression visible in the great *waka* sequences and anthologies of the Kamakura period, can only have been impatient with the triviality of the *fushimono* technique.

Yakumo mishō (Revered notes on the art of the eightfold clouds, 1221), a poetic treatise that contains a section on the composition of linked verse, includes among its rules a few on seriation as well as on the *fushimono*.[9] The same was probably true of the majority of rulebooks listed in the Reizei House catalog. So it would appear that, from very early indeed, the *fushimono* was losing its hold on the *hyakuin*, or at least its hold as a governing principle. Historically, this drift away from a principle of coherence and toward more desultory forms of progression is complemented by similar trends in *waka* poetry. A move away from temporal and thematic organization and toward more "associational" modes of integration in the imperial anthologies is, as Japanese and Western scholars agree, one of the identifying characteristics of *waka* history in the thirteenth and fourteenth centuries. Robert Brower and Earl Miner have shown how series of poems in the *Gyokuyōshū* (Collection of jeweled leaves, 1314) and the *Fūgashū* (Collection of elegance, 1346) in particular are linked together as much by conventionally associated words, images, concepts, and rhetorical techniques as by dramatic, chronological, or temporal factors.[10] And although it may not be not entirely accurate to suggest that at this time linked verse was being influenced by movements in its parent genre—indeed, quite the contrary may have been the case—it is nonetheless true that the great *renga* poets of the thirteenth century were almost to a man *waka* poets as well. It is important to realize, therefore, that, as the *renga* reached its maturity, it was encouraged in a certain direction by a poetic world that was beginning itself to embrace the qualities of asymmetry and discontinuity that were later to become such quintessential elements of the Muromachi concept of beauty. Just as the Kamakura period at its end brought disarray and uncertainty to Japanese society via the Mongol invasions and other political and social upheavals, it brought a trend toward the ideals of constant change and disunity in the arts. And the essence of the *renga* as a genre made it ideally suited to the new age.

The new *hyakuin* was thus a product of a new age and a new aesthetic—but only in part. The foundations of the genre were still in the *waka* tradition, and in a paradoxical way its values were rooted in a firmly neoclassical attitude. What this meant was that, although change was the rule of linked verse, the scope of that change was always circumscribed. *Renga* poets inherited the vocabulary and thematics of the court tradition; to a remarkable degree, they abided by the aesthetic concepts of the imperial anthologies. Change in the genre was thus a matter of progression among known categories of thought and expression, all according to well-delineated paths of association.

If anything can be said to be absolutely basic to the essence of the mature *hyakuin*, it is these categories and associations. They are the foundation of the genre as it is known in Japanese literary history—which is to say that without them the *renga* could never have been what it came to be. Without the categories and conventional associations of the *waka* world the very thought of "linked" verses would have been an impossibility: a game without rules. Therefore it is a knowledge of these same categories and associations that must ground a classical reading. As the constituting factors of literary competence in the *hyakuin* they establish interpretation of the *renga* sequence and all its parts.

The Categories of Composition

The most basic categories of linked verse can be traced back at least to the early-tenth-century *waka* anthology, *Kokinshū*, the first, and in terms of its effect on later poetics, the most important of all the imperial anthologies. In that work the poems are organized into the following books according to lexical content and thematic emphasis: Spring, Summer, Autumn, Winter, Felicitations, Parting, Travel, Names of Things, Love, Laments, and Miscellaneous. With some changes in order but virtually none in basic definition, most of the later anthologies use the same system of classification. Poems on blossoms, willows, the bush warbler, melting snow, or northbound geese are in the Spring category in all the imperial collections; poems on hail or frost are in the Winter category, poems on mountain paths or boats bobbing on the sea in the Travel category, and so on.

Although the medieval anthologies tend to drop the Parting and Names of Things categories, all twenty-one of the *waka* collections commissioned by the imperial house contain the seasonal books and books of Love, Travel, and Miscellaneous poems. The *Gyokuyōshū*, for instance, divides its poems into books on Spring, Summer, Autumn, Winter, Felicitations, Travel, Love, Miscellaneous Topics, Buddhism, and Shinto. It is this last breakdown that seems to hold throughout the entire late medieval era, which means that these were the major categories according to which most *uta*, particularly those written for formal occasions, were composed. Beyond that, we can even say that these categories constituted the poetic mindset of the Muromachi period for poets in all genres, including the *renga*. The first imperially recognized anthology of linked verse, the *Tsukubashū* (Tsukuba collection, 1356), contains the same categories as the *Gyokuyōshū*; and *Shinsen tsukubashū*, the second and last such collection, is also divided into roughly the same thematic sections. Finally, *Renga shin-*

hiki tsuika narabi ni shinshiki kon-an tō (The new rules of linked verse, with Kanera's new ideas on the new rules and additional comments by Shōhaku), a compendium of rules dated 1501, uses the following similar set of themes in its attempts at definition and classification: Spring, Summer, Autumn, Winter, Love, Travel, Lamentation, Buddhism, Shinto, Miscellaneous.[11]

Each verse in every *hyakuin* composed in the Muromachi period was both conceived and read according to these broad thematic categories. Well known by poets and their audiences, the criteria for classification were a matter of public record: lexical content and overall thematic import marked a verse as belonging to one category or another. In this way the inherited wisdom of court poetry became the foundation for linked-verse composition.

It was these categories of composition that formed the basis of the rule of change in the *renga* as it developed, meaning that change in the genre never signified randomness in any real sense. Rather, change was gauged according to shifts in acceptable and precedented imagery and theme—as change in conventional categories of thought and expression. The verses in a *hyakuin* thus fell into classifications that were, at least to poets of the time, almost natural in their delineation. Haze, plum blossoms, or melting snow indicated Spring; a mountain temple, wisteria robes, or the word "the Law" indicated Buddhism. And, as was usually the case in medieval Japanese literary history, lexical content and the assumptions arising from that content were founded in *waka* tradition. Many, if not all, of the words in any *renga* handbook or dictionary can be traced back to imperial collections of the Heian and Kamakura periods.

Thus the dependence of *renga* canons on earlier precedents cannot be overemphasized. There is, however, a crucial difference in the way the categories of composition were used in linked verse as opposed to the way they were used in traditional *waka*. In imperial anthologies of the latter genre we find poems composed on topics, and those topics fall roughly within the framework of the categories introduced above: a poem on fireflies is in the Summer section, a poem on the Ise Shrine is in the Shinto section, and so on. But the order of the books within a *waka* anthology imposes a logical sequence among the categories that is lacking in linked verse. In the *Shin kokinshū* (New collection of ancient and modern times, 1206) the seasons follow upon one another in calendrical order—Spring, Summer, Autumn, and Winter. And even within the more thematic books of that anthology, such as Love or Travel, the progression of poems is often along dramatic or chronological lines: a love affair may be treated from beginning to end, or a journey traced through poetic space. But not so in the *hyakuin*, where such ordering is avoided as a matter of principle. Within the restrictions of the rules, any category may follow any other in a sequence of linked verses; and, even in a series of verses that share the same broad category, progression need not follow any temporal or logical pattern. Thus, while modes of progression in both genres are grounded in the idea of categories, the underlying motivations are different. *Waka* progressions move by a logic of temporality, or by notions of dramatic or spatial sequentiality; *renga* progressions move along a radical of change. It is fair to say, then, that the *hyakuin* is the more self-conscious of the two genres, for, by playing with the categories of the older *waka* classics and organizaing them in ways that are aesthetically satisfying without adding up to any total meaning, the *hyakuin* communicates its artificial nature openly. In so doing, however, it also shows its dependence on the earlier form for its very existence as a genre.

The following section from a sequence dated 1495 involving Sōgi and some of his chief disciples—notably Sōchō (1448–1532), Gensei (1443–1521), and Kensai (1452–1510)—serves well as an example of how categorization informs the *renga*. For each verse the thematic category is given, along with the lexical items that dictate what the category must be.

51	Tsurara iru kakine no shimizu kumisutete	At the icy fence I take up the pure water then cast it away. *Gensen*

Winter: ice

52	Shimo wa shitaba ni musubu kuretake	Frost forms on the lower leaves of the narrow-leafed bamboo. *Sōgi*

Winter: frost

53	Kaze suguru ato ni sayakeki yowa no tsuki	A wind passes by and leaves behind it a clear midnight moon. *Kensai*

Autumn: the moon

54	Hatsukari izura koe zo sakidatsu	The first wild geese—where are they? Voices precede their coming. *Tomooki*

Autumn: the first wild geese (returning to Japan from the continent to spend the winter)

55　Minu sora mo
　　omoiyararuru
　　aki no kure

It calls to mind
an unseen expanse of sky:
autumn at its end.
Keiboku

Autumn: the end of autumn

56　Irozukinu rashi
　　kiri fukaki yama

Colors will be showing now
on mountains deep in mist.
Gensei

Autumn: mist, changing colors

57　Kozue nomi
　　tabi no yadori o
　　wakuru no ni

Only the treetops
provide me any shelter
as I cross the fields.
Nagayasu

Travel: shelter, crossing the fields

58　Yukuyuku kawaru
　　ochikochi no sato

On and on I make my way
through village after village.
Sōgi

Travel: on and on

59　Adahito no
　　oshieshi michi wa
　　sore narade

Fickle woman:
the way she told me to come
is not the way at all.
Eshun

Love: fickle

60　Ta ga omokage ni
　　ukarekitsuran

Whose image was it
that left me so obsessed?
Sōchō

Love: image, obsessed

61　Kaze kasumu
　　haru no kawabe no
　　suteobune

Near a riverbank
hazy with spring breezes—
an abandoned skiff.
Tomooki

Spring: hazy, spring breezes

62　Tamareru mizu ni
　　kawazu naku koe

Out in the standing water,
the sound of croaking frogs.
Kensai

Spring: frogs

63   Yamada sae   The snow has melted:
        kaesu bakari ni   even the mountain paddies
        yuki tokete   are ready for tilling.
                              Sōgi

Spring: melting snow, tilling

64   Amayo no asahi   A rainy night ends with dawn
        meguru satozato   making the village rounds.[12]
                              Gensen

Miscellaneous

Read in the light of another tradition, the classifications of these verses might be quite different. Indeed, a likely possibility is that explicit categorization of this type would not be a part of the reading in the first place. But in the *renga* tradition the assigning of categories is perhaps the first task of interpretation. And, although it might be argued that there is no scientific basis for such an approach (does not the moon shine in spring as well as in autumn?), strictly scientific arguments have no place—or at least no privileged place—in the classical analysis of linked verse. In the *hyakuin*, blossoms come out in the spring, and frost covers the ground in winter.

This apparent rigidity is partially a product of the great power of precedent, for such seasonal references are also customary in *waka* collections. But what is custom in *waka* becomes rule in linked verse. In the rulebooks of the *renga* tradition, assumed categories take on a clear line of definition. A work like the dictionary *Renjugappekishū* leaves almost nothing to personal whim. Even the most obvious category is clearly defined by a list of available words drawn from the heritage of the past. Travel, to take one example, is limited in the following manner:

> travel robes, pillow of grass, inn, boat, setting off at morning, the capital, native home, stable, unfamiliar mountains, my way, passing through a toll barrier, a brief pillow (or a brief sleep), crossing through the fields (or passing through the hills), crossing over the mountains, a traveler's hut, a wife for one night (or a loose woman), a bed of fitful sleep, the Eastern Road, path, letter of passage.[13]

A quick perusal of any of the Travel books of the imperial *waka* anthologies will yield much the same list of words and phrases; the same can be said for most of the other lists in *renga* handbooks. *Renjugappekishū* is not an original work, but a compendium of conventional wisdom. Its appearance in the fifteenth century, however, was not the result of happenstance. When Kanera wrote it, he did so in response to a need, and the need arose from the composition of linked verse. What was implicit in *waka* had to be made explicit in the canons of *renga*, for only with clearly stated definitions could the game of linking verses be played in a true poetic community. In other words, moderated change, the ideal of linked-verse composition, could not become a governing aesthetic until it had an adequate foundation. Only after the categories had been delineated in a relatively unambiguous way—whether in Kanera's book or in earlier books that show the same developing consciousness—could the idea of continuous but always bounded and limited change be enforced or, for that matter, perceived.[14]

The categories of linked verse did not stop with those of the *waka* anthologies. The *waka* categories are simply the major ones—the basic topical frames into which each of the verses in a *hyakuin* was designed to fit. In addition, linked-verse poets adopted a number of more narrowly lexical categories as well. *Renjugappekishū* lists over thirty of these, ranging from Heavenly Objects to Colors. In the composition of the *hyakuin*, however, only the following are of major importance: Mountains, Dwellings, Waters, Falling Things, Rising Things, Shining Things, Nocturnal Things, Plants, Animals, Human Relations, Famous Places, Clothing.[15]

The development of these subcategories was perhaps not essential to linked verse as a genre; certainly they do not inform the *renga* as do the thematic categories of the imperial anthologies. But to the growth of the *hyakuin* into a form of artistic complexity these secondary categories were of crucial importance. Again, their part in the dynamics of the *renga* becomes most apparent in the reading of a sequence. The following verses from a *hyakuin* by Sōi (1418–1485) and Sōgi offer an example:

44	Hana ni kasanaru	In the mountain recesses,
	oku no mine mine	peak upon peak of blossoms.
		Sōi

45	Sakura chiru	Cherry petals gone,
	ato no shirakumo	now white banks of cloud remain
	hi wa kurete	at the close of day.
		Sōgi

46	Yado toiyukeba	As I search for night-lodging
	harusame zo furu	a spring rain begins to fall.
		Sōi

47	Ta ga sato ni	In whose village
	fushite ka hosamu	will I spread them out to dry?
	tabi no sode	My traveler's sleeves.[16]
		Sōgi

To the uninitiated these verses may present the continuous scene of a late spring landscape through which a traveler is wending his way. But those with a knowledge of the lexical categories mentioned above will see important change even here. The first verse introduces Plants (blossoms) in the context of Mountain recesses; the second continues this general frame with a reference to cherry petals, but also turns to the sky and Rising Things (clouds); the third verse contrasts the Rising clouds with a reference to a Falling Thing (rain) and also introduces a human Dwelling into the picture; finally, the last verse places that Dwelling in a village. Any close reading might of course raise these points, it might be argued. The thing about the *renga* tradition, however, is that, due to the lexical categories which must be monitored in the composition of a sequence, the recognition of these continuities (blossoms and cherry petals, night-lodging and village) and contrasts (clouds and rain) is not a matter of choice or chance; it is obligatory. It is in this sense that the subcategories provide an undercurrent of constant shifting and movement in any *renga* sequence. As will become apparent later, this kind of undercurrent, which a writer like Roland Barthes would perhaps want to call a "play of signifiers," since it does not necessarily reinforce thematic developments, is prized in the *hyakuin* as of value in its own right.

Not all of the subcategories of linked verse have an explicit source in *waka* sources. Rather, they seem to represent rudimentary semantic categories—an attempt to organize phenomena and ideas into a coherent system of understanding. Many of the subcategories, in fact, are borrowed directly from early Japanese dictionaries. Minamoto no Shitagō's *Wamyō ruijushō* (Japanese readings: a categorized list, 938), for instance, divides its entries into many of the categories that later become the lexical categories of linked verse: Human Relations, Waters, Dwellings, Plants, Insects, and so on.[17] And, since virtually all classical Japanese dictionaries are topical in format, it appears that *renga* poets simply appropriated most of the subcategories of their genre from already existing lexical systems. As was the case with almost all scholarly endeavor in the classical period, these systems were a reflection of the world of *waka*. Made by *waka* poets using Chinese models that were also often written by poets, these systems were intended for the reference of verisifiers first of all.

The philosophical concept that underlies all of these categories, thematic and lexical alike, is *hon'i*, or "the essence of things." In court poetry *hon'i* is a concept that appears most frequently in the judgments of poetry contests as a strictly prescriptive notion: a poem on fireflies is to adhere to the "essence" of that topic and not introduce extraneous or inappropriate material into its conception—meaning at the very least that the poem should be set in summer and at night. In other words, *hon'i* is itself a kind of instrument of categorization. Almost every image and idea in the court tradition carries with it a burden of precedent, a more or less well-defined essence, and this burden is generally synonymous with its *hon'i*. Thus it is that in linked verse the wild geese always signify spring or autumn, and never winter, and that the word "pledge" implies love. Although there are some deviations from these rules of precedent, they only attest to the presence of a recognized norm.

Usage of the word *hon'i* in linked-verse criticism is varied. In some instances it is used to refer to authorial intent, in others to a general sense of propriety and decorum.[18] Most often, however, the term appears in a context not far removed from its usual usage in *waka*—as an openly arbitrary concept defining the "essence" of a word, idea, or category by an implicit appeal to the authority of precedent. Reading through medieval essays on composition, then, one comes away with the impression that some words are *by nature* in the Love category, others in Buddhism, others in Travel, and so on. To take things a step further, certain words are designated for use in one month and certain others for use in another, as we find in Sōgi's *Shogakushō* (Notes for beginners, date uncertain):

Things Appropriate to the Second Lunar Month

Pheasant, cherry blossoms, young grasses, to turn soil under, returning geese (this being appropriate to the Third Month as well), hazy fields, the idea of waiting for the blossoms, burned-over miscanthus (or miscanthus on charred fields), the east wind (this carrying over into the Third Month also)[19]

This list pertains only to the composition of the *hokku* (the beginning verse of a *hyakuin*), in which, according to the canons of the genre, the season and month of a work's writing must be clearly shown. Nevertheless, the list provides evidence of just how far *renga* poets were willing to go in confining the vocabulary of their art within neat compartments of reference. It shows the essentially *idealistic* thinking of the genre, the same sort of thinking that prompted Sōgi, again in *Shogakushō*, to insist that the phrase "scattering cherry blossoms" must be perceived as blossoms in a state of disarray on the wind, while the phrase "falling cherry blossoms" must on the contrary represent a scene of blossoms floating gently to earth.[20] Many of the entries in *renga* rulebooks are cast in the same tone as Sōgi's statement, and all have the same foundation in the idea of essences.

In a sense, then, linked-verse poets were themselves early lexicographers who saw their task as to define and classify a word's essential nature in terms of precedent. One great difference between the *renga* lexicographer and his more "scientific" counterparts in both the West and the East, however, was that he seems to have been more aware of the arbitrary and linguistic nature of his activity. To the *renga* poet, *hon'i* was more an aesthetic concept than a logical one. Perhaps the lucidity of his vision was due to his unique position in a decaying value system: it would have been difficult indeed to argue for the absolute veracity of court aesthetic (or lexical) standards when the court itself was in peril of extinction. If this is an accurate estimation of the attitude of most *renga* poets, however, it is clear that their awareness of the complicity involved in their definitions did not lead to cynicism, or even less to a diminishment in their devotion to court ideals. The tumult of the times may even have served to intensify their beliefs. For whatever reason, one thing seems certain: linked-verse poets knew that, when they assigned words to the categories of the *waka* tradition, they did so for openly poetic reasons. It is for this reason that a *renga* master can give us the following definition of love:

> The essence of love is to grieve when no visit promises, to yearn for one's lover after parting, to pine away the evening when he is late in coming, to deplore the spread of gossip—in short, to exhaust one's heart in various ways. This is the essence of love.[21]

This is a purely literary accounting, a definition of love as a category of poetic expression. As such, it appeals to literary precedents, such as these words from *Tsurezuregusa* (Essays in idleness, 1332), rather than to life experience:

> The man who grieves over a love affair broken off before it was fulfilled, who bewails empty vows, who spends long autumn nights alone, who lets his thoughts wander to distant skies, who yearns for the past in a dilapidated house—such a man truly knows what love means.[22]

The similarity between these quotations may argue for considerable direct influence. More important, however, this similarity shows another kind of intertextuality—a common conception of love that is, to put the matter forcefully, untroubled by the demands of the real world, content to deal with romanticized patterns. Linked-verse poets, as well as elegant recluses like Yoshida no Kenkō (1283–1350), author of *Tsurezuregusa*, undoubtedly knew something of the joys of love along with its sorrows; likewise, they probably knew the experience of physical intimacy. But in their writings a more refined and limited vision of love prevails. Waiting, parting, lies, resentment, grief, and yearning—these are the words one finds under the heading Love in *Renjugappekishū*.[23] In a *renga* sequence, love is always a matter of sadness and consternation, and it is always an affair of the heart.

      If the poet's awareness of his own idealism is not adequately represented in this example, there are countless others available for study. In *Yodo no watari* (Yodo crossing, 1495), a verse-by-verse analysis of one of Sōgi's solo sequences written by the poet himself, Sōgi notes, for instance, that, while it may be that in real life many people leave fine circumstances to take up the hermit's life, in *waka* and *renga* only those with a burden of despair should retire from the world.[24] In other words, the world of poetry demands poetic conception, in this case a conception based on the category of Lamentation. And this kind of self-conscious idealism is even more evident in the writings of poets living in the century after Sōgi's death. The great master Satomura Jōha (1524–1602) sums up the definition of *hon'i* in terms whose orientation is unmistakable:

> In spring, great winds may blow and rainstorms arise, but to make the winds calm and the rainfall gentle—this is to adhere to the essential nature of things. Again, spring days may on occasion be short, but in the *renga* it is the rule to describe them as long and langorous. By the same token, the essential nature of the word "blossom" (*hana*), unless otherwise qualified, is always cherry blossom.[25]

In the final analysis, the idea of *hon'i* is perhaps much more than the basis for the categories of linked-verse composition, for it may be seen as an articulation of a literary system that looks to precedent and decorum for its rationalization. In this sense the term can be perceived as an underlying concept in virtually all genres of medieval court literature. Nowhere is that concept more apparent in its effect, however, than in the organization of *waka* vocabulary into *renga* categories. In the process of time, the vocabulary of linked-verse poets expanded and grew; likewise, some new categories of expression came into being. But throughout its long history the *hyakuin* never separated itself from the idea of essences, or from the division of poetic experience into traditional classifications of meaning.

Conventional Associations

The *waka* tradition, with its vocabulary and aesthetics, was the condition of the *renga*'s historical possibility. Only after the categories of the *waka* world had been defined and elaborated did the game of linking verses develop into a lasting genre of court poetry. Thereafter, however, all that remained for the evolution of the full *hyakuin* was the gradual formulation of principles that could dictate how verses could be combined in sequences—principles of connection, or *tsukeai*. And here, too, it was the precedents of *waka* history that acted as a guide, for the links between verses in the *hyakuin*, even during the early years of the genre's development, were no more a product of random associations than were the definitions of Love and Travel described above. Instead, these links were generally the product of certain established patterns of "linking." Thus the link that joins verses in a sequence might be temporal (night to morning, late autumn to winter), spatial (mountains to plains, sea to land), dramatic (a conversation between lovers, a farewell between traveling companions), thematic (complaint giving way to resignation, conflict coming to resolution), or purely linguistic (homophone to homophone, pictograph to pictograph). At a more fundamental level, however, the links in any *renga* sequence are usually based on conventional lexical associations inherited from the *waka* canon. These associations, called *yoriai*, were as vital to the development of the genre as was the idea of *hon'i*, and a knowledge of them forms another part of one's competence as a reader of the *hyakuin*.

The oldest associations can be traced back to the beginnings of native Japanese poetry in the *Man'yōshū* (Collection of ten thousand leaves, ca. 759). Clouds and blossoms, rain and tears, frost and white hair—all of these were established in the earliest days of court poetry, first as simple metaphors and later as conventionalized *yoriai*. With time, however, most such associations came to be perceived as stemming from more specific literary foundations. By the mid-Heian period the presence of two words in the same famous poem, for example, could set them apart forever as associated words.[26] In this way the place name Akashi and the word "morning mist" were yoked together in the communal mind of the poetic tradition by virtue of their appearance together in the following poem from the *Kokinshū*, believed by most medieval critics to be a composition of the great Kakinomoto Hitomaro (fl. ca. 680–700):

Honobono to	In the dim light
akashi no ura no	of the spreading morning mist
asagiri ni	on Akashi Bay,
shimagakureyuku	a boat fades behind the isles
fune o shi zo omou	and my heart follows in its wake.[27]

That two such words—a "bay" and "morning mist"—should become linked in the minds and later in the poetry of medieval Japan may seem entirely natural in retrospect. But the move from metaphorical associations to associations based on famous poems is in fact one more evidence of the commanding dynamic of medieval poetry, and especially of linked verse—namely, precedent. No necessary relationship joins "morning mist" and "Akashi Bay." The basis of the link between the words is simply the power of tradition. So heavy is the weight of that tradition, however, that, whether actual allusion to a foundation-poem (*honka*) is intended or not, the association remains. Not open to choice, at least when it comes to interpretation, *yoriai* are obligatory, binding, and necessary. The mere presence in two adjacent verses of Akashi Bay and morning mist is enough to link the verses inextricably. Thus, even if the relationship between two concepts or images may be artificial, that relationship is all the same unequivocal, provided, of course, that it is based clearly on precedent.

Almost all *yoriai* had fairly explicit literary sources in the beginning. The *Renshōshū* (Collection of sample associations), a late Kamakura book written as an aid to poets, gives *waka* precedent for all of the 168 conventional associations listed in its pages.[28] And, although some later books do not bother to list their sources, implied in the notion of "association" is often the idea of a specific literary derivation. The following, for instance, is a quotation from *Renga yoriai* (Notebook of conventional associations in linked verse, 1494), a lexicon designed for the use of poets in the Higashiyama era:

> Zither: One links the place name Suma to this word because of a scene in *Genji monogatari* in which the Gosechi Dancer, passing by Suma on her way back to the capital from Tsukushi, hears Genji playing a zither.[29]

Genji monogatari (The tale of Genji), famous poems from the imperial *waka* anthologies, Chinese and native legends, and even the Chinese classics served as the sources for conventional associations. As with the categories of composition, however, it was not personal whim that decided the matter. Only associations that had been recognized by the practitioners of *waka* and *renga* throughout their common history could become legitimate *yoriai*. This means that almost all *yoriai* in Muromachi records date from the Heian and early Kamakura periods in terms of their true "origins." Linked verse itself, therefore, or even the most famous of Nō plays, could never become the foundation for a recognized association. The classical period was the source of all precedents.

Beginning with the *Renshōshū*, there are numerous indexes of conventional associations which enumerate the *yoriai* that inform much of the linking in any *renga* sequence—an historical fact that once again shows the general rule of the new genre's evolution: what was implicit in *waka* becomes explicit in linked verse. The most detailed of these books is Kanera's *Renjugappekishū* of 1476. Consisting of 907 separate entries, which have themselves been divided into a variety of lexical categories, Kanera's book is an exhaustive list of the basic *yoriai* which it was the business of every *renga* poet to know. As such, the work fits well into the context of Kanera's entire scholastic effort, and into the tone of the Muromachi revival of which it was a part. *Renjugappekishū* is a compendium that takes into consideration the entire vocabulary of the court tradition. Unlike some other *yoriai* lexicons, however, it does not always include references to the sources of the many associations it lists. Modern scholars have nonetheless been able to find precedents for many of the associated words Kanera gives, making it apparent that the book represents a scholarly effort more than a creative one. An example from Kanera's lists gives an idea of the comprehensiveness of the work:

> 549 If the word "dream" is used,
>
> to see, to be startled awake, to open one's eyes, to return,

> vain, ephemeral, to retell, to put together, the past (ancient), the world, oneself, image, straight path, floating bridge, floating grass, butterfly, Cathay, blossom, Spring and Fall. In general one should link with night-words.[30]

In some cases the sources of these associations are obvious: to see, to be startled awake, to open one's eyes, the past, image, and the category night-words all fit into a normal semantic relationship with the idea of dreaming—the kind of normal relationship that can be documented in many classical origins. And, although some of the other associations are less clear on the surface, scholarship has been able to establish a few of them through reference to *Genji monogatari*, a few more through allusion to imperial *waka* anthologies, and one of them to the great Taoist classic, *Chuang-tzu*.[31] All of the associations are thus founded in traditional perceptions, making Kanera's work no less than others of its type a guide to the conventional wisdom of the medieval world.

The significance of *yoriai* in linked-verse composition cannot be easily summarized, but it is safe to say that to poets of the genre these associations were a source of both creative energy and restraint. Relying on such a store of "linked" words and concepts, the *renga* poet could find any number of suggestions for his task as a participant in a *hyakuin;* but at the same time he was inhibited by the obligatory nature of the *yoriai* system. For, although a poet could abandon conventional associations and link verses in other ways, the inherently conservative nature of the art made consistent avoidance of those associations a near impossiblity. The limited vocabulary of the genre meant that escape from *yoriai* was inconceivable. Perhaps for this very reason connections between verses in a sequence always involved more than "linked" words—as will become apparent in the reading of Sōgi's solo sequence, the art of connection is a complex one involving many factors—but at the same time were dependent on such associations to ground the process of interpretation.

The place *yoriai* have in classical interpretation is also difficult to discuss in abstract terms. Only a reading of an entire sequence can show the subtle ways in which conventional associations dictate the direction of a reading, always confining meaning within well-defined traditional boundaries. To give one example, the common metaphorical relationship between clouds and blossoms would in some interpretive traditions be anything but determinate—which means that its validity in a given case would have to be tested, probably by reference to a dominant thematic trend within the literary work where it appears. But, since in linked verse there is no such thing as thematic unity within a sequence of more than two verses, associations are correspondingly more absolute. More than serving interpretation, they tend to guide it:

| 8 | Kumo o shirube no
mine no harukesa
Sōchō | So distant are the peaks
that the clouds must be my guide. |
| 9 | Uki wa tada
tori o urayamu
hana nare ya
Sōgi | My frustration is due
to the sight of those flowers:
how we envy the birds![32] |

Each of these verses is understandable as an independent statement, the first presenting a travel scene in which a disoriented man looks to the distant clouds as his guide toward the mountains and the second a cry of envy directed toward the birds who can so easily fly to the flowers. But what joins the verses in a comprehensive declaration? Without the necessary association of clouds and blossoms a reconciliation between the verses would be difficult indeed. There are no other links joining the two scenes. Only when the flowers are taken as a metaphor for the clouds can the two verses be said to make poetic sense. It is the *yoriai*, then, that initiates and virtually completes the interpretive act in this case. And, while this is not true in every verse of every *hyakuin*, it is true, nonetheless, that the presence of such associations in linked verse has the effect of grounding the interpretive process in an inherited system of relations. Conventional associations literally "link" the verses of a sequence together, joining what might otherwise appear as disparate scenes and ideas into an order of signification. Again, connections between verses may only begin with *yoriai*, but only seldom do those connections escape such interpretive grounding.

Conventional associations are one of the naturalizing forces at work in the *renga* genre. Binding the *renga* sequence in a system, they provide a method of integration and progression but limit its possibilities for random growth. Because they are so numerous, these associations are never totally predictable; but neither do they offer the surprise of free association. Thus their function is more conservative than revolutionary. Along with the categories of the *waka* tradition, they ensure that the *renga* will remain a language of communication in which meaning is produced and naturalized according to communal codes of interpretation.

Early Rules and Rulebooks

As will become apparent in the reading of Sōgi's solo sequence, there is much more involved in the understanding of the *hyakuin* than Kanera's lists of categories and associations. The interpretation of links between verses—and this is the central interpretive act in a conventional reading of the genre—demands not only knowledge of these fundamental underpinnings but also powers of reasoning and imagination, knowledge of customs and literary motifs, and acquaintance with a host of other conventions too numerous to mention. But, in tracing the evolution of the categories and associations of the *waka* tradition, one can at least come to a recognition that there is more to the history of linked verse than the usual list of major works and authors would suggest. Histories of the genre quite rightly point to a number of factors that influenced its development: the example of the hundred-poem sequences of the *waka* world, the poetry contests of the court, and even Chinese linked verse. Yet more basic than any of these "direct" influences in the development of the dynamics of *renga* art were certain habits of mind; and the latter are less well represented by specific works from the past than by the analysis of concepts such as *hon'i* and *yoriai*.

These basic concepts, so important to the understanding of the *renga* in philosophical as well as rhetorical terms, also make it possible to say something new about linked verse—that it is a kind of meta-language, a second-order semiological system built upon the foundation of *waka* vocabulary and thematics. Many of the verses of any *hyakuin* can be related back to specific precedents, as examples above have shown. More important, however, is the fact that all the verses in a sequence, when taken together, acknowledge a great debt to the past. Few *renga* verses are truly original in their surface expression.

It is perhaps for this reason that from early in its history the *renga* developed an aesthetic, clearly at work in the rulebooks, that is as much musical as literary.[33] Since the themes of poetic thought in the Muromachi period were in an exhausted state after centuries of use, the *renga* seems to have developed along lines of an almost extra-thematic nature. First, it emphasized not the statements of individual verses so much as the connections between them, drawing attention to empty space in the fashion of Zen landscape paintings. And, leaving the individual link, the genre also emphasized factors that might be called "kinetic" rather than semantic: pace, seriation, rhythm, and orchestration seem to have been as important to medieval *renga* masters as thematic statement or rhetorical richness. This does not mean that semantic value was of no consequence in the creation of the *hyakuin*, since each verse in a sequence was in fact required to have an independent meaning. Yet it is true all the same that the art of *renga* was the art of combination and arrangement. If the impact of thematic content in the genre was not emptied of force, then, one can at least say that that force was nevertheless blunted by the weight given to other dimensions of composition. In the new genre an old vocabulary was appropriated for use in a new system of expression, and that system tended to draw attention to itself.

In another culture, or at another time in the history of Japan, the impoverishment of a thematic tradition might easily have led to parody or even to symbolism. In the conservative literary world of medieval Japan, however, it led to the art of pastiche which is so apparent in so many of the aesthetic creations of the Muromachi period. Parody ridicules the past too openly, and symbolism too often obscures it behind new layers of meaning, but the pastiche only reorganizes the past according to new formal principles. So the *hyakuin*, although it may now seem an almost modernistic art form (witness the sentiments of Octavio Paz: "... the element of combination which governs the renga coincides with one of the central preoccupations of modern thought, from the concerns of logic to the experiments of artistic creation"),[34] did not constitute a betrayal of traditional values to the poetic world of its own time. Indeed, in terms of its thematics it reinforced those values and was considered a kind of aesthetic schooling for aspiring *waka* poets of the middle and lower classes. The genre was seen as simply a recasting of traditional values in a new mold.

Thus the *hyakuin* evolved in a climate of thematic poverty and was obliged to seek part of its identity in a nonsemantic sphere. Many of the organizing principles of the *hyakuin* relate more to pace than to "meaning." Intended to ensure balance and variety in the progression of a sequence, these principles made skillful arrangement an object of artistic attention. And the rules of composition, nearly all of which concern the categories and associations discussed above, are best seen in this light. They arrange elements in a dynamic system that makes the reading of the genre an exercise in literary gymnastics.

The first important statement of rules for linked-verse composition is contained in *Yakumo mishō*, the thirteenth-century *waka* treatise mentioned above in connection with *fushimono renga*.[35] And although most of the rules contained in that work have little direct application to the genre in its maturity, even from this early articulation, a few general principles emerge with clarity. The first is that each verse in a sequence should be independent, both grammatically and semantically— that it should represent a total poetic conception and not merely a fragment. This meant that each verse had to stand on its own; no verse could be simply one part of a thematic series. The second principle that becomes clear from a reading of *Yakumo mishō* is similar: that no one conventional theme (Spring, Love, Travel, and so on) should continue over more than a few verses in a series. The ideal of linked verse, at least in the eyes of Emperor Juntoku (1197–1242), the author of the treatise, was that all categories of the court tradition be represented in each hundred-verse sequence, with no one category boasting anything like dominance. And the final principle is that the repetition of categories or of specific "links" is not consistent with the ideals of the art: "It is bad to introduce the same thing too many times in a *hyakuin*." The vocabulary of linked verse was of course limited, as were the categories of composition; but the ideal of variety remained in place. "One composes linked verse," says Emperor Juntoku, "by continually moving the sequence in unexpected directions."[36]

After *Yakumo mishō*, the history of the rules takes the form of a gradual accumulation of detail. In the late Kamakura and early Muromachi periods the simple principles gave way to great catalogs of prescriptions demanded by poets actually confronted with disputes in the *za*, or linking session. On the surface these catalogs seem both incredibly complex and hopelessly trivial. But the earlier ideals of linked verse were never discarded by later rule-makers. Indeed, the aim of the new rules was nearly always to realize the abstract ideals of earlier poets: to preserve balance in the presentation of ideas and images while at the same time creating a sense of constant change and variety in every sequence. Thus it became vital, over time, that certain central images of the court world—blossoms and the moon, for instance—be restricted in their usage. Tradition almost required that such images be given special treatment, while the idea of thematic discontinuity demanded that this treatment be moderated and controlled within a larger pattern. This contest between the thematics of the court poetic heritage and the kinetic, somewhat antithematic aims of the *renga* aesthetic informed the rules' gradual evolution from general principles to specific prescriptions. Finally, the rules made the genre into a form of poetry dominated by a peculiar aura—the aura of disordered order, the literary equivalent of the Zen landscape garden. So, although the effect of the rules on any specific example of *renga* art may appear to be one of randomness, behind that randomness is concealed an ordering and organizing dynamic.

Another way to express this peculiar identity is to search for an analog. The closest complement to the *hyakuin* in Japanese literary history is the Nō drama, another product of Muromachi culture. As in the *renga*, the Nō play strings together classical themes and images according to a pattern of pastiche. But, because its structure allows for more variations than are possible in linked verse, even the Nō is a poor analog for the *hyakuin*. The complexity that emerges from the union of Nō's intertwining systems of presentation—music, miming, and chanting—is impossible in the *renga*, the rules of which offer less freedom. The rules are thus absolute by virtue of their arbitrariness, much like the rules of chess or *go*. In other words, they are *the rules of the game;* and as such they are, at least in the larger sense of the term, incontestable. Once again they return us to the metaphor of play. Binding the act of composition in a system, they are themselves often a source of creative tension.

Past a certain point, the rules of linked verse do not lend themselves to easy schematization. But the basic ideas of seriation, intermission, and repetition are simply explained. Restrictions on seriation limit the number of verses in which thematic or lexical categories may appear in sequence (Spring and Autumn, for instance, may each appear consecutively in only five verses); restrictions on intermission serve a complementary function by dictating how many verses must separate different appearances of the same word or category (appearances of the word "wind" being separated by at least five verses, and of the category Falling Things by at least three); finally, restrictions on repetition simply limit the number of times certain words may appear in a full sequence of one hundred verses ("peony" once, "life" twice, "willow" three times, and so on). These are the most fundamental rules of the genre. Above and beyond them, however, there are hundreds of rules that are not so easily classified. In their variety these represent the multiplicity of ideas, images, and themes which it is the aim of the *hyakuin* to contain as a structural whole. Since these more detailed rules differ from period to period, they can only be approached through one of the specific rulebooks left by poets as a guide to their collective competence. And it is therefore to one of these texts, specifically to a text published in 1501, just a year before Sōgi's death, that a conventional reading must turn for concrete support in the task of interpretation.

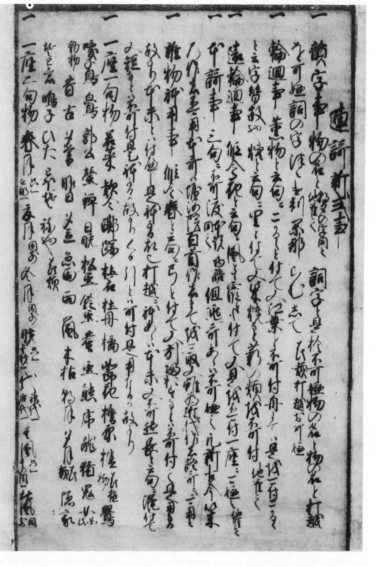

A leaf from the Hasedera text of *Renga shinshiki*, dating from the late fifteenth century. Photograph courtesty of Benseisha Publishers.

CHAPTER THREE

The Rules of Composition
Shōhaku's Renga Rulebook of 1501

This is my feeble translation,
time-bound, of what was a single limitless Word:

Stars, bread, libraries of East and West,
playing cards, chessboards, galleries, skylights,
    cellars,
a human body to walk with on the earth

Jorge Luis Borges
From "Matthew 25:30"

ONE INDICATION of the close genetic relationship be-
tween the *uta* and linked verse is that most of the early rules of the genre
come to us from the hands of *waka* poets. Although other thirteenth-
century examples have unfortunately not survived intact, we know that,
soon after *Yakumo mishō*'s appearance in 1221, such men as Teika and his
son Tameie (1198–1275) were busy compiling rulebooks of their own for
use in court linking sessions.[1] And in ensuing years other court poets also
contributed to the growth of *renga* conventions. Yet the first truly significant rulebook to appear in full written form after the Shinkokin age was
a compendium of rules put together by two men who are more often regarded as poets of linked verse exclusively—Nijō Yoshimoto and his tutor,
Gusai (d. 1376?).

In actuality, both Yoshimoto and Gusai composed *uta* as
well as *renga;* the former must in fact be counted among the major *uta*
poets of his time. But still there is some justice in the popular reduction
of these men to early *renga* masters, for the work they accomplished did
serve to establish linked verse as a court genre. Their rulebook, entitled
Ōan shinshiki, may not have been "new" in basic conception.[2] Yoshimoto's
purpose in writing it was probably less to create new rules than to standardize old ones.[3] But the historical importance of the 1372 work cannot be

minimized. Introducing the basic prescriptions of the tradition (among them restrictions on seriation, intermission, and repetition), it set the trend for all later rulebooks, which adopt an identical stance toward their material and use the same basic framework and terminology. Otherwise it might be said that it was only in terms of sheer bulk that Yoshimoto's work represented a new development in the history of the rules—although here once more such a contribution cannot be discounted. *Yakumo mishō* contained just fifteen remarks on composition; *Ōan shinshiki,* in any of its numerous textual forms, amounts to a categorized list of over a hundred restrictions and conventions. This fact alone led to a considerable expansion of the *renga* domain.

Another way in which the 1372 rulebook set the trend for later work was in its eclecticism. Coming to final form after a long process of compilation, *Ōan shinshiki* was clearly the product of a labor of study and not of original creation.[4] Indeed, Yoshimoto himself voiced the attitude of most medieval poets toward the rules in a statement that may be taken as a credo for later generations: "As time passes, styles change; and there is no need to adhere always to old precedents. But neither may one simply follow one's own preferences or incline too far toward one's own prejudices. Rather, one must look to the rules in use among the masters of one's own time."[5] At first glance this declaration may appear to be somewhat open-ended in its implications; but, since the masters of the medieval age were largely conservative by training and disposition, their predilections were for the standards of the past. As a result, the rules of the genre retained their traditional character in all periods. The final authority in matters of dispute resided in a community, but this same community defined itself in relation to tradition.

In their design and in their eclectic focus, then, Yoshimoto's rules provided a pattern for all subsequent rulebooks. Their statements on topics ranging from the proper use of foundation poems (*honka*) to more esoteric information on the proper categorization of obscure vocabulary emerged as the model for the rules of later periods in *renga* history. One might even say that all later contributions to the rules read as footnotes to *Ōan shinshiki,* although some of those footnotes turned out to be much longer than others.

For about seventy years after its appearance, *Ōan shinshiki* seems to have served, in court circles at least, as the standard rulebook. But as the *renga* grew in popularity so did the need for more detail in the rules. Yoshimoto himself added several appendixes to his original work, and other poets, too, wrote their own handbooks for composition. Thus, while the authority of Yoshimoto's effort as a whole was seldom challenged, the adequacy of his work to the task of regulating *renga* sessions—especially in the provinces, where the art was increasingly in vogue among the middle classes of Muromachi society—was put into question constantly. This led to a series of short "additions" to the rules, no one being seen as complete or final, but all adding to the general confusion of the *renga* world. And yet it was not until the 1450s, well after the death of even Yoshimoto's younger disciples, that there was a more concerted attempt to revise the rules in accordance with contemporary practice. And then the man who put his hand to the work was none other than Yoshimoto's own grandson, Ichijō Kanera.

Author of numerous studies of court lore and literature as well as of *renga* reference books such as *Renjugappekishū*, Kanera was one of the foremost scholars of his century and a prominent figure among the cultural elite of court society. He was the heir not only to his grandfather's library but the latter's social position: both chancellor and regent in his time, he was the confidant of emperors, literary and sometimes political tutor to the great military families of the capital, and teacher to a whole generation of younger scholars and poets. It was perhaps less his erudition than his pride, however, that motivated him in his revision of Yoshimoto's rules, since he is known to have been eager to surpass his grandfather's considerable achievements as a scholar.[6] As might be expected, his status as Yoshimoto's literal and figurative heir won wide acceptance for his additions to the rules, called rather unpretentiously *Shinshiki kon-an* (New ideas on the new rules, 1452). Incorporated into Yoshimoto's work as an appendix, Kanera's new rules became the basis for serious *renga* composition throughout the later part of the fifteenth century.[7]

Similar to the rules of 1372, the *Kon-an* was not simply the product of one man's efforts, nor did it represent only one man's opinions. It was another statement of changes in the rules over time. Before writing the work, Kanera is reported to have consulted with the greatest *renga* master of his day, Takayama Sōzei (d. 1455), and it can be assumed that he asked the opinions of other important poets too.[8] So the contents of the *Kon-an* represent a consensus, reflecting a growing need for more complete rules. Most of the comments in Kanera's work are additions to Yoshimoto's lists. The words "bird," "fire," and "jewel," for instance, are added to things that may appear three times in a *hyakuin;* similarly, Kanera adds a few words to the list of things that must be separated by at least one verse—the category of Plants and the words "thicket," "autumn paddies," and so on. Other entries emend slightly or clarify Yoshimoto's statements in the light of current practice. The framework of the earlier rulebook, on the other hand, remains intact, making Kanera's text entirely what its title proclaims it to be—a group of new rules for a new age.

These additions, however, were clearly important in their own time. Above all, they were authoritative statements in a literary climate that demanded authority above all else. While their influence on the essence of *renga* art may have been minimal, then, the effect of Kanera's suggestions on the day-to-day composition of *renga* sequences was no doubt considerable. They were not laws, of course, because senior poets were always free to accept or reject them according to their own habits and prejudices. But Kanera's reputation guaranteed his work respect among the highest practitioners of the art. At the very least, the *Kon-an* increased the number of words to which the restrictions generally applied, thus bringing more vocabulary—usually but not always from the imperial *waka* anthologies—into the process of conventionalization.

The next major rulebook to appear after Kanera's *Kon-an* was also a footnote to Yoshimoto, albeit a more extensive one. Bearing the prolix title *Renga shinshiki tsuika narabi ni Shinshiki kon-an tō* (literally, "The new rules of linked verse, with additions, new ideas on the new rules, and other comments"), it was compiled in 1501 by Shōhaku (1443–1527), a disciple of Sōgi. As with Kanera's work, Shōhaku's is a compendium of the rules current in his time. In his case, however, the time was the age of the *hyakuin*'s maturity as an art form—the age of Sōgi, Kensai, Sōchō, Sōseki (1474–1533), and, of course, Shōhaku himself. Perhaps for this reason, the rules of 1501 have long been considered the definitive rules of the *renga* tradition.

Although the exact manner in which Shōhaku compiled his rulebook is not entirely documented, after a detailed comparison of texts and much tracing of the poet's activities during the last years of the fifteenth century, Kidō Saizō has concluded that the 1501 work was the result of a labor of emendation by various people that had begun as early as 1482. In the spring of that year, Sōgi and Sōi, a prominent warrior-poet of the older generation, had met at Arima hot springs in Settsu to compile a short appendix to Yoshimoto's and Kanera's rules. Shōhaku, acting partly as Sōgi's student and partly out of his own need as a master of the art, took up the process of redaction later, gathering rules from various sources written after Kanera's time with the idea of producing a definitive rulebook. His work, which represented another great increase in the number of individual items in the rules, reached completion nearly twenty years later, in 1501.[9]

One might expect of Shōhaku, after his many years of study and compilation, a thorough revision of the rules; but once again a different approach to the task of emendation was taken. Rather than an open revision, Shōhaku's work is an interlinear commentary—sometimes a critical commentary—on the rules of Yoshimoto and Kanera. To read the rulebook of 1501 is to read Yoshimoto, Kanera, and Shōhaku, along with some anonymous voices, in a kind of running discussion or argument. Preserving the rules in both their original and emended forms, *Renga shinshiki tsuika narabi ni Shinshiki kon-an tō* is thus a complex and at times confusing text—one that has contributed greatly to the reputation of linked verse as a rule-bound genre. But the work's greatest fault is also its greatest virtue, for it allows the reader a chance to see exactly what kind of changes had taken place during the first century and a half of the rule's existence.

Shōhaku's comments are once more primarily additions and clarifications. Occasionally he emends an earlier statement without any attempt at justification, but more often he indicates changes in practice and perception openly. In the following example, for instance, he takes Kanera's side in an argument over a matter about which Kanera himself seemed to show some equivocation:

Yoshimoto: Once one has linked "wind" or "spring haze" to a blossom verse, one should not repeat the same link again in the same *hyakuin*. This rule holds even if the links are widely separated. And the same holds for all other cases of this sort.

Kanera: In modern times we do not necessarily prohibit the repetition of links such as the one described above between "wind" or "spring haze" and a blossom verse.

(Shōhaku: Current practice abides by this direction.)

Kanera: It may well be, however, that we should follow *Ōan shinshiki* in this matter.[10]

This sort of "conversation" between the three authors makes for a frustrating experience in reading. Out of such a reading, however, emerges a clear picture of the rules of Shōhaku's day. Shōhaku's comments often show that opinion was divided upon word usage and categorization, indeed, his work primarily attempts to put an end to such disagreements. Numerous words are added to each of Yoshimoto's original lexical and thematic categories; and the lists of words restricted as to seriation, intermission, and repetition have grown apace. Yet the categories themselves remain unaltered, showing once again the conservative nature of the *renga* tradition in its most practical manifestation. Shōhaku's contribution to the growth of the rules was one of quantity primarily, and not of quality.

The new rules of 1501 seem to have been widely accepted as the new standard for *renga* composition. Partly this was because they represented the combined wisdom of all the major figures of the tradition, including Gusai, Yoshimoto, Sōzei, and Kanera, not to mention the contemporary masters Sōgi and Shōhaku. But the rapid acceptance of the new rulebook also says something about the state of linked verse in the early sixteenth century. By this time linked verse had become a recognized institution with semi-official masters in most major castle towns, many of them disciples of Sōgi or his senior students. And the vehicle of composition, the *hyakuin*, was also by this time an increasingly well-defined genre—a fact to which the continued development of the rules itself attests. Since the environment of linked verse in Shōhaku's time was more rigidly controlled than it had been even in Kanera's time, uniformity in both composition and interpretation was more easily enforced.

Given the implications of this social context, one is not surprised to find that during the sixteenth-century *renga* poets elaborated considerably on Shōhaku's initial efforts. Beginning with Sōboku (d. 1545) the process of proliferation reached grand proportions, with many poets publishing their own commentaries on the rules, which usually included additions as well as interpretations. By 1600 there were perhaps five or six times as many words contained in the rules as there had been in 1501. *Mugonshō* (Silent notes), published in 1598 by a disciple of Jōha after an exhaustive survey lasting some twenty years, represents the culmination of this trend.[11] Essentially a dictionary of the rules that arranges them according to the *iroha* order used in so many Edo-period reference works, *Mugonshō* is encyclopedic in scope. And since it makes frequent clarifying references to Shōhaku's work, it is an invaluable aid to the interpretation of the rules in earlier periods as well.

Even after *Mugonshō,* the process of rule-proliferation continued. *Ubuginu* (Baby's first clothes), a mid-Edo work compiled by an unknown poet, runs to fully two hundred printed pages.[12] Its bulk, however, shows more than anything else the oppressive triviality into which the *renga* tradition fell after the end of the Muromachi period. There are no great *renga* masters after Jōha—although literary genealogies list the names of poets writing in the genre into the twentieth century. The word used by scholars to describe *renga* even during Jōha's time is "stagnation." Thus the rulebooks and handbooks of later years, for all their copiousness, are of interest now only for what they can tell us about earlier days—primarily the days of Sōgi, his teachers, and his students.

The most important work for reading *hyakuin* of the *renga*'s golden age is clearly Shōhaku's rulebook of 1501. For this reason I have chosen to include it in full as preparation for Sōgi's Komatsubara *dokugin.* Esperanza Ramirez-Christensen has referred to the rules as a "grammar" of the genre—a metaphor that is entirely apt.[13] Originally Shōhaku wrote his rules as a help to poets and referees faced with the practical job of making difficult decisions in the atmosphere of a *renga* linking session. But the rules can also be a guide to the classical reading of a sequence—to reconstructing the most basic interpretive strategies involved in any approach to the *hyakuin* as a genre.

Most of the terminology employed in the translation is self-explanatory, and special problems are addressed in the footnotes. But a few items deserve special attention. The first is the phrase *uchikoshi o kirau,* generally rendered in my text as "to clash."[14] Unless otherwise qualified, this phrase means that two words or ideas must be separated by at least two verses because they are too close to each other in meaning, reference, pronunciation, or association. Thus homonyms, synonyms, and words in the same lexical category are often judged to "clash" with each other.

A related term that warrants comment is *rinne,* "repetition" or "recurrence." Originally this was a Buddhist term referring to the transmigration of souls; and it retains part of that meaning in linked verse, where it is a pejorative indicating the improper recurrence of a lexical category, word, or linking technique. As Sōboku says in *Tōfū renga hiji* (Secrets of linked verse in the current age, 1542), to be able to avoid *rinne* is the mark of a true master of the genre: "What sort of master is truly skilled in the composing of sequences? The truly skilled masters are all alike in making certain that a sequence contains no improper repetition."[15] Thus *uchikoshi o kirau* and *rinne* both point to the most basic principle of *renga* composition by insisting that every *hyakuin* represent a true progression of ideas and images. "Linking" is accomplished by joining a verse to its predecessor; beyond this, however, movement in a sequence must always be forward.

Two other words that need comment are "sheet" and "side." The former refers to the *renga kaishi*, the sheet of paper upon which the verses of a linked-verse sequence were usually recorded. Four such sheets were used for a *hyakuin*, according to the following breakdown: Sheet 1, 22 verses (8 on the front side and 14 on the back); Sheet 2, 28 verses (14 on each side); Sheet 3, 28 verses (again 14 on each side); and Sheet 4, 22 verses (14 on the front side and 8 on the back—an exact reversal of Sheet 1). Although most of the rules deal with the more limited kinds of "clashing" described above, some words or categories are prescribed in a broader context involving the sheet or the side of a sheet. Not surprisingly, these more sweeping prescriptions are almost all attributable to Kanera or Shōhaku, who seem to have had a more complete appreciation of the demands of composition in the full *hyakuin* form.

The translation follows the format of the 1501 text as closely as possible, with little attempt at reorganization but some effort toward clarification. For convenience, the sections of the work have been numbered, and the contents are as follows: Section I deals with the question of rhyming in a linked verse; Sections II and III give practical examples of *rinne* and instructions on how to avoid it; Sections IV and V discuss the proper limits of allusion to court poems and tales; Section VI attempts to explain the "clashing" of so-called "essential" and "attributive" vocabulary; Sections VII through XI list words and categories that are prescribed as to occurrence (that is, "things that may appear only once in a *hyakuin*," and so forth); Sections XII through XV list restrictions on intermission (that is, "things that must be separated by more than one verse," and so forth); Section XVI, the longest and most confusing part of the text, deals with a number of disparate problems ranging from the simple categorization of unusual or ambiguous words to more complicated questions of "clashing." Section XVII introduces the rules of seriation; and the final section, XVIII, returns to the question of "essential" and "attributive" words, giving lists of relevant vocabulary items associated with the major lexical categories.

The various sections are not always consistent in the ways they treat problems, and one word may appear in several sections and contexts. But to reorganize the text in a way that would still retain the interlinear character of the comments of Kanera and Shōhaku would be practically impossible, as well as untrue to the very nature of the rulebook. For convenience, I have included a complete glossary to the work in an appendix, listing English words as they appear in the translation, their romanized Japanese counterparts, and Chinese characters. Since the rulebook tends to treat words that presented special problems for *renga* poets rather than general vocabulary, the glossary is something less than a complete guide to the words and images of linked verse. Yet it does present the most important words of the tradition—dew, snow, blossoms, clouds, wind, and so on—and may perhaps be regarded as a basic introduction to the *renga* lexicon.

One concession I have made to clarity is to provide attributions of authorship by means of a play format, something that the rulebook itself does not do. In addition, I have used brackets to indicate parenthetical remarks by Kanera or Shōhaku on Yoshimoto's original text—as opposed to situations in which they have simply added words to existing lists. Single asterisks signify Shōhaku's clarifications, interpretations, and criticisms of Yoshimoto's comments; double asterisks signify the more complex (and less frequent) situations in which Shōhaku has emended or added to Kanera's criticisms of Yoshimoto. Finally, I have used semicolons to demarcate category or word groupings in the original text. All thematic and lexical categories, as well as Japanese transliterations, are italicized; the first letters of independent entries in lists are capitalized for easy reference, while independent words or phrases referred to parenthetically or in complete sentences are in quotation marks.

The New rules of Linked Verse, with Kanera's New Ideas on the New Rules and Additional Comments by Shōhaku

I Rhyme[1]

Yoshimoto: Verses ending with the names of things, as well as those ending with compounds such as "morn and eve," do not clash with verses that end with inflective words. But verses ending with the names of things should be separated from each other by more than one verse.

[*Shōhaku: Words such as *shigure*, "showers," or *yūgure*, "nightfall," do not clash according to current thinking.[2]]

Yoshimoto: The final inflections *tsutsu, keri, kana, ramu, shite,* and all others of the same sort should be separated from each other by more than one verse.

[**Kanera:** In modern times, *kana* is allowed in the first verse of a sequence, while its variant form, the "request" *gana,* may also be used once. No other uses are permitted.]

[**Shōhaku: The "request" *gana,* if used at all, should appear only after the end of the first sheet.]

II Recurrence

Yoshimoto: If one has linked *kogaru*, "to burn," to the word "incense," then one should not introduce "red leaves" in a subsequent third verse, but instead use a word such as "boat." This is because "boat" makes for a change in the meaning of *kogaru*.[3] By the same token, if one has linked "town" to a verse containing the word "smoke," then one should not use "brush-burning" or any reference to any kind of firewood in the third verse. And the same holds for all other cases of this sort.

Shōhaku: If one has linked "cloud" to "evening shower," then it will not do to use "lightning" or "thunder" in a third verse; likewise, it will not do to link "Mount Fuji" to "snow" and then use "icehouse" in a third verse. And the same holds for all other cases of this sort.

Kanera: In modern times there are those who contend that one should not link the word *omokage*, "image," to a word such as "dream" and then follow with "blossom" or "the moon" in a third verse, supposedly because the latter present such

41

strong "images" themselves. There is no reason for such a restriction, however; in the past such progressions were not avoided.

III Remote Recurrence

Yoshimoto: Once one has linked "wind" or "spring haze" to a blossom verse, one should not repeat the same link again in the same *hyakuin*. This rule holds even if the links are widely separated. And the same holds for all other cases of this sort.

[**Kanera:** In modern times we do not necessarily prohibit the repetition of links such as the one described above between "wind" or "spring haze" and a blossom verse.]

[**Shōhaku:** Current practice abides by this direction.]

[**Kanera:** It may well be, however, that we should follow *Ōan shinshiki* in this matter. And it is certain that one should not link *yo*, "the world," to the word "bamboo" and then later in the same sequence link the homophonous *yo*, "night," to "bamboo" again.[4] This kind of linking is also a case of remote recurrence.]

IV Allusion to Foundation Poems

Yoshimoto: Allusion to a foundation poem should not extend over three consecutive verses, and the same holds for allusions to legends or tales. Such extended allusion need not be avoided, however, if there is an available "escape-poem."[5] As a general rule, one should not allude to poems by poets writing after the *Shin kokinshū*.

[**Shōhaku:** It has been decided more recently that poets writing as late as the *Shoku gosenshū* (Later collection continued) may be used in allusion.[6]]

Yoshimoto: Instead, one should use poems by poets writing up to the time of the *Horikawa-In hyakushu* (The hundred-poem sequence of Retired Emperor Horikawa).[7] For the purpose of establishing precedent, however, one may refer even to contemporary authors.[8]

[**Kanera:** In the case of poets writing up to the time of the *Horikawa-In hyakushu*, one may allude to their poems even if they appear in modern imperial anthologies. But if a foundation poem is relatively unknown, it is best not to use it in linking. Only in appeals to precedent may one refer to obscure poems.]

42

V The Statement of Go-Fukō-on[9]

Yoshimoto: *Genji monogatari* is a work of such magnitude that one should extend allusion to it over at least three verses. Only two consecutive verses, however, should refer to the same incident within the tale.

[*Shōhaku:** Although Yoshimoto is reported to have made this statement, we do not condone it. In alluding to foundation poems and legends, as the rules state, one should avoid seriation over three consecutive verses. Should this not apply all the more in the case of allusions to the same tale?[10]]

VI Essences and Attributes: Extracategorical Cases[11]

Yoshimoto: If one has linked "longbow" to the word *haru*, the latter acting as a pivot-word meaning both the season spring and the verb "to string," then one should not follow with "pull," "recoil," or "push" in a third verse. This is because these last three words are all attributive. The word "tip," on the other hand, would be suitable in a third verse because it expresses an essence. Again, one should not link "rope" to a word like "long" and then use the word "short" in a third verse, since the latter is also an essence. Instead, one should use "pull" or "to wind," both of which are attributive.

VII Things That May Appear Only Once in a *Hyakuin*

[*Shōhaku:** Here only a selection of things is listed. Any striking or conspicuous word should be restricted to one appearance in a sequence. This rule therefore holds for all words of a nature similar to those which follow.]

Yoshimoto: Young Greens, Globeflower, Azalea, Iris, Peony, Orange Blossom, Maidenflower, Cypress Grove, Sumac (all of the above being in the *Plants* category); Bush Warbler, Calling Bird, [12] Kaodori[13] (a word in the *Spring* category); Wood Thrush,[14] Firefly, Cicada, Cicala, Pine Cricket, Bell Cricket, Field Cricket, Insect, Bear, Tiger, Dragon, Wild Boar (things of this sort being in the *Animals* category); Demon

[*Shōhaku:** This word clashes with words in the *Living Things* category.[15] There is an old theory that has "demon" as a variety of insect, but one must question whether the supernatural can be so easily defined. Is there any need to go to such lengths in definition?],

Yoshimoto: Woman

[****Shōhaku:** This word is in the same category as the last one.];

Yoshimoto: The Past, Ancient, Nightfall, Yesterday, Evening Shower, Passing Shower, Rain

[****Shōhaku:** In recent years, "rain" has been classed among things that may appear twice in a *hyakuin*.],

Shōhaku: Fulling Block,

Yoshimoto: Storm

[****Shōhaku:** Again, this word is now classed among things that may appear twice in a *hyakuin*.],

Yoshimoto: Withering Wind,[16] Morning Moon, Evening Moon, Hermitage, Environs, Bird Rattle,[17] Clapper,[18] Pivot Door,[19] Bedchamber.

Yoshimoto: These things and others like them should be restricted to one appearance in a sequence.

Kanera: Pine Cricket, Bell Cricket, Field Cricket, and Insect (*Ōan shinshiki* treats each of these separately as among things that may appear only once in a *hyakuin,* but in modern times the practice is to allow the word "insect" plus one additional "named" insect—meaning "pine cricket," "bell cricket," and so on. And even when one is composing by design according to *Ōan shinshiki* one must make sure that "insect" and words such as "pine cricket" and "bell cricket" do not come up on the same sheet, and again that "insect" and words such as "field cricket" and *hataori*[20] do not come up on the same side.); Spring Rain, Drizzle, etc. (These are both types of "passing showers."); Raindrops, Rainy Night (Either of these words may be used once without being counted as an instance of the word "rain."); Horse (The word "pony" counts the same as "horse." But the word "horse" in the saying "The will is a horse, the heart a monkey"[21] or again in the metaphorical expression ". . . like a horse passing by a crack in the wall"[22] should not be counted as an instance.)

[****Shōhaku:** The word "pony" may be used in addition to the word "horse." These two words are like *tazu* and *tsuru*.[23]]

Shōhaku: Slow Day (And "long day" may not be used in addition.); Spring Chill (And even a slightly different phrasing, such as "take on a chill," should be counted as an instance.);

Autumn Chill (Again, this idea may appear only once—
even if phrases such as "growing chilly" or "the chill of
night" are used instead.); Edgestone (a word in the *Dwellings*
category); Bed. (The "beds" of birds or beasts do not count
as instances in this case.)

VIII Things That May Appear As Many As Two Times in a *Hyakuin*

Yoshimoto: Dawn (once as such and once in the phrase "that dawning"[24]);
Reign (as in "The Reign of the Gods," "our sovereign's
reign"); Spring Wind (once as such and once in the phrase
"wind of spring").

[*Shōhaku:** There is no need to change the phrasing from "spring wind"
to "wind of spring." In recent times this has simply been
regarded as a word that may appear two times in a sequence.];

Yoshimoto: Autumn Wind, Pine Wind (the same applying in these cases
as for "spring wind"); Rains of the Fifth Month[25] (once as
such and once in the word "plum rains"[26])

[*Shōhaku:** Some think it unnecessary to count "plum rains" as an
instance of "rains of the fifth month."];

Yoshimoto: Evening; Today; Hut (once read as *io* and once as *iori*[27])

[*Shōhaku:** Again it is all right not to change the phrasing in this way.];

Yoshimito: *Furusato* (once meaning either "old capital" or "home town,"
and once meaning "home" in the context of *Travel*[28]); Hill
(once as such and once in the name of a *Famous Place*); Pond
(with the same restriction as noted for "hill"); Harbor
(again, with the same restriction); Lodge (once meaning
"house" and once in the context of *Travel*)

[*Shōhaku:** Besides this word there is the word "lodging,"[29] which may be
used in phrases like "a bird's lodging" or "a lodging for the
dew."[30]];

Yoshimoto: Garden (once as such and once in a word such as "garden
precepts"[31])

[*Shōhaku:** In addition to simple "garden" one may use "temple garden"
or "garden of the imperial residence." But "garden precepts"
is something entirely different.];

Yoshimoto: Wild Geese (once in *Spring*, once in *Autumn*)

[*Shōhaku:** The word "tarrying wild goose"[32] should be counted as among
these instances.];

Yoshimoto: Monkey (once as such and once in the synonym *mashira*[33]); The word "travel" (once as such and once in a compound like "travel robe")

[*Shōhaku: In recent times we do not go so far as to make this latter distinction.];

Yoshimoto: Life (once as such and once in connection with the "life" of an insect, etc.); Old Age (once as such and once in connection with birds, trees, etc.); Man (once as such and once in a phrase like "the man in the moon," etc.[34]);

Shōhaku: The Sao Princess;[35] The Princess of the Bridge.[36]

Shōhaku: In the case of all of the two-instance things noted thus far, the two allowable instances of any one thing should not appear in the same sheet.

Yoshimoto: The words *narinikeri, omoishi ni,* and *mono o* (Words of this sort may be used twice in a sequence, but the placing of the word in respective verses should be different.); Lovingly/Loving, Resentment/To Resent (Such words should be inflected differently in each instance, as suggested by these examples. And the same holds for all other cases of this sort.)

[**Kanera:** But there is really no need to require different inflections here.]

Kanera: Showers (once in *Autumn* and once in *Winter*); Morning (once as such and once in the word "this morning");

Shōhaku: Crane (once as *tsuru* and once as *tazu*[37]);

Yoshimoto: Taking Leave (once in connection with "blossoms")

[*Shōhaku: and once in the context of *Love*];

Shōhaku: Image (once as such and once in connection with "blossoms" or "the moon");

Yoshimoto: Lonely (once as such and once in another inflection);

Kanera: Jewel String of Life[38]

[**Shōhaku: This word should not appear in the same sheet as the word "life." The "life" of an insect or another animal, however, should be considered as outside this restriction.];

Shōhaku: Treetops (once as such and once in connection with "pines" or "blossoms," with the epithet "Autumn of the Treetops"[39] also counting as an instance); *Inaba,* "rice plant" (once as such and once in the synonym *oshine*); Dust (Besides simple "dust" one can use words like "this world of dust."[40]); The Law (Besides the Buddhist "Law," one should use the civil "law." But after the word "law" has been used, it is not appropriate to introduce the title "Teacher of the Law."[41]); Peak (Even if this word appears in the name of a *Famous Place*, it should count as an instance.); Ocean (once as such, once in the name of a *Famous Place*. Epithets such as *Watatsumi*[42] do not count as instances of "ocean."); Field; Meadow (One of the two instances of this word should be in the name of a *Famous Place*.); Eaves; Fence (with no need to use the reading *kakio* one time and *kaki* another); Hedge (once as such and once in the phrase "hedge of mist"); *Pining Love, Fulfilled Love, Parting Love,* and so on (Each of these subcategories may be used two times in a sequence, and the same holds for other cases of this sort.); Afar; The negative predicate *wa nashi* (once in a long verse and once in a short one[43]); The negative predicate *mo nashi* (the same applying here as for *wa nashi*); Word (once in the phrase *koto no ha*, "leaves of words." But "way of the word" need not count as an instance here.); Straw Mat (once as such and once in words like "Mat of the Law."[44] Also, words such as "mat of moss" and "mat of grass" should count as instances.); Gaze; Cool (One instance of this word should be in a season other than *Summer*.).

IX Things That May Appear As Many As Three Times in a *Hyakuin*

Yoshimoto: Spring Moon (once as such, once as "dawn moon" in a *Spring* context, and once as "new moon" in a *Spring* context); Summer Moon (the same applying here as for "spring moon"); Winter Moon (again with the same restrictions)

[****Shōhaku:** "Dawn moon" may be used once outside of an *Autumn* scene. It is best that "new moon" appear only once among the four seasonal contexts. Some say that two or three such instances are acceptable, but this is a dubious notion.];

Yoshimoto: The Gods (once as such, once in a phrase like "The Reign of the Gods," and once in the name of a specific god[45]; Blossom (This word should not appear twice in the same sheet. "Counterfeit" blossoms,[46] however, do not count toward the allowed number of instances.)

[**Kanera:** In modern times the word "blossom" has come to be counted among things that may appear four times in a *hyakuin*. And "late blossoms"[47] should be counted among these instances.]

[**Shōhaku: The compound "blossoms and red leaves"[48] should also count as among the allowed instances. If one side of a sheet contains the word "blossoms," then "cherry blossoms" should not be used on that same sheet: the words clash. And the same holds for "blossoms of the heart" and other "counterfeit" blossoms. There are some who claim that "blossom" should still be counted among things that may appear only three times in a *hyakuin*, but this is a misguided notion. Whether the word appears in three or four verses is a matter of little consequence.[49]];

Yoshimoto: Wistaria (once as such, once in the family name Fujiwara,[50] once in a season other than *Spring*)

[*Shōhaku: There are those who say that this word need not be used once in a season other than *Spring*.];

Yoshimoto: Willow (once as such, once in "green willows," and once in the context of *Autumn* or *Winter*[51]); Cherry Blossom (once as such, once in "late cherry" or "mountain cherry," and once in connection with "red leaves"[52])

[*Shōhaku: Again, there is no harm in using "cherry blossom" twice instead of using "late cherry" or "mountain cherry" in its place.];

Yoshimoto: Red Leaves (once as such, once in connection with cherry or plum blossoms, and once in the phrase "red leaves of grass"[53])

[*Shōhaku: The phrase "bridge of red leaves"[54] should not be counted here as an instance.];

Yoshimoto: Falling Leaves (once as such, once in the context of "falling pine needles," and once in the context of such words as "molting willows"); Reeds (once as such, once in *Summer* or *Winter* instead of *Autumn*, once in the context of "burnt-over fields")

[*Shōhaku: The word "shore reeds"[55] should not appear in the same sheet with simple "reeds." But "reeds" should indeed be used once in a season other than *Autumn*.];

Yoshimoto: Miscanthus (once as such, once by means of a synonym such as *obana*,[56] and once by means of either the word "charred stubble"[57] or the word "thatched roof"[58]); The Capital (once as such, once in the name of a *Famous Place*, once in the context of *Travel*); Salt (once as such, once in connection with "salt-burning,"[59] once by means of the homophonous *shio*, "tide");

Shōhaku: Cascade (once as such, once in the name of a *Famous Place,* once by means of the synonym "falling rapids."[60] "Cascade of blossoms" and "cascade of tears" are not counted as instances here.);

Yoshimoto: Shore (once as such, once in the name of a *Famous Place,* once in the word "the far shore"[61]); Letter (once in the context of *Love,* once in the context of *Travel,* and once in the context of literature)

[**Kanera:** The word "jeweled missive"[62] should be counted as among these instances.];

Yoshimoto: Hunting (once in connection with hawks, once in connection with quail, and once in connection with *Beasts*); Cock (once using the phrase *niwatori,* once using the word "night bird," and once using another synonym)

[*Shōhaku: The word "night bird" is simply another name for "cock." Taken together, synonyms should account for two instances of the word in question.];

Yoshimoto: Deer (once as such, once by means of the word "fawn," once by means of the synonym "hart"[63])

[*Shōhaku: Words such as *kaseki* and the phrase "to present a stag" are in the *Miscellaneous* category.[64]];

Yoshimoto: Wheel (once as such, once in the phrase "Wheel of the Law,"[65] once in "water wheel")

[*Shōhaku: The word "handcart" should also be counted as among the three instances in this case. "Water wheel" comes up only rarely.[66]];

Yoshimoto: After the phrase "blossoming grasses" has been used once in a sequence, it should only appear again in a new phrasing, such as "hut in the blossoming grasses" or "pillow of blossoming grasses."

[*Shōhaku: But if "blossoming grasses" has been used already, another phrasing may only be used once.];

Shōhaku: Lamp (once as such, once in the word "hanging lamp,"[67] once in "Lamp of the Law"[68]); Alone (once as such, once in the context of *Love,* once in connection with "pines" or "the moon").

X Things That May Appear As Many As Four Times in a *Hyakuin*

Yoshimoto: Snow (Besides this word, "spring snow"[69] may also be used once. But "counterfeit" snow is note counted here as an instance.)

[*Shōhaku: In recent times, "snow" has come to be classed as something that may appear four times in a *hyakuin*. "Spring snow" should not appear in the same side as "snow."]

[Kanera: "Icehouse snow" should be classed in the *Spring* category, just as "Fuji's snows," and neither of these should appear with the other in the same sheet. The same holds for "snow" in any other season but *Winter.*]

[*Shōhaku: These days "snow" may appear as many as four times in a *hyakuin*, with "spring snow" counting in this number, just as in *Ōan shinshiki*.[70]];

Yoshimoto: Dawn Moon (once in each of the four seasons)

[*Shōhaku: This word has already been referred to above.[71]];

Yoshimoto: Barrier-Gate (once as such, once in the name of a *Famous Place*, once in connection with *Love*)

[*Shōhaku: Another instance may involve the idea of "halting" either autumn or spring.[72] And indeed one instance should involve *Love, Autumn,* or *Spring.*[73]];

Yoshimoto: Ice (once as such, once in the word "icicle," once in "moon-ice"[74]

[*Shōhaku: or in "icy tears"],

Yoshimoto: once in connection with "frost" or "snow")

[*Shōhaku: "Icicle" and "ice needle" should account for only one instance between them. And the word "icehouse" is not counted as an instance of "ice."];

Yoshimoto: Bell (once as such, once in connection with vespers, once in the context of *Buddhism*, once by means of a synonym)

[*Shōhaku: These distinctions, as between a usage involving *Buddhism* and a synonym, are not always clear. But when the context makes definition obvious, there is no need to pursue the matter further.[75]];

Kanera: Sky (Here the phrase "relying on the empty sky"[76] should not count as an instance.)

[**Shōhaku: Nor do *sorame*, "empty illusion," or *soragoto*, "idle words," count as instances. But the word "midair" should not appear in the same sheet as "sky."];

Kanera: Shrine (twice in the context of *Shinto*, twice meaning "imperial residence." But one of these instances should involve a *Famous Place.*);

Yoshimoto: The word "morning" in "morning wind," "morning frost," and so on (These words should not appear in the same sheet.); The word "evening" in "evening wind," "evening frost," and so on (the same rule applying here as for the previous item);

Kanera: Bird (once as such, once in the word "spring bird," once in "little birds" or "flock of birds," and once in the compound "birds and beasts." Birds referred to in the context of hunting, birds that sleep on the water, and the word "night bird" should not be counted as instances here.[77]); Fire (with the "fire" of "firefly" not counting as an instance); The word "jewel" ("Counterfeit" jewels[78] and euphemisms involving the word "jewel" should be counted as instances in this case.);

Shōhaku: The word "leaf" ("Bamboo leaves," "leaves of grass," and other such words should be separated from this word by at least five verses.);

Kanera: The word "sleep" (as it appears in words such as "traveler's sleep" or "sleeping alone." The verb *nuru*, "to recline," is outside this restriction.);

Shōhaku: The word "heavens"; The word "shop"[79]; The word "door" ("Pivot door," "barrier-gate," "valley door," and other words of this sort should not appear in the same sheet as "door.").

XI Things That May Appear As Many As Five Times in a *Hyakuin*

Yoshimoto: The World (once as such, once in "the floating world" or "this world of ours,"[80] once in connection with *Love*, once in "the former world," and once in the "the next world")

[*Shōhaku: Since it is difficult to distinguish "the floating world" and "this world of ours" as "named" instances of "world,"[81] the rule now is simply that two of the five instances should be in the *Lamentation* category. The Buddhist "world" should be referred to either in the context of "the former world" or "the next world."];

Yoshimoto: Plum Blossom (once as such, once in "red plum," once as a "winter tree," once in "green plum," once in connection with "red leaves")

[*Shōhaku: "Green plum" and "red leaves of the plum" appear only rarely.[82]];

Yoshimoto: Bridge (once as such, once in "Palace Bridge,"[83] once in "rope bridge," once in the name of a *Famous Place,* once in the word "floating bridge")

[*Shōhaku: The word "Palace Bridge" is really in a category of its own. And there should be just one instance of "floating bridge," whether as such or in the phrase "floating bridge of dreams."[84]].

XII Things That Must Be Separated by More Than One Verse

[**Kanera:** plus a number of things that should not appear together in the same sheet.]

Yoshimoto: Cavern, Barrier-Gate, Hermitage, House, Residence (all of which clash with words in the *Dwellings* category);

Kanera: *Dwellings* and Paddy Hut,

Shōhaku: *Dwellings* and Village or Hedge of Mist (the same applying here as for the previous list);

Shōhaku: Shoreline Eaves[85] (There are various opinions about this word, but depending on context it may clash with *Dwellings*.); *Furusato,* when used to mean "imperial residence," and words in the *Dwellings* category (And *furusato* must be separated from the word *sato,* "town," by at least five verses.);

Yoshimoto: Mist and words in the *Falling Things* category; Haze and the word "dim";

Shōhaku: Smoke from pines, bamboo, grass, or water and words in the *Rising Things* category; Words like "those who dwell in the clouds"[86] or "garden in the clouds"[87] and phrases like "smoke rising from the breast" or "smoke rising from one's thoughts" (the same holding here as for the previous word); "Running Hail"[88] and words in the *Falling Things* category;

Yoshimoto: A time of day and the same or another time of day ("nightfall," "daybreak," and so on); Moon and the word "day"; sun and the word "month"; Seed-Scattering, Fields Changing Color, Winter-Withered Fields or Mountains, etc., and words in the *Plants* category; Bogwood (the same holding for this word as for those in the previous list);

Shōhaku: The Color of the Mountains, The Color of the Fields (Both of these generally clash with words in the *Plants* category, but the final decision should depend on the context of the verse in question.);

Kanera: Words in the *Plants* category and any of these: Grass-Cutting, Fodder

[**Shōhaku:** And these last two words must be separated from the word "grass" by at least two verses.],

Kanera: Garden Orchard,[89] Thicket, Autumn paddies, or other words of this sort

[**Shōhaku:** "Autumn paddies," if used in conjunction with "wild geese" or "deer," does not clash with *Plants* at all, but if a phrase such as "chasing deer from the paddies"[90] is used with it, then the verse will indeed clash with *Plants*.];

Yoshimoto: Bamboo and any sort of greenery;

Shōhaku: Heart of Pine, Heart of Cedar[91] (These should be separated by at least two verses from words in the *Plants* category.); Seedling Bed (This word does not clash with *Plants,* but still it should be separated from words in that category by at least two verses.); New Sprouts[92]; Reed Hut or Reed Fire, when used in a withered *Winter* setting, and words in the *Waters* category;

Yoshimoto: The place-name Ukishimagahara[93] (This clashes with words in the *Mountains* category.)

[*Shōhaku:** But it is itself not in that category.];

Kanera: Words in the *Human Relations* category and other words in the same category;

Yoshimoto: Old Age and The Past; Fulling Block and any sort of clothing

[*Shōhaku:** And the word *kinu,* meaning "robe," should be separated from *kinuta,* "fulling block," by at least five verses.];

Kanera: Words in the *Living Things* category and the word "sacrifice"

[**Shōhaku:** And depending on the content of the verse, "sacrifice" may indicate the *Shinto* category.];

Kanera: The Release of Living Things[94] (a word in the *Waters* category);

Shōhaku: Stable (This word should not appear in the same side of a sheet with "horse" or "pony."); The metaphor "something for the horse"[95] (with the same restriction as noted for "stable"); The place-names Naniwa in Tsu and Toba in Yamashiro[96] (These clash with *Famous Places*.); Verses that include words like Shinobu no Urami or Shinobu no Wabi[97] (These clash with words in the *Waters* category, and at least three verses should separate such words from *Famous Places*. After the beginning of another sheet, one may use Shinobu no Yama[98] or Shinobu no Oka,[99] but not Shinobu no Ura again. The same holds for all other cases of this sort.).

Shōhaku: All of the things mentioned thus far in section XII should be separated by more than one verse.

Yoshimoto: Cloud and To Cloud Up;

Shōhaku: Warm Day and Tranquil;

Yoshimoto: Cool and Chilling;

Shōhaku: Cold and Chilling;

Yoshimoto: The phrase "piercing the soul" and Cold; Ancient and Home Town[100]; Treetops and End;

Shōhaku: Pine and Day of the Rat[101];

Yoshimoto: Sound and Voice or Echo

[*Shōhaku: And depending on the context of the verse, "voice" and "echo" may also clash with the place-names Otowayama and Otonashigawa.[102]];

Yoshimoto: To Look Back and To See; Evening and the "end"[103] of *Autumn* or *Spring*; Woodcutter and Tree; Image and Shadow; Shadow and Shade

[*Shōhaku: And "shadow" also clashes with "beneath," "under," and "hidden." Whether it clashes with "under," however, finally must depend on context.[104]];

Yoshimoto: Distant and Faraway; Wet Sleeves and Tears;

Shōhaku: Tears and Dew on the Sleeves;

Yoshimoto: To Cry and Tears (The "crying" of birds and beasts should not be counted in this case.); Parting and To Return (because in the context of *Love* these two words mean the same thing.); Parting and The Morning After[105]

[*Shōhaku: And if both verses are in the *Love* category, these words should not appear in the same side.];

Yoshimoto: Musing and Fire[106] (although these may not clash in certain contexts); The negative suffix *nu* and the affirmative suffix *nu*

[*Shōhaku: The negative *nu* is so indispensable that now it is agreed that it may be used again as early as the very next verse.];

Yoshimoto: The negative suffix *zu* and the verbal *su;* The past suffix *shi*[107];

Kanera: Dream and Reality; Waking and Dreaming; Dawning and Daybreak; Today and either Yesterday or Tomorrow; Bow and Arrow ("Bowlike moon" and "arrowlike year"[108] do not count as instances here.)

[**Shōhaku: But still these last two words should not appear in the same sheet with "bow" or "arrow," respectively.];

Shōhaku: Rain Cloak and Rain Hat;

Kanera: Evening shower and the word "to come to a close"[109];

Shōhaku: Evening and the word "late and soon"[110]; Morn and Eve and the word "to come to a close"; Break of Day and Morning ("Break of day" does not clash with evening time-words.); Twilight and Evening ("Twilight" does not clash with morning time-words.); Distant and Afar; Window and Door; Proverb and Word or such other terms (These all clash with each other because they are "sayings."); Dark and To Grow Dark; The compound Light and Shadow and the compounds Noon and Night, Moon and Sun[111] (If only one word from this last compound—"moon" by itself or "sun" by itself—is present, then there is no need to hesitate. And the same holds for "noon" when used by itself, or "night" when used by itself.); The compound *nowaki*, or "typhoon," and either of its constituents—*no*, "fields," or *waku*, "to put asunder" (This word is written with the characters for "violent wind" in Shitagō's *Wamyō ruijushō*[112]); Withering Wind and Tree; Green and Green Growth; Clan Way and Storm[113]; The place-name Kiso[114] and the word *ki*, "wood" (This place-name is written with different characters in *Shūchūshō*[115] [Notes to keep in one's sleeves.]); Fields or Mountains and the word *hotori*, or "vicinity"[116]; Heavens and Sky; the place-name Awaji and Path[117] (And if one uses the word "mountain path," the separation between it and Awaji should be at least five verses.); *Ariake*, or "around dawn," and *ari*, the verb "to be" (These words should be separated from *ake*, "to open up," by at least five verses.); The compound *iriai*, or "sunset," and either of its constituents—*iru*, "to enter," or *au*, "to join"; Voice of the Reeds (This word should be used without direct reference to the wind, as in court poetry, and it should be separated from the

word "wind" by at least two verses.); *Nageki,* or "pains," and
any word in the *Plants* category that contains the word *ki,*
"tree," should be separated by at least two verses[118]; Thirty
Years of Age or Forty Years of Age and the word "year" (The
digital numbers, such as "seventy" or "eighty," do not clash
here.); *Tamashii,* or "soul," and the word *tama,* "bead" or
"jewel" (If one refers to "soul" by the expression "my jewel
string of life," then the latter must be separated from *tamashii* by at least five verses.); Gaze and To See (The former
does not clash with "eye."); *Katami,* or "keepsake," and To
See (And the former does not clash with "gaze."[119]); The
word *yumeyume*[120] (This should be separated from *yume,*
"dream," by at least two verses. It is not, however, in the *Nocturnal Things* category.); *Mono omou,* "to be lost in
thought," and either of its constituents—*mono,* or "thing,"
and *omou,* "to think"; Grief and Grievous; Grief and Bitter
or Sad; *Nagori,* "taking leave," and either of its constituents—*na,* or "name," and *nokoru,* "to remain behind"; To
Think About and To Think[121]; *Sukunaki,* or "scarce," and
the negative *naki; Hakanaki,* or "ephemeral," and the negative *naki* (Linking these words together in consecutive verses
should indeed be avoided, but current thinking is that they
do not clash when separated by one verse.); The word *shiru,*
"to know," and *shirushi,* "mark," or *shirube,* "guide"; The
word *aramashi,* "future prospect," and the verb *ari,* "to be"
(According to some there is no clash here at all.); Where,
When, What, Why, Wherefore, How, and Which (If a different one of these interrogative words is used in a second
instance, then they need only be separated by two verses.);
nari and *nari, nare* and *nare, naru* and *naru*—all inflections
of the copula (These are the sorts of words that should be
separated by at least two verses.[122]); *nari, nare,* and *naru*
(These should not appear consecutively in successive verses,
but they may appear separated by one verse. They do not
clash with the word *naru,* "to become."); To Search Out and
To Visit (These may or may not clash, depending on
context.);

Yoshimoto: Jeweled Missive and Word

[*Shōhaku:** Depending on context, there may be no need for hesitation
here.];

Yoshimoto: Japanese Poetry and Leaves of Words

[*Shōhaku:** the same applying here as for the previous word];

Yoshimoto: The Way of Shikishima and Japanese Poetry [123]

[*****Shōhaku:** These words should not appear in the same sheet.];

Yoshimoto: Lie and Truth; To Be Born or To Die and Life; Years of Age and Old Age

[*****Shōhaku:** Depending on context, these last two may not clash.];

Yoshimoto: Old Man and Old Age; Parent and Child.

Shōhaku: All of the above, from "jeweled missive" on, also clash if they appear in adjacent verses.

Shōhaku: On the matter of excess syllables[124] (One must question the wisdom of using excess syllables in consecutive verses. Such verses should be separated by at least one verse. As *waka* treatises point out, verses with excess syllables should not be used unless it is necessary for a particular effect.[125]);

Kanera: Cicala and Cicada; The Past and Ancient;

Shōhaku: Maple Tree and Red Leaves;

Kanera: The World and The Floating World or This World of Ours; The Former World and The Next World; Words with the word "to abandon" in them—To Abandon the World, Abandoned Soul, and so on; The Eastern Road and The Eastern Cottage[126] (None of the above, from "cicala" on, should appear with each other in the same sheet.);

[******Shōhaku:** Waking From]

Kanera: Sleep and Bedchamber or To Recline[127];

Shōhaku: To Sleep and To Recline

Kanera: These last words clash if they appear on the same side;

Kanera: To Take on a Chill and Cold

[******Shōhaku:** If these are both used in the *Winter* category, they should not appear in the same sheet.];

Kanera: To Abandon the World and Hermit of the Priestly Way, since the latter is one who has abandoned the world[128]

Kanera: These words, from "to take on a chill" on, should not appear on the same side

[******Shōhaku:** or even on the same sheet.];

Shōhaku: The World when used in the context of *Love* and The World when used in *Lamentation* or *Buddhism* (These should not appear on the same side.); The number "one" (Although there are many times when this word is indispensable, it should not be used twice in the same side. The other counting numbers should not be used twice in the same sheet—or at least so it is said these days, and with good reason.); Three-syllable Words[129] (These should not appear on the same side.); The honorific prefix *mi* (as in "Honored Presence," "Palace Bridge," and so on. Depending on the way the word is used in a verse, however, there may be no need to avoid using this prefix twice in the same side.); The word *koro*, or "the time of . . ." (If it appears as the last word in a verse, this word may be used only once in a sheet. Used elsewhere, it belongs to the category of words that must be separated by at least five verses.[130]); Old Age and White Hair (These clash if they appear on the same side.); Tracks of the Brush and Bird Tracks[131] (These too clash if they appear on the same side.); The word *ato*, "remains," when used in the sense of "ruins," should not appear twice on the same sheet. Used in any other sense it belongs to the category of things that must be separated by at least five verses; Boulder and Rock (These should not appear on the same side.); Sand and Rock or Boulder (These should not appear on the same sheet.); *Sasa*, "bamboo grass," and the synonym *shino* (the same applying here as for the preceding item); *Take*, "bamboo," and the synonym *suzu* (These should be separated by at least three verses.); The word "gods" and *kagura*, "Shinto music" (These should not appear on the same side.); The Ninefold Enclosure[132] and The Capital (These should not appear on the same sheet.); The Capital and The Great Shrine[133] (the same applying here as for the previous item).

XIII Things That Must Be Separated by At Least Three Verses

Yoshimoto: The Moon, The Sun, Star (and other things in the *Shining Things* category); Rain, Dew, Frost, Snow, Hail (and other things in the *Falling Things* category); Haze, Mist, Cloud, Smoke (and other things in the *Rising Things* category); The *Trees* category and the *Grasses* category; The *Insects* category and the *Birds* category; The *Birds* category and the *Beasts* category;

Shōhaku: One *Famous Place* and another *Famous Place;* The Tanabata Festival[134] and The Sun or The Moon (because Tanabata is also the name of a star.).

XIV Things That Must Be Separated by At Least Five Verses

Yoshimoto: Instances of the same word; Instances of the following words and subcategories: Day, Wind, Cloud, Smoke

[*Shōhaku: Instances of this last word should in fact be separated by at least seven verses.],

Yoshimoto: Field, Mountain,

Shōhaku: Bay,

Yoshimoto: Wave, Water, Path, Night, *Trees, Grasses, Birds, Beasts, Insects;* Instances of the following categories: *Love, Travel, Waters, Dwellings;* Instances of the word *kure*, "to come to a close"; Instances of the *Lamentation* category

[*Shōhaku: A note on the words associated with this category is in order. The Past, Ancient, Old Age, Death, and Living do not belong to the category; The World, Parent and Child, Moss Robes, Ink-Dyed Sleeves, Hermitage, Abandoned Soul, Grieved Soul, and Life, on the other hand, do mark a verse as in the *Lamentation* category. In other words, even if the idea of lamentation is present in a verse, it will not be considered as in that category if it does not contain an explicit reference. The verb "to be born" is not in the *Lamentation* category. And, although recently "ink-dyed robes" has been classed in the *Buddhism* category, the term does not really refer to Buddhist robes, but only indicates the robes' color.[135] Mototoshi puts "ink-dyed robes" with "moss robes"; thus it would seem best to follow *Ōan shinshiki* in this matter.[136]];

Yoshimoto: Instances of the *Shinto* category; Instances of the *Buddhism* category; Instances of the word "sleeves"; Instances of the *Clothing* category; Mountain and the name of a *Famous Place* located in the mountains; Bay and the name of a *Famous Place* located on a bay;

Shōhaku: *Hara,* or "stand" (But if one changes the content of the stand — say from "stand of pines" to "stand of bamboo grass," for example — then the instances need only be separated by five verses.);

Kanera: *Asazukuhi*, or "morning sun," and *yūzukuhi,* or "evening sun" (These words clash with "sun" or "moon.")

[**Shōhaku: There are those, however, who insist that these words simply refer to the morning and the evening sun, and see no problem here.[137]].

XV Things That Must Be Separated by at Least Seven Verses

Yoshimoto: The same seasonal category; Instances of the following words: Moon, Pine, Bamboo, Paddy, Robe, Dream, Tears, Ship

[**Kanera:** On the word "ship" (It is equally necessary that words like "the Ship of Amanoiwa" and "the Ship of the River of Heaven"[138] be separated from "ship" by at least seven verses, although these last words are not in the *Waters* category. And the place-names Funaoka Mountain and Mifune Mountain, both of which contain the word *fune*, or "ship," should be separated from the latter by at least five verses.)];

[**Kanera:** On the word "robe" ("Robe of haze" and "Robes of the Weaver Maiden" should be separated from "robe" by at least seven verses, although again these two words are not in the *Clothing* category. The place-names Koromogawa and Koromode Grove, both of which contain the word *koromo*, or "robe," should be separated from the latter by at least five verses.)];

[*Shōhaku: On the word "pine" (The place-names Pine Island and Pine-Bay Mountain should be separated from the word "pine" by at least five verses.); On the word "paddy" (The place-names Ikuta Grove, Tanakami Grove, and Ukita Grove, all of which contain the word *ta*, or "paddy," should be separated from the latter by at least five verses.); On the word "bamboo" (The place-names Takeda and Takekawa, both of which contain the word *take*, or "bamboo," should be separated from the latter by at least five verses, following the examples given above.)].

XVI Some Additional Words of Advice

Yoshimoto: Waves of Blossoms, Cascade of Blossoms, Clouds of Blossoms, Shower of Pine-Wind, Shower of Autumn Leaves, River Rainfall,[139] Moon-Snow

[**Kanera:** With the inclusion of a *Summer* word, this last word is not in the *Falling Things* category.],

Yoshimoto: Moon-Frost

[**Kanera:** the same applying here as for the previous item],

Yoshimoto: Door of Cherry Blossoms, Robe of Leaves.

Yoshimoto: All of these compounds clash with both their constituents.[140]

Yoshimoto: Snowfall of Blossoms (This clashes with *Plants* but not with *Falling Things*.), Rain of Tears (This does not clash with *Falling Things*.), Blossoms on the Waves (This clashes with *Waters* but not with *Plants*.[141]),

Shōhaku: Snow on the Waves (This is in the *Winter* category. It clashes with both "snow" and "waves.").

Yoshimoto: The ways in which these "counterfeits"[142] clash are not always the same. These days we use this standard: if the compound is likely to cause confusion, then it will clash with both its constituents; but if it is not likely to cause confusion, it will not clash with both constituents.[143]

Kanera: Dew on the Sleeves

[****Shōhaku:** One theory says that if there is no explicit indication that "dew" is to be taken for tears in a verse, then it should not be classed in the *Love* category.];

Kanera: Tears of Dew (This word clashes with words in the *Falling Things* category.);

Yoshimoto: Shower of Tears (This may be used once to refer to literal "rain.")

[***Shōhaku:** Since it is in the *Winter* category, "shower of tears" clashes with words in the *Falling Things* category. If "showers" has once been used in a *Winter* context, then it is best not to use "shower of tears."];

Yoshimoto: About the Essential and Attributive words in the *Waters* category: If one has linked "bay," to "waves," one should not use "water" or "salt" in a subsequent third verse, but instead use "marsh reeds," some sort of waterfowl, "boat," or "bridge," because the latter are all Neutral words[144];

Yoshimoto: The place-names Suma and Akashi[145] (These are in the *Waters* category. The place-names Ueno and Oka,[146] however, are not, and the same holds for other cases of this sort.); The place-names Naniwa and Shiga[147] (These are not in the *Waters* category, and the same holds for other places of this sort.);

Yoshimoto: Iris, Sweetflag, Marsh Reed, Lotus, Komo Reed,[148] To Cup Water in One's Hands, Water Pipe,[149] Icehouse, Washing Water (All of these are in the *Waters* category.);

Shōhaku: Capital Bird[150] (also a word in the *Waters* category);

Yoshimoto: Thatched Hut,[151] Net of Haze, Paddy-Plowing, Cloth-Bleaching, Inkstone-Water,

Kanera: River of Tears

[**Shōhaku:** If used as a place-name, this last word clashes with words in the *Waters* category.[152]],

Kanera: Moon-Ice, Sleeve-Drenching Waters, Ice Needle, Ice-Beads on the Eaves, Seedling Bed, Rice Seedling.

Yoshimoto: These words, from "thatched hut" on, are not in the *Waters* category.

Yoshimoto: Barrier-Gates located in the mountains clash with words in the *Mountains* category; Barrier-Gates located on bays clash with the word "bay"; Bridge of Stones,[153] Firewood, Brushwood, Monkey, Falling Rapids[154] (These words are not in the *Mountains* category.); The place-name Uji no Kawashima[155] (This is not in the *Mountains* category.)

[*Shōhaku: And the same holds for other river islands.[156]];

Kanera: Hase Temple (Because this is a temple located at a barrier-gate in the mountains,[157] it belongs to the *Mountains* category, and the same holds for other cases of this sort.); Kiyomi Temple (Because this temple is located at a barrier-gate on a bay,[158] it belongs to the *Waters* category.); Naniwa Temple[159] (This is not in the *Waters* category.); Kiso Road and Suzuka Road[160] (These place-names and the phrases "the recesses of Yoshino" and "the recesses of Ono" are not classified in the *Mountains* category.[161]); Crane Grove[162] (This is in the *Plants* category.); Vulture Peak[163] (This is in the Essential class of *Mountains*.)

[**Shōhaku: Neither Crane Grove nor Vulture Peak were originally restricted in this way, and it would seem best to follow earlier practice in this matter.];

Kanera: Woodsman, Charcoal-Burning, Mountains of Snow (These words are not in the *Mountains* category.); The place-name Muro no Yashima[164] (This clashes with neither *Mountains* nor *Waters*.);

Shōhaku: Mount Fuji, Mount Asama, and Mount Katsuragi[165] (These are the only words classed as Neutral in the *Mountains* category.); The place-name Matsushima, or "Pine-Island" (It was said that this place should not be in the *Mountains* category, but since it is not on land,[166] recent thinking has put it in both *Mountains* and *Waters*.); Taminoshima, Mishima (These are places in Settsu and Izu, respectively, and neither is in the *Mountains* category.[167]); Mountain of Love[168]

(Depending on the way it appears in a verse, this may refer to a *Famous Place.*);

Yoshimoto: Late Cherry Blossoms, Flowers of the Pine,[169] Burnt-Over Field of Reeds,

Kanera: Bird's Nest (This word is in the *Spring* category. The "nests" of waterfowl, however, are in the *Summer* category, and the word "crane's nest" is in the *Miscellaneous* category.),

Yoshimoto: Pheasant

[**Kanera:** This word is in the *Spring* category even if one refers to it by means of a synonym. When it is used in the context of a hunting site, however, the category is *Winter.*],

Shōhaku: Cracks in the Ice, Rough-Hewn Year,[170]

Kanera: The Kasuga Festival[171] (And both Kasuga Festivals are in the *Spring* category, since the spring festival is the most fundamental.),

Shōhaku: The Southern Festival (This is the Extraordinary Festival of the Iwashimizu Hachiman Shrine.[172]), The Announcement of Provincial Appointments,[173]

Kanera: "Running Hail,"[174]

Shōhaku: The Suma Lustration[175] (This is also called The Lustration of the Snake.[176] It is in the *Spring* category.), Flower of the Heart,[177] White-Tailed Hawk,[178] Long-Tailed Hawk.[179]

Yoshimoto: All of the above, from "late cherry blossoms" on, are in the *Spring* category.

Shōhaku: Crossing Shiga Mountain (One theory has this in the *Spring* category, but recent thinking does not place it in *Spring.*);

Yoshimoto: The Festival of the Gods,[180] Taking the *Sakaki* Branch,[181] Iris, Peony (Conventional *waka* topics[182] treat "iris" and "peony" sometimes in the context of *Spring*, sometimes in the context of *Summer*. According to *Keibutsushō* (Images of the seasons),[183] both belong in *Summer*.), Molting Hawks and Caged Hawks.

Yoshimoto: All of the above, from "The Festival of the Gods" on, are in the *Summer* category.

Kanera: The Hirano Festival[184] (This is in the *Summer* category.), Bush Warbler (If used with "wood thrush," this word should be classed in the *Summer* category.),

Shōhaku: Trout (This is in the *Summer* category, but the word "young trout" is in the *Spring* category and "rusty trout" is in the *Autumn* category.),

Kanera: The Long Rains at Suma[185] (This is in the *Summer* category.)

[**Shōhaku: This interpretation is incorrect. "The long rains at Suma" should not be in the *Summer* category.],

Kanera: Pure Water (This word is in the *Miscellaneous* category. But in conjunction with *musubu,* "to cup water in one's hands," the word should be classed in the *Summer* category.)

[**Shōhaku: By itself, however, "to cup water in one's hands" is in the *Miscellaneous* category.];

Yoshimoto: Cicala, Lightning, Dove Whistle,[186] Catalpa,[187]

Shōhaku: Paulownia,

Yoshimoto: Withered Tips,[188] Ivy, Plantain, Moss Fern,[189] Putting on a Thatched Roof,[190] First Bird-Hunt[191]

[*Shōhaku: and also "opening the birdcages"[192]],

Yoshimoto: Hunting with Young Hawks, Quail Robes[193] (This word is not in the *Animals* category.), Thatch,[194] Dew on Withered Fields, Blossoms on Withered Grasses,

Shōhaku: First Storm, Dewey Frost, Dewy Drizzle,

Kanera: The Announcement of Capital Appointments,[195] The Sumō Wrestling Matches,

Shōhaku: The Release of Living Things (This is in the *Shinto* category.), Starry Night (This word should be separated from "moon" by at least five verses.[196]),

Yoshimoto: Autumn Robes (These are worn during the Tanabata Festival.), Pleading Threads[197] (This also is connected with Tanabata.),

Shōhaku: Grasses Where the Shrikes Hide[198] (This phrase is in the *Plants* category.),

Kanera: Plover (When used in conjunction with "wild geese," this word should be classed in the *Autumn* category.),

Shōhaku: Laying the Fan Aside (This phrase may be in the *Autumn* category, depending on the context of the verse.),

Yoshimoto: Chilling

[*Shōhaku: There are those who claim that in some contexts this word does not indicate *Autumn,* but there are also cases in which it is used in a forced manner because the *Autumn* season is so important.[199]],

Shōhaku: Chill of Night, Piercing the Soul.

Yoshimoto: All of the above, from "cicala" on, are in the *Autumn* category.

Yoshimoto: Light Snow, Shower of Tears, Garden Fires,[200] Robe of Leaves,[201] The idea of Falling Leaves "dyeing" something,

Shōhaku: The Northern Festival (This is the Extraordinary Festival of the Kamo Shrine.[202]),

[*Shōhaku: The Festival of]

Yoshimoto: Abounding Light[203] (This word is not in the *Nocturnal Things* category.),

Kanera: Purification Robes,[204] Sun-Shaded Cords[205] (Both of these two words are in the *Shinto* category.), Spring Coming in the Midst of the Old Year.[206]

Yoshimoto: All of the above, from "light snow" on, are in the *Winter* category.

Yoshimoto: Camelia,

Kanera: Oak,

Yoshimoto: Mugwort, Vine, Cogon Grass,[207] Forgetting Grass, Gossamer, Gull, Grebe (and also "floating nest"[208]),

Shōhaku: New-Pine Growth.

Yoshimoto: All of the above, from "camelia" on, are in the *Miscellaneous* category.

[*Shōhaku: "New green-growth" and "young green-growth,"[209] however, are in the *Spring* category.];

Yoshimoto: Salt-Hut,[210] Shinto Shrine, Buddhist Temple,

Shōhaku: To Leave Home and Family[211] (This word is in the *Buddhism* category.), Town *Kagura.*[212]

Shōhaku: These words, from "salt hut" on, are not in the *Dwellings* category.

Yoshimoto: The Capital, Palace Bridge, Hundred-Layered,[213] Above the Clouds,[214] The Ninefold Enclosure[215] (These are not in the *Dwellings* category.)

[*Shōhaku: nor are they *Famous Places.*];

Yoshimoto: Bamboo Blinds

[*Shōhaku: This is in the Attributive class of the *Dwellings* category.],

Yoshimoto: Floor, Imperial Seat.

Yoshimoto: These words, from "bamboo blinds" on, are in the *Dwellings* category.

Yoshimoto: Pillow of Grass, Brush Door, Pine Gate, Cedar Window,[216] Sedge Hat,[217] Bamboo Hut, Grass Hut, Floating Wood, Driftwood, Brushwood, Brush-Gathering,[218] Trees and Grasses depicted in paintings

[**Kanera:** Depending on how trees and grasses in paintings are used, they may indicate a seasonal inference.],

Kanera: The titles of folk songs[219] (with the same applying here as for trees and grasses depicted in paintings), Robes that are blossom or tree colored (Such robes are not in the *Plants* category, but, depending on the color involved, a season may be indicated.[220]), Tree-Cutting,

Shōhaku: Pathmarker, Reed Mallard,[221] The phrase "a crane in the reeds,"[222] Palace in the Bamboo[223] (This is a *Famous Place.*).

Yoshimoto: None of the above, from "pillow of grass" on, is in the *Plants* category.

Yoshimoto: Sweetflag Under the Eaves, Pine Mountain in Sue,[224] Pillow of Bamboo Grass, Mat of Rice Stalks, Mat of Moss, House in the Mugwort Patch,[225] Weed-Choked House,[226] House of the Evening Faces,[227] Mat of Grass,

Kanera: Grass-Cutting.

Kanera: All of the above, from "sweetflag under the eaves" on, are in the *Plants* category.

Yoshimoto: Mud Hen

[**Shōhaku:** This is a type of waterfowl.],

Yoshimoto: Firefly, Mosquito Incense,[228] Straw Mat, Pillow, Bed (The word "floor" indicates a daytime context.), Returning to Sleep,[229]

Shōhaku: *Kagura,* The Gloom of Night, Fishing Fires.[230]

Yoshimoto: All of the above, from "mud hen" on, are in the *Nocturnal Things* category.

Yoshimoto: Sleeping Waterfowl,[231] "Moonlike" Heart[232]

[**Shōhaku:** This word is in the *Buddhism* category.],

Yoshimoto: Quail's Bed, The Darkness of the Heart,[233] The phrase "that dawning,"[234] World of Dreams,[235] The Constant Flame,[236] Full Dawning,[237] After Dawning,[238] Faint Dawn Light,[239] Emergence of the New Moon, Setting of the Dawn Moon,

Shōhaku: Hazy Bellsound.[240]

Yoshimoto: None of the above, from "sleeping waterfowl" on, is in the *Nocturnal Things* category.

Kanera: Bonfire (And even if the word "shadows" is used in conjunction with "bonfire," the verse will not be in the *Nocturnal Things* category.);

Shōhaku: Moonlit Evening (This is not in the *Nocturnal Things* category.), Gloaming (This is not a time of day.[241]);

Yoshimoto: Evening and *Higurashi*, "cicala,"[242] Showers and the word "time,"[243] the compound place-name Kasuga and either of its constituents—"spring" or "day," Orange Blossoms and the word "blossoms," Thunder, or *Kaminari*, and the word *kami*, "gods"

[*Shōhaku: Here it says that these last two words do not clash, but this is an unfortunate interpretation. Certainly these two words should be separated by at least two verses.],

Shōhaku: Morning Glory and the word "morning" (But again there are those who do not agree that these do not clash.), Sun and Daytime, Lightning and Moon or Sun.

Yoshimoto: None of the above, from "evening and *higurashi*" on, clash with each other.

Yoshimoto: Under-Cord, Shoulder Sash (These are in the *Robes* category.); Sash, Cap, Shoes, *Kinuginu*[244] (These are not *Robes*.)

[*Shōhaku: But they do not clash with words in that category.];

Yoshimoto: The Robes of the Sao Princess (Again, this is not in the *Clothing* category.).

Yoshimoto: If a simple *Autumn* verse is followed by a verse that involves both *Autumn* and *Love*, then one should not return to a simple *Autumn* scene in a third verse (the same holding for all other cases of this sort); If "timber" is linked to "decayed wood," then one should not use a place famous for timber in a third verse; If one links "grove" to the place-name Ikuta,[245] then one should not introduce another place famous for its grove of trees, even as a "hidden topic"[246]; One need not hesitate to use "black pine" near the word "tree"[247]; The words "pillar of black pine" and "door of black pine" should be separated from the word "tree" by at least five verses (because the former are used as lumber.); Azalea, White Hydrangea[248] (These are both in the *Trees* category.); Wisteria (This is in the *Grasses* category.); The epithet *ama* *obune*, as in . . . "mooring at Mount Hatsuse" (This clashes with words in the *Waters* category if it is connected with "boat."[249]); The Sao Princess (This is in the *Spring* catgory.), The Tatsuta Princess[250] (This is in the *Autumn* category.), The Mountain Princess (This is in the *Miscellaneous* category.)

[Shōhaku: And none of these last three words is in the *Shinto* category.];

Yoshimoto: The categories *Transience, Lamentation,* and *Reminiscence* (Taken together, these categories should not continue over more than three verses.);

Kanera: If elements of *Buddhism* and *Lamentation* are present in the same verse, then the next verse should be clearly in the *Buddhism* category;

Yoshimoto: Verses ending with particles such as *te, ni, o,* and *ha* should not be linked to each other[251];

Kanera: Eastern Dances,[252] "The Sought-After Child"[253] (These are in the *Shinto* category.);

Yoshimoto: The Shrine in the Fields[254]

[Shōhaku: The same applies here as for the previous item.];

Shōhaku: The *kagura* title "Field Cricket" (The same applies here as for trees and grasses depicted in paintings.[255] But this title should not be used to indicate the *Autumn* season. Instead, the *Shinto* category should remain foremost.); Cherry Seabream,[256] Cherry Shell[257] (These should be in the *Spring* category, as their names suggest.); "Cherry-Blossom Man,"[258] Paddy of Cherry Trees[259] (These are in the *Plants* category.); Plucking Young Greens (This is in the *Spring* category.); Outing in the Fields[260] (This is not in the *Spring* category.); Flowers of Words (the same applying here as for the previous item); To Grow Warmer (The "warming" of the sun is in the *Spring* category.); Warming of the Waters (This is in the *Spring* category.); The verb "to haze over" (This is different from the noun "haze," but since it is little more than an extension of the latter, it does clash with words in the *Rising Things* category. And if it is used with the meaning of "haze" it should be considered in the *Spring* category.); New Leaves (There are two theories about this word: one puts it in *Spring*, the other in *Summer*. When coupled with "blossoms," it should be considered in the *Spring* category. But since *Summer* is the more natural category in most circumstances, the word should in general be put in the *Summer* category.); Hunting by Torch[261] (This word is in the *Summer* category. It involves the hunting of beasts.); Bridge of Red Leaves (Because this refers to a bridge in the River of Heaven,[262] it does not belong to the *Plants* category. In some cases, however, it should be separated from words in the *Plants* category by at least two verses.); First Tide,[263] Colored Birds[264] (These are in the *Autumn* category.); Passion Flower[265] (This is a *Plant* in the *Autumn* category.); Love Grass[266] (This is not in the *Plants* category.); Cloth Dyed in Moss-Fern Design[267] (The same applies here as for the previous item.); Snowy Temples, Frosty Brow (These are not in the *Falling Things* category, nor are they in the *Winter* category.); Night Growing Late, Dew Accumulating (These are not in the *Nocturnal Things* category.); Imperial Lustration[268] and To Purify,[269] *Kawazu,* "frog," and *kawa,* "river," *Tsurenaki,* "hard-hearted," and the negative suffix *naki,* Fishing Fire and Boat, Fishing and Boat or Fisherman, etc. (None of the above clash.); *Yūmagure,* "dusk" (This does not clash with *ma.*[270]); Trickling from the Mountains, Trickling from the Eaves (These do not clash with *Falling Things.*); On the matter of clashing between "old" and "young" (There is no reason these should clash. The difference is only a matter of whether one is young in years or well endowed with them. The situation is not the same as the case between "parent" and "child" or between "bow" and "arrow," which do clash.); Deep and Shallow, Distant and Near (These are words ending in *ki,*[271] and there are many like them. Some say they clash, but they do not—even if used in adjacent verses.); The words "what" and "how many"[272] (These clash in adjacent verses, but otherwise there is no restriction.); The decorative prefix *sa,* as in *saoshika,* "stag," or *sayo,* "night," and the decorative prefix *o,* as in *obune,* "skiff," or *ozasa,* "dwarf bamboo" (the same applying here as for the previous item); Hawk and Hunting (These do not clash in adjacent verses.); The Hearths of the People[273] (This does not clash with words in the *Dwellings* category.); The "opening" of the day and "opening the door" (These clash only in adjacent verses.); Yokawa[274] (This is not in the *Waters* category.); Stand of Mugwort[275] (This is not in the *Mountains* category.); Mountain Rustic[276] (This is not in the *Mountains* category, but it should be separated from the word "mountain" by at least five verses.);

Yoshimoto: Mountain Bird

[**Shōhaku:** The same applies here as for the previous item.[277]];

Shōhaku: Skirt of the Mountain (This need not be counted in the *Mountains* category.); Dragon (There are some cases in which this is treated as if it were a *Beast,* but it is really something quite in a separate category. As the Master said, "This is one thing I know nothing about."[278]); Heron (This is not in the *Waters* category.); Sedge (the same applying here as for the previous item); Boat (Both "seaway" and "ferry boat" are in the *Travel* category, but either one may not be considered so in certain contexts.); Phrases such as *sakazuki no hikari,* "moonlight from the *sake* cup," in which "moon" figures either metaphorically or as a pivot word,[279] should be separated from the actual word "moon" by at least two verses. And such phrases make the verse in which they appear belong to the *Autumn* category; Kickball Garden[280] (It is said that, if this word is used to mean something much the same as simple "garden," then it should be counted as an instance of the latter; but is this not a dubious idea?); The name of one province and the name of another province (These should be separated by at least three verses.); The name of a province and a *Famous Place* (These should be separated by more than one verse.); The name of a provincial "sea"[281] (These are *Famous Places.*); "Named" Gods (These are not *Famous Places.*); The word Azuma, "the East," and Highway, etc. (These two clash.[282]); After using the word Morokoshi, "Cathay," to refer to the mainland, one should use "the T'ang Kingdom" in a second instance.

XVII Seriation

Yoshimoto: *Spring, Autumn, Love* (These categories may continue up to five verses in a series.)

[*Shōhaku: But *Spring* and *Autumn* should not be introduced at all unless they continue over at least three verses. And it is a shame to drop *Love* after only one verse.[283]];

Yoshimoto: *Summer, Winter, Travel, Shinto, Buddhism, Lamentation* (with both *Transcience* and *Reminiscence* counting here as well), *Mountains, Waters,* and *Dwellings* (These categories may continue up to three verses in series.).

XVIII Essences and Attributes

Yoshimoto: Hill, Peak, Cave, Mountain Crest, the Foot of the Mountain, Slope, Mountain Pass, Valley, Island

[**Shōhaku:** This word clashes with *Waters* also.],

Yoshimoto: Barrier-Gates located in the mountains.

Yoshimoto: All of the above are in the Essential category of *Mountains.*

Yoshimoto: Rope Bridge, Cascade, Timber, Charcoal Kiln.

Yoshimoto: Things of this sort are in the Attributive category of *Mountains,* and the same holds for all other words of this kind.

Yoshimoto: Ocean, Bay, Inlet, Harbor, Dike, Shore, Island, Offing, Beach, Tideland,[284]

Shōhaku: Shorebank,

Yoshimoto: Water's Edge, Swamp, River, Pond, Spring, Sandbar.

Yoshimoto: All of the above are in the Essential category of *Waters.*

Yoshimoto: Wave, Water, Ice, Salt, Icehouse.

[**Kanera:** These are in the Attributive category of *Waters*]

[****Shōhaku:** along with other things of this sort.].;

Shōhaku: Even a phrase such as "the source of the pure waters" should be classed in the Attributive category of *Waters;*

Yoshimoto: Floating Wood, Ship, Current, Salt-Burning, Salt Hut, any kind of Waterfowl, Frog, Plover, Iris, Sweetflag, Marsh Reed, Lotus, Water Oat, Sea Pine[285]

[**Kanera:** This last word is in the *Summer* category.],

Yoshimoto: Sea Grass[286]

[**Kanera:** "Young sea grass" is in the *Spring* category and "harvesting sea grass" is in the *Summer* category.],

Yoshimoto: Seaweed, Floating Grass,[287] Fisherman, To Cup Water in One's Hands, any kind of Fish, Fishnet, Pole-Fishing, Washing Water, Water Bucket.

[**Kanera:** All of the above, from "floating wood" on, are in the Neutral category of *Waters.* Since there are some discrepancies on this matter in *Ōan shinshiki,* one must exercise caution here.[288]]

Yoshimoto: Eaves, Floor, Town, Window, Gate, Hut, Door, Pivot Door, Roof Tiles, Wall, Next-Door, Fence.

Yoshimoto: These are all in the Essential category

[***Shōhaku:** Of *Dwellings.*].

Yoshimoto: Hermit's Cavern,[289]

Shōhaku: Shrine (This word is not in the *Dwellings* category.),

Yoshimoto: Garden, Environs.

Yoshimoto: All of these, from "hermit's cavern" on, are in the Attributive category.

Yoshimoto: Person, the personal pronoun "I," *Mi,* or "self," Friend, Father, Mother, the word "who," Border Guard.

[**Shōhaku:** Things of this sort]

Yoshimoto: are in the *Human Relations* category.

Yoshimoto: Master,

Shōhaku: Alone, Go-Between (the same holding here as for the previous items); even the compound "parent and child" is in the *Human Relations* category.[290],

Yoshimoto: Taking the Moon as a Master, Taking the Blossoms as a Master, Scarecrow,[291] The Mountain Princess, Dryad,[292]

Shōhaku: the counter *futari,* or "two people."

Yoshimoto: These are not in the *Human Relations* category.

Kanera: Master of the Blossoms, Friends of the Moon (These phrases are not the same as "taking the blossoms as a master" or "taking the moon as a friend."[293] Depending on how they are used, they may indeed belong in the *Human Relations* category).

CHAPTER FOUR

Reading by the Rules
The Basic Operations of a Rule-Based Interpretation

Words, after speech, reach
into the silence. Only by the form, the pattern,
can words or music reach
the stillness, as a Chinese jar still
moves perpetually in its stillness.

T. S. Eliot
From "Burnt Norton"

AN ILLUSTRATION attributed to the late fifteenth-century artist Tosa Mitsunobu (dates uncertain) gives us a rare glimpse of the *renga* master at work.[1] The drawing, one in a collection depicting the major professions of the time, shows an elderly man with a shaven head and a priestly demeanor sitting upright on his heels in the standard pose of the artist. In front of the poet, seated at a short table on which is placed a folio already partly covered with verses, is a boyish figure whom we may take as a young disicple acting as recorder. Ink-stone and writing brush are at the ready, awaiting the poet's next attempt. Although the scene is hardly a dynamic one, it does serve to confirm the impressions one receives about *renga* composition from written sources. The large formal meetings held in the mansions of the nobility and the warrior elite could be boisterous affairs, as witnessed by the existence of a short document co-authored by Sōgi and Sōi enjoining against lapses in taste and decorum in the *za*.[2] But the greatest *renga* sequences were produced in more sedate and informal surroundings. Marked less by ostentation than by simplicity, the artistic environment favored by the *renga* master shared more with the understated aesthetic of the *wabi* tea ceremony than with the grand spectacle of the court poem-contest.

Records of the *renga* master (or of his students) in the act

Renga Master with Scribe, an Edo-period copy from the late Muromachi *Shichijū-ichi ban shokunin uta-awase*. Caption: "As yet there is not a flower verse in this sheet." Photograph from Gunsho Ruijū.

of reading are, needless to say, more scarce than those showing him in the act of creation. Then as now, reading was a solitary activity, and one that did not inspire much critical or artistic description. Yet, in another way, reading in the fifteenth century—at least the reading of linked-verse sequences—was not at all the sort of activity it is today, in Japan or in the West. For in Sōgi's time *hyakuin* were most often read as a kind of *keiko*, or practical education aimed at the enhancement of creative skills. And this meant, of course, that sequences were generally read by the rules. Although some texts were probably read for pleasure, most were read for instruction in the art. Ancient commentaries (*kochū*), written by poets soon after the works themselves were produced, provide evidence that the most famous sequences of the canon were preserved and read as artifacts.[3] But even here the technical tone of the commentaries is an indication that they were intended primarily for the enlightenment and training of novice poets who had been taught to read, as well as to write, according to shared conventions. Memorized by all aspiring poets, the rules formed a natural grounding point for Muromachi readers. And they can, of course, do the same for readers today.

The most fundamental way in which the rules dictate a reading is by focusing attention back upon themselves, and in so doing creating anticipation about how the variations possible in composition will be realized in a particular sequence. In short, every *hyakuin* read according to the rules is an interpretive exercise. Because each link presents a new situation in which the reader must readjust his views within the bounds of convention, the reader is caught up in a process of constant anticipation, recognition, and readaptation. If presented with a text in which Spring has continued for five verses, he must expect a change, and concentrate his attention on how that change comes about. At the same time, however, he may have to pay heed to sequencing in a lexical category, or to the alignment of "restricted" words, or to possible "clashing" between words in various verses. In this way the rules of composition dictate the focus of interpretation by dominating the reader's mind at the point of impact with the text. And yet all of this is to no thematic purpose—a fact that once more sets the traditional interpretation of linked verse apart from most other strategies of reading. Conventional interpretation of the *hyakuin* is, in other words, self-conscious in ways that one encounters only rarely in the literary world. Aimed at the simple rehearsal of the interpretive process throughout all the verses of a sequence, the expectations created by the rules do not lead to the kind of final thematic summing-up one anticipates in readings of the novel or even lyric poetry; instead, the main goal of a rule-based interpretation of linked verse is the reflexive of one working out the set of problems posed by the rules themselves. Again one returns to the metaphor of play, to the idea of the text as a kind of literary game. The outcome of a classical reading is nothing less than an intellectual correlative to the *jouissance* of poets assembled in the *za,* where the first concern was always with art as a kind of performance.

The means by which a conventional reading proceeds are too numerous to list without reproducing Shōhaku's rulebook. And the most basic of classical strategies—the act of "linking" two independent verses in a way that makes a semantic whole—can perhaps only be studied by recourse to the practical evidence of a *renga* sequence. But a few of the more basic interpretive "biases" implicit in Shōhaku's rulebook can be stated as operations. Not discrete but rather interdependent, these operations complement and supplement each other just as the rules of any game. In the interpretation of any particular verse they cannot always be isolated. For strictly exegetical purposes, however, they may be termed as follows: Categorization, Distancing, Allusion, and Orthodoxy.

CATEGORIZATION

There is nothing implicit about the preoccupation of the 1501 rulebook with categorization. Many of Shōhaku's remarks are no more than notes establishing category; some sections of the rules—"Some Additional Words of Advice," for example—are almost totally lists of words in various thematic and lexical groupings. Thus, categorization is also a fundamental feature of a classical reading. Without preliminary categorization of every verse in a *renga* sequence, in fact, a rule-based reading cannot take place. And, as was mentioned earlier, this categorization is not a casual activity but a highly formalized feature of interpretation that must place each verse in one of the established categories of the *renga* tradition.

The examples of categorization given in Chapter 2 are fairly uncomplicated. But categorization is not always so straightforward. One must learn the dynamics of the operation in order to approach a sequence with confidence. In most cases, the primary criterion used in classifying a verse as to thematic category is content, usually lexical content. Words such as "wood thrush," "fan," "cicada," "trout," or "peony" mark the verses in which they appear as in the Summer category, while "inn," "grass pillow," "path," and "boat" place verses in the context of Travel. This means that seasonal and non-seasonal categories may overlap in some cases—producing verses of Winter Travel, Spring Shinto, and so on—but only when corroborating vocabulary is present. Furthermore, it is only when such vocabulary is absent that overtly thematic considerations come into play in categorization. About this matter Shōhaku is very clear: "Even if the idea of lamentation is present in a verse it will not be considered as in that category if it does not contain an explicit reference."[4] There can be little doubt that by "explicit reference" he means vocabulary. Each verse in a sequence must therefore be taken less as a whole than as a sum of its parts.

One implication of this approach is that it is verses of a

more abstract nature (notably those in the categories Love, Lamentation, and occasionally Buddhism) that present most of the problems in classification. But, even in problematic cases, a conventional reading is not without resources, for the rules themselves do much to dictate category in the context of an actual *hyakuin*. Knowing, for instance, that rules of seriation or intermission prohibit (or, on the other hand, demand) the appearance of a particular category, the reader can hardly transgress against his knowledge. The assumption of a conventional reading, in other words, is that the rules will be obeyed. In linked verse every text is an edited text. And, even when the rules do not seem to offer a final statement on the category of a verse, the concept of *hon'i* can always be called in as an arbiter of last resort. A rustic mountain scene cannot be read as Lamentation, returning to Shōhaku's statement, unless it either employs traditionally "marked" vocabulary or expresses a sense of abandonment, desolation, or deep regret in unmistakable terms. Whereas in other genres categorization may be a rather vague and undirected process synonymous with a general "understanding" of the text, in the classical reading of linked verse it is precisely the opposite. The handbooks and rulebooks of the art, all drawing on classical sources, detail classifications in terms that are relatively unambiguous. The task of the reader resides less in creative thinking than in recognition.

There are other categories in the rules: lexical categories such as Falling Things, Rising Things, Plants, and Animals; and then there are the categories set up by the rules themselves—things that may appear only once in a *hyakuin*, and so on. But here the reader has even less choice in classification. Although works like *Renjugappekishū* and the rulebook of 1501 may disagree on rare occasions, only seldom is a true "judgment" required of the reader. Instead it is the reader's competence that is constantly challenged in the reading of a *renga* sequence—his knowledge of a catalog, an inherited lexicon.

The following link by Sōboku provides a good introductory exercise in the most fundamental of conventional operations.

Wakarete nochi wa	Since that final parting
yume mo hakanashi	even my dreams are fleeting
Katami to ya	One spring blossom—
haru ni hitohana	a reminder of the past,
nokoruran	it remains behind.[5]

Taken as a whole, Sōboku's verse presents a fairly simple scene of a single blossom left as if to remind the speaker of the swift passage of spring: seeing this last remnant of the season, he says, makes all that has passed seem a fleeting dream. Yet the first verse, when read as an independent statement, is clearly not in the Spring category. The word "parting" is found in Kanera's list under Love; and it is also treated as such in Shōhaku's rules.[6]

And, since "dream" too is usually used in the context of a classical tryst,[7] the category of the first verse is clear: it is a Love verse, followed by a scene that recasts it in the context of Spring.

Not all verses fit so nicely into one category or another. But even when vocabulary does not provide an unequivocal indication of theme, decisions follow from other factors. Although the first verse of the following link from Shōhaku's personal anthology contains no word from the Love lists of the rulebooks, it is nonetheless a romantic scene:

Ariake made to	Before break of day, he said—
iishi tsuki ka wa	but is this not the dawn moon?
Namida nado	My tears will not cease
shigi no haoto ni	with the last fluttering beats
tsukisuran	of the cold snipe's wings.[8]

In linked verse, as in the court tradition, only lovers wait forlornly at day-break. Here the scene is of a lonely lady greeting the dawn moon with tears that will not cease even after the proverbial hundred morning beats of the snipe's wings.[9] The presence of the moon in the verse may mean that the categorization must be Autumn Love; that the verse is an expression of courtly romance, however, is beyond dispute.

A final example from a sequence by Shōhaku and Sōseki, this one presenting more problems than are usually encountered in an actual reading, will provide a summary case in categorization:

67	Shibashi bakari ni	For only a brief moment
	kasumu yūtsuyu	haze obscures the evening dew.
		Sōseki
68	Nodokeki mo	So serene a sound:
	mi wa iriai no	yet my own end is also tolled
	kane no koe	by the vesper bell.
		Shōhaku
69	Hitori namida o	All alone I shed my tears
	otosu yamazato	in this mountain village.[10]
		Shōhaku

The first verse in this sequence, containing vocabulary from both the Spring (haze) and Autumn (dew) categories, presents us with our first problem. But its environment within the sequence provides one early indication of what the classification must be. Verses 62 through 66, not translated here, trace the following progression: Autumn (the moon)—Autumn (mist)—Autumn (first tide)—Autumn (red leaves)—Spring (blossoms). In order to avoid breaking rules of seriation and intermission, therefore, the verse must be categorized as Spring. And, as if this were not enough, *Mugonshō* gives a general principle to guide in the interpretation of verses that present "conflicting" vocabulary. Quite by chance, the principle is found under the word "haze":

> When "haze" and "mist" occur together, the category is Spring. In such cases it is common for the verse to be classi-fied according to the more dominant image. "Haze" does not appear in autumn; on the other hand, mist—although gener-ally considered an autumn phenomenon—does appear in the spring as well. In both Chinese and Japanese poetry mist is used in vernal as well as autumnal contexts. Thus, since "haze" is the dominant of the two words, any verse contain-ing both "haze" and "mist" should be classed in the Spring category. And the same holds for other cases of this sort.[11]

Further evidence of such thinking abounds in linked-verse criticism. Thus we have the following by Sōgi in *Sōgi sode no shita* (Notes from Sōgi's sleeve pocket, date uncertain): "If one uses 'snow' and then employs Autumn imagery, the category is still Winter. 'Snow' is dominant."[12] Adapting the principle to Sōseki's verse, Spring must again be judged to win over Autumn as a thematic category. For while dew, like mist, is generally con-sidered an Autumn image, it is nonetheless true that both in poetry and in nature dew falls in spring as well. Haze, to borrow *Mugonshō*'s argument, is the more dominant of the two images in Sōseki's scene.

Because the rules state that Spring must continue as a cate-gory over at least three verses each time it is introduced, a conventional reading will come to the next verse with the expectation of a continuing Spring theme—an expectation answered with the word *nodokeki* ("serene," "calm," or "tranquil").[13] But the verse presents another theme at the same time, which at first one might suppose to be Buddhism. The word "bell" alone, however, is not enough to cast the scene into a Buddhist framework, as we will remember from Shōhaku's comment on that word in the 1501 rulebook.[14] *Mi* (literally "self" or "body" but here translated with the per-sonal pronoun "I"), however, offers a good clue as to the import of the verse. Listed among the words in the Lamentation category in *Renjugap-pekishū*, the word is most often used in reference to the sad state of one abandoned and grieving. Taking the dew of verse 67 as a metaphor for the ephemerality of human existence, then, we can read the link as the musing of an old man as he hears the onslaught of his own demise in the echo of the bell over the spring landscape.

Verse 68 is thus a mixture of Spring and Lamentation, which means that the verse succeeding it may take any one of three options in its own self-definition: it may continue both categories, con-tinue Lamentation and drop Spring, or drop both categories and go on to a new theme. (Rules of seriation dictate no lower limit for Lamentation, and with verse 68 Spring has continued over its obligatory string of three verses.)[15] So the last verse in the sequence is under only one real constraint—that it not reintroduce Autumn, a category dropped only four verses before. Otherwise the verse is limited only by the necessity of linking itself to verse 68, which it accomplishes smoothly by presenting an additional view of the old man already introduced. The link between verses, however, cannot influence the act of categorization, and this fact leaves even a conventional reading in a dilemma brought about by another pair of ambiguous words—"tears" and "alone." Both of these are listed in Love and Lamentation in handbooks; both are used in a variety of contexts that defy easy categorization. Thus the verse in which they appear is an enigma, a true pivot that can be turned to different purposes.

In such cases, a final decision can sometimes be arrived at by reference to the next verse in a sequence, which must bear a thematic relationship to its predecessor, thus constituting a kind of interpretation in itself. But verse 70 in the sequence in question is a Travel verse that provides little help in explaining the "original" meaning of Shōhaku's lonely tears:

Narōran
mine kosu kaze mo
tabimakura

One gets used to it—
the wind crossing the high peak
over my travel pillow.[16]

Sōseki

Here the lonely tears are those of a traveler passing through a remote mountain village. Were the tears clearly those of a recluse or an abandoned lover, the category of verse 69 would come within the bounds of definition. But what called forth the tears of that verse to begin with is in no way suggested by the addition of a traveler to what has become a crowded interpretive scene.

Shōhaku's verse thus retains its ambiguity after all the means of conventional reading have been exhausted: no word places it in a single framework, nor does any rule of progression demand that it be seen in a particular category. Yet, the verse's ambiguity is still limited in scope. The verse contains no seasonal reference, no hint of Buddhism, and no indication of Travel. So it is either an expression of forlorn Love or a more vague lament—two ideas that seem to imply each other in any case. Even if the category of the scene remains undecided, its meaning is transparent. The faint note of uncertainty it leaves with the reader is both product and function of a highly conventionalized mode of interpretation.

These three verses also present a number of words that must be placed into appropriate lexical groupings if the rules are to complete their work: a Rising Thing (haze) and a Falling Thing (dew) in 67, an instance of Human Relations (*mi*) in 68, and another of the latter (*hitori*, "alone"), along with a Dwelling (mountain village), in 69. Here the reader's role is once again limited to recognition. But any account of interpretation in linked verse must avoid the temptation to dismiss recognition of categories as a minor and preliminary act. It is recognition, after all, that grounds the whole idea of competence; without it, the inner complexity of the hundred-verse sequence, which consists largely in the concatenation of categories and the sequencing of words and images, would remain forever obscure. Accurately defined, recognition is perhaps not an intellectual activity, but it is nonetheless a basis for intellection as well as for artistic appreciation.

DISTANCING

No principle is more conspicuously defined in the rules than that of "clashing." "Dream" and "reality" clash if they are not separated by at least two verses, "rain" and "hail" if they are not separated by at least three, instances of the same word if they are not separated by at least five, and so on. One of the more prominent concerns of Yoshimoto, Kanera, and Shōhaku is that synonyms, associated words, and homonyms be kept apart in the progress of a sequence—that they adhere to what a classical reading may call the operation of "distancing."

On the most fundamental level it might be said that the idea of distancing is no more than a restatement of *Yakumo mishō*'s standard of independence. If every verse in a sequence must stand on its own, it can do so only by opening up a space between itself and the verse to which it is linked, not to mention earlier verses. And this is true even of verses that seem on the surface to be linked rather closely together by shared seasonal orientation or associated vocabulary. The following verses by Senjun (1411–1476) and Shōei (fl. ca. 1470) from *Mino senku* (One thousand verses at Mino, 1472) offer a good example of the subtle distancing that occurs between close verses:

Kokoro sae	Our spirits too
chisato ni meguru	range over a thousand leagues:
tsukiyo kana	Ah, moonlit night!
Senjun	

Shigure ato naki	No trace remains of past showers—
aki no kogarashi	only a cold autumn wind.[17]
Shōei	

These are the first two verses of a *hyakuin*, and as such may be expected to share a common context.[18] Both are in the Autumn category, both are basically descriptive, and each develops around one natural image–the moonlit night in Senjun's verse, and the storm winds in Shōei's. Yet a classical reading will see the differences between the verses at the same time that it links them in a complete statement. As close as the two scenes may seem, interpretive strategy can create a space between them as surely as it can join them. To begin with, one can notice the difference in weather, Senjun's verse connoting tranquility and Shōei's the natural violence of a storm; then one can call attention to the change in temporal setting between verses from deep night to a neutral scene without indication of time of day; finally, one can contrast the tone of the verses–Shōei's stark and anxious attitude diverging sharply from Senjun's excited optimism. Thus the relationship between even these closely related verses may be seen as a complex one. As it is the task of every verse in a sequence to enact change, it is the task of a conventional reading to re-enact a corresponding change in interpretation–to search for additions, deletions, and reinterpretations.

Even adjacent verses are therefore affected by the operation of distancing. *Renga* treatises in fact often include a section on *dōi no renga*, "verses of identical meaning"–a pejorative designation applied to verses that simply repeat the tone or content of their predecessors without meaningful change.[19] But there is a limit to the extent to which the idea of distancing is applied to "linked" verses, which must be closely joined if the genre is to be true to its name. It is in the case of verses separated by an intervening verse that distancing comes into play as a fundamental feature of classical interpretation. The whole intent of the rules is to make sure that such verses do not "clash." Consequently, *yoriai* that might be obligatory in adjacent verses are generally ignored when they appear in separated verses, unless of course the elements of the *yoriai* happen to be specifically designated as "clashing" vocabulary in the rules themselves.

That this kind of distancing was a general rule in composition represented by more than the numerous restrictions on "clashing" listed in the rulebooks is apparent from any number of abstract statements made in treatises and handbooks. To give but one example, one may turn to Sōchō's *Nagabumi* (Long letter, 1490), which offers the following as two of the most important working standards of the genre:

> 1. Compose in such a way as not to return to the penultimate verse.
> 2. Link in such a way as to not repeat the identical meaning of the previous verse.[20]

Evidence that the idea of distancing also affected the reading habits of *renga* poets is less easy to discover, although occasionally the influence of the principle is discernible in annotations and commentaries. One case is the following comment taken from Sōboku's verse-by-verse commentary on a sequence composed by Sōchō and himself in 1527:

22	Aware no toki ya furusato no haru	What an impressive season: spring in my native village. *Sōboku*
23	Nobe chikaki kakiuchi sakeru sumiregusa	Within the fencerows along the edge of the field all is violets. *Sōchō*
24	Ueken hito o omou yamabuki	The globeflowers raise a question: who planted them long ago? *Sōchō*

There will of course be those who think this last verse too close (*shitashisugitaru*) to the "native village" of the next-to-last verse. But as a single verse it presents an independent scene. It makes one feel one is looking from a distance at violets and globeflowers planted alongside a fence.[21]

Since Sōboku was one of Sōchō's disciples, one is tempted to dismiss his words as an example of apologetics. But the fact that he feels the need to defend Sōchō against such anticipated criticism is itself evidence of his acceptance of distancing as an interpretive strategy. In adjacent verses, "native village" and the idea of planting flowers would be a natural *yoriai*—and this much Sōboku nearly admits. Because here the verses are separated, however, he is able to insist that such an association is not a *necessary* feature of interpretation. The task of the reader, in other words, is to forget the next-to-last verse and keep to the work of forward movement.

The final effect of distancing on the reading of a sequence is best illustrated by another example, this one from one of Sōboku's own solo works:

38	Kari naku tsuki wa ariake no sora	Geese cry as they pass the moon in the sky of early dawn.
39	Aki samumi sawa no hotaru no mizu kakurete	Amidst autumn's chill the fireflies in the marshes stay low in the pools.
40	Kadota honomeku kaze wataru nari	A breeze passes on its way— just a hint in the paddies.[22]

Most interpretive systems would be tempted to see these verses as constituting a whole scene: an autumn landscape with geese above in the predawn sky and fireflies below in the marshes and paddies. But to read the verses in such a way is also to blunt the effect of the two links that they comprise. If the scenes are fused, in other words, small changes are lost. A conventional reading, for instance, will notice that the last verse has no seasonal reference, thus finding a minor "break" with 38 and 39. Likewise, a reader following the advice of *renga* handbooks will put more emphasis on certain details that a "totalizing" interpretation might over-look, that is, the faint hint of light suggested in the final verse. A holistic interpretation might not see that light because of the overarching presence of the early-morning moon; but a conventional reading, since it must distance itself from the first verse of the sequence, will look for the source of the faint light elsewhere—in the glimmer of roving fireflies. Thus, while the aim of one interpretive approach is to de-emphasize progression and emphasize unity, the aim of the principle of distancing is the opposite—to concentrate interpretive energy on the spaces between verses and to allow for the minute distinctions that create a sense of constant change and variety in the *hyakuin*.

An extension of the idea of distancing that is also of great importance in a classical reading is the linking technique of *torinashizuke*, or "recasting." There is no mention of the concept in Shōhaku's 1501 rule-book, nor is the strategy that develops from it implied so directly as are categorization or distancing itself. Yet the idea of "recasting" verses is, nonetheless, a clear product of the rules' bias against unity. When the reader applies Sōgi's principles of reading so as to neither return to the penultimate verse nor reproduce the meaning of the verse immediately previous, he is in essence submitting to the notion of "remaking" every verse in a sequence. Hence the phrase "just a hint" in verse 40 of Sōboku's solo sequence refers to a hint of wind in its own narrow context, but to the faint light of low-flying fireflies when put into dynamic play with the marsh scene of verse 39. And this is only a minor example of recasting. The following verses by Sōgi and Sōi offer a more arresting and obvious instance of the same phenomenon:

7	Inaba moru	From a makeshift hut
	kariho no io ni	a farmer guards his rice-crop:
	me mo awade	eyes wide through the night.
	Sōi	

8	Yadori ya izuru	Out of his lodging he comes
	hito sawagu nari	in a rush to get away.[23]
	Sōgi	

Here again a direct interpretation recommends itself: we see a lonely farmer, guarding his crops at night, who contrasts his own soli-tude with the warmth of a nearby inn. But such an interpretation lacks complexity; it is too static. Sōgi, who has left us his own annotation of the entire sequence from which these verses are taken, joins the verses in a more interesting and less predictable way. "Unable to sleep because of the crop-guard's voices," he says, "a traveler leaves his inn."[24] Thus the subject of "eyes wide through the night" is no longer the cropguard but the unfortunate traveler, who finds himself awakened by the noise of voices chasing animals from neighboring paddies—a reading that would perhaps not occur to the casual interpreter but which does represent a true "recasting" of the first verse in new terms.[25] And it is also a reading that prepares the reader for what happens in the next verse of the sequence, which Sōgi labels explicitly as a *torinashi* link:

9	Fusu tori o	The hunter's voices
	karikoe chikaki	draw closer to a still bird
	yama no kage	in the mountain shadows.[26]
		Sōgi

In this link the traveler of verse 8 becomes a bird scared into flight by hunter's voices—or such at least is the burden of Sōgi's commentary.[27] And, although this particular interpretation need not be accepted as final or even definitive, it is nevertheless a strong indication of what one *renga* master considered to be a superior way of "linking" verses. A more common-sense approach might simply join verses in a sequence; but a classical reading, based on principles such as distancing, interprets in such a way as to produce changes in meaning from link to link. The idea of an absolute and unchanging meaning is in this sense inimical to the very nature of linked verse as a genre. In the *renga* tradition, meaning is a function of context above everything else: ambiguity is all.

ALLUSION

Since linked verse takes an inherited vocabulary for its foundation, it cannot help but be an "allusive" genre in the general sense. Every conventional association can be traced back to classical precedents, every conventional phrase can be seen as a reference to the court tradition. Even place names mentioned in the rules—Toba in Yamashiro, Naniwa in Tsu, Shiga Mountain, Ikuta Grove, and so forth—carry with them a weight of poetic association that linked verse must bear. In addition to this vaguer sort of allusion, however, most *renga* sequences contain more specific citations from the past. Sōgi puts the matter succinctly in *Asaji* (Cogon grass, 1500?): "No verse in any linked-verse sequence will depart from the vocabulary of foundation poems [*honka*]; but it is important also to understand how to refer to a specific poem."[28]

The allowable sources of allusion are clearly enumerated in the 1501 rulebook, which states that only poems by authors writing before the *Shoku gosenshū* (1251) may be used as foundation poems in the composition of linked verse.[29] This general rule seems to have held for prose sources as well. As statements by poets from Yoshimoto to Sōboku make clear, only Heian tales were admissible for open reference in the *hyakuin*. Although Muromachi literati read and studied *Heike monogatari* (Tales of the Heike), *Tsurezuregusa,* and other great works of their own time, allusions to such medieval classics were not sanctioned in the *za*. The world of linked verse was dedicated to a more distant past.

The very notion of searching the classical canon for possible allusions is itself of importance in the progress of a conventional reading. For one thing, this search helps to bind the genre in a known tradition. Moreover, the stipulation that only works of the distant past can be allowed as sources for allusion exerts a further narrowing effect on a classical reading. This means, to begin with, that the *renga* can never allude to itself; past classics of linked verse, no matter how important in the history of the genre, are simply not available to the reader who reads by the rules. Thus what seems like an obvious relationship between two *renga* verses must pass without notice.

Oshimi kanashimi   Regretfulness and grief:
utsuru haru aki   the passing springs and autumns.
                          Nōa

Oshimikanashimu   They bring us regret and grief—
haru aki no sora   the skies of spring and autumn.
                          Sōgi

The first of these verses, written by Nōa (1397–1471), is from an anthology compiled by Sōgi himself in 1476; it is also one of the verses found in *Shinsen tsukubashū,* another work organized by Sōgi's hand.[30] That Sōgi knew the verse, and knew it well, is therefore beyond dispute. But still a conventional reading of Sōgi's poem will not see Nōa's as a source. Instead, it will indicate a common ancestor in the following lines from the *San t'i shi* (Poems in three styles), a collection of T'ang dynasty poems compiled around 1250.

Day by day I watch from the bank
    as the waters flow by;
Before spring's regret has passed.
    the grief of autumn is upon us.
In the hills, the old house
    is now without inhabitants;
Roaming in the world's dusty ways,
    we have both gone grey.[31]

A popular anthology among Muromachi poets, the *San t'i shi* was a collection that Nōa, a learned art curator and *renga* steward of the shogunal government, and Sōgi, a Zen monk who could boast a long acquaintance with Chinese literature, would have known well. Indeed, it is not unreasonable to assume that both poets had this particular poem in mind when they composed their own laments about the passing seasons. Yet at the same time one cannot believe that Sōgi's verse was written without Nōa's influence. That a conventional reading of the *renga* overlooks this fact is clearly a matter of choice and design. In linked verse, allusion is used as a conservative force—one that confines the search for precedents to a classical canon. It is as if *renga* poets divided their heritage into two large periods: the golden past and the iron present.[32]

The place of allusion in the practical task of interpreting verses is once again illustrated best by reference to a few examples. The first, a verse by Senjun, alludes to a poem by Shun'e (fl. ca. 1160–1180) from the *Shin kokinshū:*

Ibukiyama	At Mount Ibuki
shigururu yuki no	the foothills below the snow
fumoto kana	are bathed in showers.[33]
Senjun	

Miyoshino no	At fair Yoshino
yama kakikumori	clouds gather in the mountains
yuki fureba	and drop their snow
fumoto no sato wa	while below in the foothills
uchishiguretsutsu	villages are bathed in showers.[34]
Shun'e	

Mount Ibuki is a mountain on the border between the ancient provinces of Mino and Ōmi; and the Yoshino Mountains are the site of a famous Shingon temple complex south of the capital in Yamato. Aside from this difference in geographical setting, there is really little difference between Senjun's verse and its twelfth-century predecessor. The allusion, which might more aptly be called an echo, indicates precedent and little more. It becomes a part of a classical reading in only two ways: by legitimizing Senjun's verse in terms of the court tradition and by providing a slight variation that, while of little thematic significance, may still be said to contribute to the verse's overall effect. In a word, the allusion adds to the verse a sense of historical depth but in no way changes its basic meaning.

When a foundation poem is used literally to "link" verses together, the results are occasionally more complex—and certainly a more explicit concern in interpretation. The following verses provide a case in point:

Uguisu tsuguru	A warbler proclaims the dawn
yokogumo no sora	from a cloud-bank in empty sky.
Kasumi yori	From the spring haze
hatsuka amari no	the late crescent moon breaks out
tsuki idete	into the open.[35]

Kensai

These verses are joined by spring imagery (the warbler and the haze) and by celestial imagery (clouds and the crescent moon). But Kensai's intent was no doubt to link the verses by reference to a *Shin kokinshū* poem by Fujiwara no Teika—one of the most famous poems of the entire court tradition:

Haru no yo no	On this spring night
yume no ukihashi	the floating bridge of my dreams
todae shite	has broken away:
mine ni wakaruru	and lifting off a far peak—
yokogumo no sora	a cloud-bank in empty sky.[36]

Teika's poem has elicited as much critical commentary as some of Shakespeare's sonnets, and with equally uneven results. Since it appears among the Spring poems of the collection, it may be read most simply as a rumination on the quick passing of a dream on a spring night. But, along with other poems of Teika's early years, it has often been mentioned as coming close to being a "nonsense poem" (a *daruma uta*), and one can see why. An example of the *yōen* style, which aims for an aura of ethereal and enigmatic elegance, the work simply refuses to yield to paraphrase. The spring night, the floating bridge of dreams (a reference to the final chapter of *Genji monogatari*, which leaves the fate of Ukifune and the ending of the story in uncertainty), and the clouds in the morning sky are all symbols of ephemerality, to be sure; yet the poem is as much a locus of energy as a meaning. The dream and the clouds, both breaking away from their grounding points in a kind of fragile symbiosis, are correlatives of syntactic tensions within the poem that seem ready to explode, reducing the poem to nothing—which is precisely the meaning of its final word, *sora*. And when Kensai alludes to the poem he seems to recognize the undefinable qualities that make it what it is, for he borrows its tensions and its basic form but says virtually nothing about its meaning. Alluding essentially to the poem rather than to its theme, he creates a variation in which Teika's dream becomes a crescent moon breaking into the open as a warbler proclaims dawn; but the *renga* poet stops short of entering into an intellectual dialogue with his courtly forbear. His more prosaic poetic statement is meant as an independent artistic expression that can be appreciated at least partly for the subtlety with which it draws upon a great poem from the past.

No commentary of the fifteenth century lingers over the philosophical implications of an allusion. Even treatises that deal with the proper use of foundation poems in rather detailed terms, works such as Senjun's *Katahashi* (Fragments, 1476?) and Sōgi's *Asaji*, emphasize the technical mastery of allusion as a stylistic technique—that is, whether the vocabulary or the meaning of a poem should be borrowed, which words of a poem should be adopted per se and which should not, and so forth. What is appreciated in allusion is less intellectual than stylistic in nature: originality in treatment, control of linguistic resources, and virtuosity. The aim, it would seem, is generally to appeal to great works of the past for authority. And, since the mainstay of medieval poetry is the descriptive mode, semantic variation by the alteration of a few words or images is a near impossibility. Once again, signification itself, rather than its outcome, receives most attention in the classical interpretation of linked verse. By means of allusion every *hyakuin* is firmly anchored in a classical vocabulary, a classical value system, and a classical frame of semantic reference. But, by passing over these same allusions without philosophical elaboration, the *renga* as a genre releases its energy for service to the real masters of the art—change and movement. Even in the case of the greatest of classical sources, *Genji monogatari*, the rules are quick to remind us that allusion must not be allowed to dominate the progression of a sequence. Similar to most other principles of composition, the most fundamental goal of allusion, both as a technique of composition and as an operation in interpretation, must be variety. Paradigmatic references to a host of past works and writers break the syntax of any *renga* sequence—but always at random and unexpectedly, never according to a preconceived pattern of display.

ORTHODOXY

It might be said that a sense of orthodoxy is at the heart of the rulebook's approach to everything from word-definition to the proper limits of allusion. The idea of orthodoxy, however, is more essential to the classical identity of linked verse than even so bold a statement might suggest. Most fundamentally, it is orthodoxy as an attitude which dictates that the *renga*—once a parlor game—be taken seriously. Binding it always to the poetic values and tastes of the court heritage, orthodoxy as an operation of interpretation directs a reading ideologically. The effect of this binding process is apparent in all facets of the form's conventions. Even the concepts of *yoriai* and *honi,* which form the historical foundations of the genre, testify to an underlying insistence on authority and precedent.

Historically speaking, it is as easy to relate the development of linked verse to the future as to the past. Although a descendant of the court *uta,* linked verse is clearly the forefather of *haikai*—the more light and less decorous form of linked verse that achieved greatness in the hands of Bashō (1644–1694) and his disciples. Evidence suggests, in fact, that from Sōgi's days onward serious linked verse had to share its medieval world with a more boisterous and comic counterpart, a genre that in general obeyed the formal and structural rules of *renga* but allowed itself more freedom in the choice of vocabulary and theme.[37] Yet one of the most obvious biases of a classical reading is the one against *haikai* interpretation. Orthodoxy demands that the serious *renga* be read according to serious conventions.

What this means in the context of a classical interpretation is that most *renga* texts are marked by what one might call ruptures or fissures—places where a likely or possible interpretation is simply not recorded. The following verses from the most famous of all sequences, *Minase sangin hyakuin*, provide an example:

30	Fukikuru kaze wa koromo utsu koe	It comes on the autumn breeze: the sound of robes being fulled.
		Sōgi
31	Sayuru hi mo mi wa sode usuki kuregoto ni	Even on cold days I have only these thin sleeves against the nightfall.
		Sōchō
32	Tanomu mo hakana tsumagi toru yama	An uncertain livelihood: gathering wood in the hills.
		Shōhaku
33	Saritomo no kono yo no michi wa tsukihatete	I had not lost hope, but now my way through the world has come to nothing.
		Sōgi
34	Kokorobososhi ya izuchi yukamashi	What a wretched situation. Is there nowhere left to go?[38]
		Sōchō

When the Minase sequence was composed in 1488, Sōchō, the youngest member of the poetic trio, was just 41 years old, and his contributions to the work have traditionally been criticized for their lack of maturity. Verse 34 has come in for particularly strong comment. Earl Miner, for instance, singles it out as the first in a series of stanzas by the young poet which are in his opinion "over-subjective, moralistically simple or sentimental."[39] And some Japanese commentators, too, have criticized the verse for producing no real change in a series of verses that have become mired (*tsumaru,* or "stuck," being the technical term) in a forlorn thematic development.[40] It occurs to no one, however, to interpret Sōchō's verse in a way that would be entirely natural in some other strategies: as a self-conscious recognition of the poet's predicament meaning "I am at a loss: How can I break out of this pattern?" Such a reading certainly improves our opinion of Sōchō's talents; and it also conforms to our knowledge of his tastes, which tended toward the comic and the informal. But to read the verse as such an editorial comment is nothing if not a *haikai* strategy. Standards of orthodoxy in Muromachi Japan dictated a less playful reading, which is well represented by the words of the earliest commentary on the sequence. There Sōchō's verse is paraphrased to mean: "My hopes dashed and my fortunes ruined, where shall I go now for help?" Thus the speaker is a lonely figure from the *waka* tradition—an abandoned lover, perhaps, or a woodsman not unlike the one introduced in verse 32, but most assuredly not the poet himself, whose personal comment on the linking process would constitute a break in the seriousness of what has been considered one of the sacred texts in the *renga* canon.

Classical readings of *renga* texts are generally marked by the absence of such *haikai* interpretations—or indeed by the absence of any analysis that makes the verse seem unorthodox. Occasionally, however, this attitude of orthodoxy becomes explicit. The diary of Sanjōnishi Sanetaka (1455–1537), for instance, records the complaints of Sōgi about an unorthodox reading of one of his links. Sanetaka first notes the link and then quotes the master's objections:

Namida o ba	Even the demons
oni mo otosu to	are given to shedding tears,
kiku mono o	or so it is said.
Kawara no ame no	Raindrops fall on the rooftiles—
akatsuki no koe	voices in the light of dawn.

People have praised this link; but the way they praise it makes it into *haikai,* and this is most inappropriate. My intent in the verse was to say, first of all, "I too shed tears, just as the rain falls at dawn on the mountain temple." The word "rooftiles" was simply added to link with "demon," as is the custom in linked verse. To attribute feelings (*kokoro*) to the non-human world (*kokoro naki mono*) in this way is after all an established practice of the *waka* tradition.[41]

One can only guess at the substance of the *haikai* interpretation alluded to by Sōgi at the beginning of his self-defense. But one can be sure at least that it centered around the word *oni,* "demon"—one of the striking or conspicuous words restricted by the 1501 rules to only one appearance in a hundred-verse sequence.[42] More than likely the unorthodox interpretation presented that supernatural being in a comical posture, taking the rain of the second verse as his tears. What Sōgi objects to, however, is less the meaning of the link than the humor people see in it. To link "rooftiles" to "demon" is entirely customary, he protests, adding a reference to *waka* precedent for support.[43] And his stance becomes even more clear a few lines later when he reminds Sanetaka (and readers of that courtier's diary) that *waka* poets routinely attribute feelings to other non-human creatures such as birds—the implication being that readers have no business laughing at a purely conventional rhetorical technique. Once more the reader is made aware of an attitude, almost a dogma: verses of serious intent must be interpreted in that same spirit.

That such unorthodox interpretations of serious verses existed in Sōgi's time is evidence of the vitality of *haikai* as an alternative tradition. But ancient commentaries make it clear that in general a sense of orthodoxy governed *renga* interpretation just as surely as it governed formal *renga* composition. More unequivocally than any of the other operations of a conventional reading, the idea of orthodoxy binds linked verse within a well-defined value system. And in so doing it returns us to the very foundation of the genre in the *waka* tradition, reminding us that the first rule of *renga* is that it must remain itself—a conventional text dominated by traditional lines of thought and expression.

ADDITIONAL OPERATIONS

Categorization, Distancing, Allusion, and finally Orthodoxy—these four conventional operations act on each verse of a *hyakuin* to produce a classical interpretation. Yet it would be a mistake to assume that only four operations can account for all the features of a reading. As will become apparent later, any approach to a literary text involves a host of expectations that can be identified only in the actual process of reading. Furthermore, no approach can claim to be complete if it ignores the non-semantic aspects of the text. One can hardly conceive of an interpretation of romantic poetry without due attention to rhythm and rhyme, for instance. Nor can one complete a study of *renga* conventions without mention of that genre's more musical features—pace and pattern.

Jo-ha-kyū

Pace is a feature of most literary genres. We refer to it when we characterize a novel as slow-moving or a poem as tedious or uneven. But seldom do critical considerations of pace go beyond such generalizations, unless they are used to support a dramatic trend—slow pacing being subordinated to the idea of suspense, fast pacing to the idea of resolution, and so on. In linked verse, on the other hand, pace serves a more innocent but nonetheless vital function: rather than drawing attention to thematic events, it simply modulates the speed of the sequence in order to produce maximum aesthetic effect. In other words, it performs a task that is literally musical. When composed, every *hyakuin* was a concert, a performance that demanded pacing. Thus quick-moving seasonal sequences had to be balanced against more complex and deliberate love sequences, and arresting linking techniques had to be moderated by more smooth and uncomplicated transitions. One might even say that the insistence of the rules on a constant concatenation of categories had pacing as one of its unstated ends. Recognition of these variations in tempo and complexity is as much a part of a classical interpretation as recognition of categories and allusions.

Pacing seems to have been an integral consideration in *renga* composition from the beginning. An ideal scheme of pacing was in fact established by Yoshimoto in the late fourteenth century along with many of the other conventions of the genre. Borrowing from the world of court music, Yoshimoto erected a standard for the progress of the *hyakuin:* the first 22 verses were to constitute a quiet prelude (*jo*), the next 23 a break away (*ha*) from that smooth series, and the last 50 an exciting presto (*kyū*) section characterized by fast-moving combinations of simple and complex verses.[44] Although the specifics of this particular breakdown were radically changed by later ages, the basic principle of pacing remained important for all generations of *renga* poets. Every linked-verse sequence followed a pre-established ideal of modulated speed and movement that in some ways took the place of the dramatic and thematic development characteristic of so many other poetic genres.

Although there is no mention of *jo-ha-kyū* in the rulebook of 1501, other *renga* handbooks and treatises of the late fifteenth century prove that the principle was of vital significance to poets of the time. Kanera, Senjun, Sōgi, Kensai, and Sōboku all give it substantial treatment in their works. From what they say we can reconstruct the schemes current in sessions of the Higashiyama era—schemes that are quite different from Yoshimoto's, as the following comparative chart will help to make apparent.[45]

```
              1  10 22          50        78  92 100
Yoshimoto  /---Jo----/-----Ha-------/---------Kyū-----------/
Senjun     /-Jo-/--------------------Ha----------------/-Kyū-/
Sōboku     --Jo---/------------Ha--------------/----Kyū------/
```

Along with these changes in the division of the *hyakuin* into sections, late-fifteenth-century *renga* poets also altered the definitions of ideal pace within each. The *jo*, for instance, was to be a calm prelude to the sequence, and one more restricted in content: Kensai states that the beginning section should contain no verses in the categories Love, Lamentation, Buddhism, Shinto, or Famous Places—which means that most late-fifteenth-century *hyakuin* will begin with seasonal imagery presented in a smooth, simple, and unarresting sequence.[46] And the *ha* section of linked verse composed in Sōgi's time was likewise somewhat different from its fourteenth-century predecessor. It was the more experimental part of the sequence, corresponding in its vitality and variety to the *kyū* section as it appears to have been envisioned by Yoshimoto. But the greatest changes in definition came in the presto section of the *hyakuin*. In Yoshimoto's works this final section was reserved for the outstanding verses of a sequence: a crescendo of activity toward which the entire sequence was designed to build. But later poets came to see the final verses as a return to the smooth pace of the prelude. As Senjun puts it, "When one reaches the last side of the final sheet, one should compose at a quick pace."[47] Restrictions concerning acceptable categories did not apply to the final verses as they did to the first, but no longer was the *kyū* section a climax. Instead, it became a swift conclusion.[48]

Every sequence composed in Sōgi's time therefore presents a fairly consistent reading experience: a smooth introduction; a long series of varied scenes, categories, and linking techniques; and then a final swift denouement. Yet it must be remembered that the denouement is not thematic or dramatic; it simply presents a conclusion in terms of the pace of the sequence.

Originally the concept of pace was introduced into the *renga* in order to ensure the same kind of balance in tempo that the rules are supposed to ensure in thematics and imagery. And the effect of the *jo-ha-kyū* idea on a conventional reading is much like the effect of the other rules in that it creates expectations for the mind to fulfill. Alerting the attention of the reader to one of the non-semantic dimensions of his experience, it points out the many contrasts in the text—the smooth continuities, building complexities, sudden eruptions, twists and turns in style, texture, and technique that together make up a full *renga* sequence. In other words, *jo-ha-kyū* has a truly musical value; it is an expression of certain variations in pace that appeal to the reader for their "kinetic" energy. The enjoyment these variations lend to a classical reading is much like that engendered by a classical symphony that offers a sense of creative play within the conventions of a well-known and recognizable pattern.

In addition to the one created by the *jo-ha-kyū* ideal, any *hyakuin* presents a number of other patterns. Restricted imagery, for instance, is generally spaced with care in a linked-verse sequence. Snow, an image that may appear only four times in a sequence, will create a pattern of appearance; and on a more abstract level, the lexical categories themselves—Falling Things, Rising Things, and so forth—will do the same. This is particularly true for images that traditionally have received special attention in composition—the moon and blossoms. These images, so essential to the whole tradition of Japanese court poetry, are the only truly obligatory images in the genre, meaning that they alone must appear in every *hyakuin*. Thus where and how they appear has always been of interest in a conventional reading. Early rules state that "blossoms" must appear in each of the four sheets of a sequence; and, from at least the time of Yoshimoto, we also find the "moon" appearing in a regulated fashion—once in all but the last side of a sequence.[49] At least eleven verses of any *hyakuin*, then, are the subject of special attention and anticipation for anyone aware of the genre's conventions. A classical reading marks these, creating a pattern that again constitutes a variation on a constant theme.

Ji and Mon

A final pattern of importance in the reading of linked verse involves the placing of what *renga* poets refer to as Ground (*ji*) and Design (*mon*) verses.[50] Borrowed from the vocabulary of ancient weavers, the use of these terms in *renga* criticism also correlates well with the idea of cloth-making. Design verses are the striking verses in a sequence, Ground verses the smooth and ordinary background against which the pattern is placed.

Early *waka* writings on *mon* and *ji* tend to distinguish the two categories by reference to imagery, often defining design attempts as those containing images proper to public composition in poetry contests.[51] Thus poems on blossoms, the moon, snow, and other such decorous images were equated with design composition. And to an extent, this same bias is apparent in poets of linked verse. But it is apparent that in *renga* circles the distinction has always been more based on style and complexity of treatment than on simple content. The following quotation from Yoshimoto's *Kyūshū mondō* (Kyūshū queries, 1376) is instructive:

> What we refer to as Design in linked verse are verses of
> uncommon conception or arresting aspect, or again verses
> that present a bright and captivating style and appear to be
> well-wrought: these are Design verses. Ground verses are by
> contrast unremarkable, background verses.[52]

Yoshimoto says nothing of the moon or blossoms, indeed nothing about imagery at all. His focus is on conception, aspect, and style.

This general attitude is representative of nearly all Muromachi poets writing on the subject. Imagery is important, of course, as it must be in a tradition that emphasizes natural description. Rather than defining some images as innately striking, however, *renga* poets might say that some images—most conspicuously the moon and blossoms—lend themselves better to Design treatment than others. For as they were classically conceived, Design and Ground distinctions rested on a more technical foundation. Hence Sōboku's reference to the following link as a typical Ground effort:

Nowaki seshi hi no	After a day of storm winds,
kiri no awaresa	how impressive are the mists.
	Sōchō

Shizuka naru	A quiet bell sounds—
kane ni tsuki matsu	and reveals a village
sato miete	waiting for the moon.[53]
	Sōgi

These verses present a scene of calm beauty, which Sōboku characterizes as "vaguely captivating" (*nan to yaran omoshiroki*).[54] Yet in most respects the link is hardly outstanding in a technical sense. Despite the presence of images that in other sequences might be given more special treatment (the storm winds, the mists, and the moon), the verses provide a good example of the essence of Ground composition. The scene presented in Sōgi's verse—a village waiting quietly for nightfall—seems a perfect objective correlative to Sōchō's idea of a storm's peaceful aftermath. The link thus contains no unusual turns or twists of rhetoric or meaning. Storm winds give way to the quiet sound of a bell, mist trails through the fields around the village, and the villagers, in the midst of this calm, await the emergence of the evening moon—and all in an effortless link that declines to draw attention to its own artistry.

Even with the assistance of examples like this, it is not always easy to identify the Design and Ground verses in a sequence. Critics differ considerably on the question of how many Design verses should be inlcuded in a full sequence; and there is always a gap between the idea and its realization in a text.[55] But it seems safe to assume that no *hyakuin* will contain more than ten or fifteen truly arresting verses; likewise, those verses should be recognizable by virtue of the intensity of their expression and by their complexity, particularly in linking technique. A final statement on the subject by Shinkei (1406–1475), a true master of Design composition, provides a working credo for those wishing to follow Muromachi standards in definition: "No matter how subtle or profound an individual verse may be, it is meaningless if one does not look back to the verse that precedes it. It is through the manipulation of elements in preceding verses that one has the impression of Ground and Design."[56] Linked verse is an art of association and relation; and Design and Ground verses, too, must be recognized by their approach to the linking process.

Perhaps our most useful textbook on late Muromachi conceptions of Design and Ground is Sōboku's *Kyōchūshō* (Notes from deep within, 1530?), one whole section of which is devoted to examples of the two styles accompanied by analysis and commentary. Although rather lengthy, the passage is of such importance in the development of a proper understanding of Muromachi ideals that it warrants quotation in full.[57]

On the Concept of Ground Composition

1   Soko to shi mo naku   Everywhere the haze spreads out
     kasumu umitsura   over the face of the sea.

     Akebono no   The wild geese cry out
     nami ni wakaruru   as they take leave of the waves
     kari naite   just before daybreak.

The idea of returning geese fits well with the phrase "everywhere the haze spreads out," as well as with "the face of the sea."

2   Tabigoromo   In my travel robes
     kiri wakeyuku wa   I cut through the autumn mists—
     shigi tachite   then up flies a snipe.

     Yamaji ga sue ni   The end of a mountain path:
     tsuzuku araoda   a stretch of barren paddies.

Here "mountain path" has been linked to "in my travel robes I cut through the autumn mists" and "barren paddies" has been used to join with "snipe."

3   Furusato no   In my village home
     kakine arawa ni   the fence all but disappears
     uchikasumu   in the spreading haze.

     Nagare taedae   Water comes down in trickles
     kawazu naku nari   and frogs begin to croak.

The idea here is to link the trickling stream with the country fence. "Frog" links well with spring haze. The same time of year is indicated in both verses.

4   Tsuki honoka naru   The moon shines faintly at dusk
     yūkare no niwa   over a withered garden.

     Naku mushi no   A bug chirps away
     oto mo murasusuki   from a clump of miscanthus
     kaze tachite   as the wind rises.

Miscanthus has been introduced here to link with the word "faintly"–the association being with that word and the plumes of the miscanthus.[58] In a withered garden at dusk, a little breeze begins to blow: this is the conception of the link.

5   Nohara no sato ni   In a village on the moors
     karine suru kure   I bed down at evening.

     Mushi no ne wa   The chirp of a bug
     makura ni chikaki   comes from close by my pillow
     tsuki fukete   as the moon declines.

"Bug" fits well with "village on the moors"; and the link between the idea of the moon and bedding down for the night is obvious. Thus among these five examples none is unconventional; nothing about any of them is unusual. This is the idea of Ground composition. One should master the composition of such verses first and then occasionally produce verses of striking conception or distinctive meaning.

On the Concept of Distinctive Composition

1   Hitotsu zutsu   Leaves accumulate
    chireru ko no ha no   as one after another
    kasanarite   they scatter away.

    Hana yori ato no   After the cherry blossoms—
    hono kuraki yama   a mountain in faint darkness.

In the first verse, "as one after another they scatter away" refers to autumn leaves; but when linked to the second verse the same phrase applies to scattering blossoms. This means that "leaves accumulate" must also be taken in a new way, referring to the spring growth accumulating on the trees after the blossoms have fallen. This is a truly remarkable Distinctive verse.

2   Ushi ya ware ni mo   How wretched to find myself
    arazu nariyuku   going against my nature.

    Koke no to no   Before my moss door
    hana ni fukitatsu   the blossoms are blown about
    yūarashi   by an evening shower.

The word "moss door" indicates the house of a recluse, where one will always find blossoms. The meaning of the link is this: although one who has left the world should waste no thought on blossoms, when he sees them scattered on the winds of an evening storm, the recluse is seized with sadness. "Going against my nature" thus applies to the recluse's wretchedness over his own weakened resolve.

3   Yagate kaeran   Know that this heart of mine
    kokoro to zo shire   has been altered after all.

    Hitoyo to wa   These vows of love
    omoi amareru   are too strong to be confined
    chigiri nite   to one night alone.

Here the first verse expresses resentment toward an unresponsive person. In the link, however, the speaker is pining over a heartless lover and hoping for just one night of union, all the while realizing that he will want to meet her again. He knows that he will have been altered by the experience.

4	Kokoro ni sutenu	Of what value is a soul
	mi wa kai mo nashi	whose heart shows no resolve?
	Tanomaji mo	I vow an end—
	koto no ha made no	but my denials extend
	urami nite	no further than my words.

The first verse presents a recluse who says that there is no value in giving up the world if one does not do it sincerely. But the link recasts the first verse in the context of Love, with the speaker, resenting a heartless lover, vowing not to hope any longer for a positive response. Despite this vow, however, he knows that he will soon be courting again because there is no true resolve in his heart.

5	Kusaki orifushi	Bushes bend toward the earth
	yuki no akebono	before a snowy daybreak.
	Nowaki seshi	The storm is over
	niwa no tsukikage	and moonlight fills the garden
	yoru saete	on a chilly night.

Here the bushes bent down under a burden of snow have been recast in the link as bushes bent after a storm, and the snow of the first verse has been recast as "moon-snow"—moonlight.

Here we find developed a trend of thought already noticed in Yoshimoto, Sōgi, and Shinkei—namely, that complexity of linking technique and conception more than any other factors made a verse stand out in the minds of Muromachi poet-readers. Sōboku's examples of Ground composition are all simple and straightforward in conception, relying totally on conventional associations and commonplace relations for their effect; moreover, each link presents an uninterrupted seasonal or thematic whole, Spring being linked to Spring, Autumn to Autumn, Travel to Travel, and so on. The Design verses he mentions, on the other hand, include some striking leaps: Autumn to Spring, Lamentation to Love, and Love to Lamentation. It would seem therefore that the idea of reinterpretation, of an arresting change in context, is at the heart of Sōboku's understanding of Design composition. His commentary consistently stresses that a Design verse has taken a word in a new way, reinterpreted a phrase, or moved the meaning of a verse in an unanticipated direction. Furthermore, he says nothing about the impressiveness of images in their own right. Links 3 and 4 among his Design examples are in fact included in that category even though they contain no natural imagery at all, implying that complexity and intensity may impress despite the absence of visual symbols. A classical reading must therefore search not simply for the arresting image, but for its reception in the *renga* link.

Another thing that emerges from Sōboku's short comments is an awareness of the kind of excellence that Ground verses can attain of their own accord. That a verse is seen as part of the background does not mean it is inherently inferior in quality, for Sōboku's examples are lacking only in rhetorical complexity and not in beauty. Verse 4 of the Ground verses is taken from Kensai's personal anthology—a sure indication that it was considered a fine example of *renga* art.[59] And the last verse of the category, by Shōei, comes from *Mino senku*, one of the two or three great long sequences in the canon.[60] A complete appraisal of the place of Ground and Design verses in the *hyakuin* thus cannot dismiss the simpler verses of a sequence as of little consequence. As Sōgi reminds us, "The way of linked verse is to ponder deeply, indeed, to brood over one's links. But there are nevertheless times when, judging the needs of a whole sequence, one may produce a simple verse that surpasses a Distinctive verse in total effect."[61]

A Ground verse, then, could impress by its very simplicity. Both Design and Ground composition were, of course, necessary in the composition of a sequence, which would finally present two complimentary patterns: one of well-placed Design attempts, calculated to arrest movement and draw attention; and another, less conspicuous pattern of Ground verses designed to assist in the sequence's flow. The modulation of these patterns, the alternation of the simple with the complex, made for the most prized aesthetic effect.

The recognition of Design and Ground verses remains one of the most challenging aspects of classical interpretation. Not all poets approached the idea in the same way, and modern scholars are even more divided in their definitions. But for at least two reasons it is a feature of the reading experience that is essential to our understanding of linked verse on its own historical terms: first, because it allows us to identify points of concentration within each *renga* text; and second, because it reminds us that every linked-verse sequence was in the beginning a performance that depended as much on musical patterns of pace and emphasis as on more purely semantic factors for its success. Scholars of Renaissance literature are careful to note that criticism of that age tended to focus more on dramatic or emotional impact on an audience than on the production of meaning.[62] The same can be said of the classical approach to linked verse, another medieval genre: if the goal of a reconstructed reading is to create a correlative of the experience of composition, then the recognition of Ground and Design—and of *jo-ha-kyū*—might be said to correspond to the sighs and exclamations of poets in the ancient *za*.

Masks and Personas

In addition to the rules stated in Shōhaku's work, there is a substantial body of lore (*kojitsu*) about the composition of linked verse. There are dicta regarding the proper composition of the first three verses of a sequence, statements about the placement of moon and blossom verses, and even words of advice about how to show proper deference when composing in the presence of high-ranking courtiers.[63] To list such "secondary" conventions would be an impossible task. But one last convention of composition must be mentioned in order to provide an adequate foundation for the interpretation of Sōgi's Komatsubara sequence of 1492. Quite by chance, it is a rule that can best be approached by reference to the subgenre that sequence represents—the *dokugin,* or solo *hyakuin.*

Even in Sōgi's day, solo composition was employed primarily as a vehicle for training novice poets. But in the hands of masters like Shinkei, Senjun, and later Sōgi himself, the subgenre had gained a place in the creative life of more mature poets as well. Perhaps more than any other experience in *renga* composition, the *dokugin* allowed for the true virtuosity of those with a lifetime of practical education in the art. Solo composition thus held a natural appeal for master poets, and it appears to have attracted Sōgi especially. In Sanetaka's diary he is quoted as saying that no other linked-verse poet had composed as many solo works as himself.[64]

The rules for solo composition were identical to those for the ordinary *hyakuin.* Yet solo work can only have been a very different creative experience, more introspective and reflective, less a public performance than a private challenge. In order to compensate for this subjective tendency, some poets developed a habit of punctuating each solo sequence with a number of unusual verses. Senjun, for instance, is reported to have said that, whereas he aimed at the production of smooth and refined verses in a normal linking session, in a solo sequence he always mixed in a few "rough, frightening" scenes—presumably to give the solo sequence a character that might otherwise be lacking in a work composed by a single person.[65] In this one case, however, Sōgi seems to have rejected the counsel of a past master, for his efforts in solo composition are among the most calm and measured of all his contributions to the art. And yet this does not mean that he was unaware of the special problems posed by solo composition. His solution was simply different—another kind of *kojitsu,* also cited in Sanetaka's diary: "One should not let it show that one is composing alone, but instead vary one's styles so as to appear to be seven or eight different people."[66]

Although not in quite the same terms, Sōgi's statement about the composition of solo sequences holds equally true for communal sequences. It emphasizes an unspoken rule of the genre, which one may call the rule of anonymity. For, although one will not find explicit mention of such a convention in the rulebooks, it is clear from a perusal of the *renga* tradition that the poet in the *za* rarely spoke in his own voice. Every sequence rather presents a series of masks—not characters, or even personalities, but types that bear a strong resemblance to the stylized roles of the Nō theatre. As Konishi Jin'ichi puts it in his study of Sōgi, the whole idea of an omnipresent "author" must be abandoned if we are to understand the disjointed progress of a *renga* sequence:

> In linked verse, the thoughts, feelings, and point of view of the author (*sakushu*) are only allowed in the *hokku*, or first verse, of a sequence, which means that in the case of a hundred-verse *renga* the authors' identities are denied in the last 99 verses . . . In a certain sense these last 99 verses are in fact authorless.[67]

In a conventional reading a clear distinction must always be made between the author, whose existence has no certain place in the sequence, and the speaker, who exists as a function of the linking process. This is particularly true in the case of a solo work, where the temptation to see one author behind all the verses is understandably strong. Anonymity, not the search for narrative voice, must guide a classical reading. Rather than the vision of one poet, then, the *renga* represents an entire tradition. And when some writers use verses from an author's opus as biographical evidence—especially in the absence of corroborating information—they are bound to end by confusing mask and man.

The most ubiquitous of *renga* masks is one that is virtually a product of the genre's vocabulary. A faceless courtier, he is adept at the evocation of an aesthetic mood, and his attitude, while calm and somewhat distant, is mildly sentimental. He is educated in the classics mentioned in the rules of the genre, knows poetic geography, and is able to create his mostly descriptive verses without betraying a sense of individuality. The court tradition would call him masculine, for he is a roving consciousness. Nevertheless, he possesses none of the more bellicose traits of men in the Muromachi age. It might be best, in fact, to say that he is merely a figure from the court past, although he must above all be taken as a figment of nostalgic imagination—a construct that functions as a locus of classical perceptions. As the speaker of most of the seasonal verses in a sequence, he is the true anchor of a classical reading. His perceptions and many of his tastes, however, are shared by most of the more easily isolated masks of the *renga* repertoire.

Although few in number and limited in definition, feminine types also play a part in the linking process. The lover—waiting, despairing, remembering, or abandoned—is the most common of female speakers. Then there are the lady-in-waiting and the nun, the passionate lover and the patient wife. Most of the other *renga* masks, however, are in the male gender: the lonely traveler, the old man living in the past, the reluctant recluse, the devout priest, the loyal subject, the lamenting man of letters. The list of masks might be rounded out by mention of a character from

Genji monogatari or *Ise monogatari* (Tales of Ise), or perhaps even of an occasional hunter or woodsman, but still the list is finite. All of the masks are stylized, and all share a courtly demeanor. Peasants, although they are sometimes the subject of conversation in linked verse, seldom speak; but birds have the gift of song. No matter how elegant, however, the warblers and wild geese of a *renga* sequence derive more from the imperial *waka* anthologies and Chinese painting than from nature observed. Indeed, such a statement is valid for all the masks of linked verse, whose purpose is to conceal individuality in deference to a more universalized identity. Above all else, their function is to conceal the poet as a personality, making him a kind of medium through which the speakers of the tradition can obtain a temporary voice. "To reveal art and conceal the artist," said Oscar Wilde, "is art's aim."[68]

Since it demands the displacement of one mask by another in the progress of a linked-verse sequence, one might call this last operation of a classical reading "narrational displacement." By whatever name, its purpose is to disallow the reading of a full linked verse as autobiography. If Sōgi writes his *dōkugin* behind the guise of competing voices and identities, a classical reading is obliged to respond accordingly. Thus the final verses of his famous solo *hyakuin* of 1499 are not spoken by the poet himself so much as by the mask of an old man:

Kumo kaze mo
mihatenu yume to
samuru yo ni

Waking in the night,
I leave unfinished my dream
of clouds and wind.

Waga kage nare ya
fukuru tomoshibi

How like a shadow of myself:
a taper, slowly burning down.[69]

Because Sōgi was seventy-eight when he wrote these lines, the temptation to read them as a truly personal comment is strong indeed. And many commentators, ancient and modern, have done precisely that, seeing the final verse as Sōgi's lament over approaching death. But, within the context of the sequence in which it was written, Sōgi's verse must have a more universal validity when read by the conventions of the *renga* tradition. The idea of lonely brooding, of fond reminiscence interrupted by stark reality, is part of the stylized image of old age employed by every *renga* poet with predictability. Such stereotypes are as much a part of the *renga* ethos as are the thematic and lexical categories of Shōhaku's rulebook. All derive finally from the concept of *hon'i*. Thus it is that the same masks appear in all periods of Sōgi's long career. The following, for instance, is from one of his earliest extant works:

Mi o akikaze
kayou tamakura

Weary beneath the fall wind,
I use my arm for a pillow.

Katabukinu	The moon is sinking
tsuki ni waga yo	and with it my world too declines
fukenuran	into the deep night.[70]

An autobiographical mode of interpretation might be forced to conclude from such a link that Sōgi held the attitudes of an old man all his adult life. But a classical reading can see the link for what it was in Sōgi's time: a product of convention. In the tradition of *renga* composition, the mask of old age was as available to the young novice at forty as it would prove to be to the real old man at seventy-eight.

When Sōgi arrived in Komatsubara in the summer of 1492 he therefore came partly as a representative of a long tradition. Contemporary records show that he was a popular poet among both the elite of the capital and the warrior-barons of the provinces. Yet, as the next chapter will show, his times revered him less as a personality than as a consummate professional. His chief task was to compose linked verse for his patrons; and this was a task that demanded knowledge of a canon and command of both a vocabulary and an established rhetorical technique—in a word, mastery of the conventions of his genre. The solo sequence of 1492 stands as the best measure of his success.

CHAPTER FIVE

The Road to Komatsubara
Renga *and the* Renga *Master in an Age of Strife*

Words, words and words! What else, when men are dead,
Their small lives ended and their sayings said,
Is left of them?

Witter Bynner
From "Correspondent"

T HE SOLO SEQUENCE of 1492 was composed when Sōgi was well advanced in years, but it does not end with the ruminations of an old man. Instead, the final verse of the sequence contains a clear reference to the poet's patron, couched in terms borrowed from the *Analects* of Confucius:

Yumi toru michi zo   This is the way of the bow:
moto o tsutomuru   to work at the foundation.

A less stern statement might have provided a more pleasing ending to a work dominated by subtle descriptions of falling blossoms, dewy fields, and fractured love affairs. But, like many *renga* efforts, the Komatsubara sequence was a commissioned work produced, at least in part, as a supplication to the gods. And Sōgi therefore ends his sequence with what the gods might want to hear—a statement of military responsibility in a time that was much in need of the same.

The rules of linked verse impose upon the genre a sense of strictly defined order. Yet the world in which linked verse thrived was, paradoxically, a world of confusion and strife. There is even some evidence to suggest that Sōgi's sequence of 1492 was composed specifically as a prayer for the future of the Yukawa family on the eve of battle. If this was in fact the case, however, it appears that the prayer went unanswered, for Masaharu was soon to lose his fortunes in a disastrous campaign against the

Portrait of Sōgi, from early sixteenth century. Photograph courtesy of Kaneko Kinjirō

powerful Hosokawa house. After 1493 the ambitions of Masaharu and his clan were in a state of ruin.[1]

Masaharu's were not the only designs to end in defeat during the last decades of the fifteenth century. The period was littered with ruins, many of which found their way into the poetry of the time as powerful symbols of the evanescence of glory. In the following passage from *Oi no susami* (An old man's diversions, 1479), for instance, Sōgi quotes a verse that must have evoked poignant feelings of nostalgia for people of his day.

Sode sae nururu	Even my sleeves are dampened
michishiba no tsuyu	by dew on the grassy roadside.
Inishie no	At Uchino Fields
miya no uchino no	I look out on the old site
hara o mite	of the palace grounds.

To associate Uchino with grasses is customary. Uchino is the former site of the ancient Imperial Palace Compound. Of that once grand palace not a trace remains now, and the feeling one has looking out on the grass growing there is truly such as to drench one's sleeves. Whenever I cross through those fields I am moved again by Sōzei's verse.[2]

Heian records describe the Imperial Palace, located in the north central area of the capital, as a place of grandeur and spectacle. Within its walls were numerous richly appointed buildings—audience halls, chambers of state, living quarters for the emperor and his attendants, chapels, banquet halls, and whole strings of offices where the court aristocracy carried out their government duties. But in Sōzei's verse the compound is a field overgrown with grass. An old "town palace" (*sato dairi*) located east of the original palace grounds, the imperial residence of Muromachi times was a modest enclosure housing only the emperor and his family, which meant that officials of the court government—practically powerless in any case—were forced to conduct business from their own homes. This left only the deserted expanse of Uchino Fields to remind the medieval population about ancient days of opulence and strength. Sadly, however, such desolation was not remarkable in the fifteenth century, when a passerby lacking Sōzei's knowledge of history would have been hard-pressed to distinguish one barren field from another.

Sōgi's century had begun with greater promise. The court of Ashikaga Yoshimitsu (1358-1408), a shogun bred and educated in the ways of the old aristocracy, was bright and forward-looking in a manner courts since the early Kamakura period had not dared to be. Under Yoshimitsu's patronage the arts flourished, particularly Nō drama, *waka* poetry, and linked verse. New trade relations with China's Ming Dynasty (1368-1644) brought exotic items of art into Kyoto, as well as much-needed copper coins into the shogun's coffers. And with the unification of the long-feuding Northern and Southern courts in 1392 came a period of relative peace, especially around the capital itself. The sense of optimism that accompanied these developments continued into the times of Yoshimitsu's sons, Yoshimochi (1386–1428) and Yoshinori (1394–1441), who were also patrons of the arts.

As was so often the case in Japan's medieval age, however, the euphoria of the court classes was based less on a realistic assessment of their situation than on wishful thinking. In the provinces, fighting between warrior factions was not ended by the unification of the courts; and the shogunal government, never truly strong even in Yoshimitsu's time, was unable to control its own vassals, let alone clans in the more distant corners of the country. Not long after Yoshimitsu's death in 1408 the capital itself was being threatened by mounting forces of social and economic change that the nobility were hesitant to recognize and powerless to withstand. The full force of these changes came only some sixty years later, in the form of the Ōnin War of 1467–1477; but signs of social and political breakdown were not absent even in the time of Yoshinori—whose reign was brought to an end with his own spectacular murder during a Nō performance being staged at the home of one of his rivals. Thus, long before the Yamana and the Hosokawa began to pile their bloodied corpses in the Kyoto streets, realistic hope for rejuvenation had come to an end for the Emperor, his shogun, and their noble followers.

In the midst of this upheaval, high culture did not thrive as it had in the early years of Ashikaga hegemony. *Waka* poets, though still powerful as a class, turned more and more to nostalgic pursuits as the Muromachi deterioration progressed; as a whole they seem to have lacked confidence in themselves and in their art. And the courtiers whose ancestors in earlier generations had produced glories of elegant prose from *Genji monogatari* to *Tsurezuregusa* devoted themselves less to acts of creation and more to tasks of preservation—the copying of important texts, the writing of commentaries, and so forth. Yet—and this is another paradox of the age—this did not mean that the court had lost faith in its own heritage. On the contrary, one effect of the degradations of the Muromachi era was to give rise to a whole generation of neoclassicists who were perhaps more dedicated to their common history than had been those who created it. Their calendars often as empty as their storehouses, court scholars, poets, and artists of the late Muromachi period spent much of their time and most of their meager resources in attempts to recreate the past.

It was among these neoclassicists that Sōgi seems to have counted himself, although he could hardly claim affiliation with the court and its traditions by birth. Born into the lower orders of society, he attained his identification only through a lifetime of perseverance and study. So complete was his dedication to the traditions of the court, in fact, that in the end he seems to have disappeared into its recesses, leaving barely a trace of his personality behind. Modern biographers have expended great effort in following his movements as a *renga* master, detailing his many travels, piecing together his relationships with important families in the capital and in the provinces, and listing his honors and accomplishments. Yet in all of this they have done little more than outline his professional life. The man behind the scenes of poetry, scholarship, and travel has always remained elusive.

Some incidents in Sōgi's later life suggest that he was an uncommonly stubborn (or supremely confident) man; other incidents hint at a sense of humor. And more than one scholar has described him as humble and self-effacing, basing such a characterization on his known affection for that most delicate and unpretentious of Japanese flowers, the *yamabuki*, or globeflower.³ But when biographers are forced to use such impressionistic means to define personality, only one thing is really certain: that their subject resists easy definition. Finally, we must admit that, although we know a great deal about Sōgi's career, something about his role in society, and even a little about his tastes in everything from flowers to perfumes, we know almost nothing about the man himself. "His biography is that of a skillful poet," Donald Keene says as if in summary, "rather than that of an interesting man."⁴

Yet there are features of the man's biography that suggest an appealing and forceful personality. We know, for one thing, that he was welcomed in nearly every corner of the country by the greatest political, military, and literary figures of his time. And we also know that he attracted more disciples than any other poet of his generation. Furthermore, his wide-ranging activities as a teacher and lecturer provide support to the idea that he was a man of great charisma. So if the historical record offers us little about Sōgi's personality, it may be that the problem lies with the record itself. One suspects that the final reason for his rather bland showing in the chronicles of his time is a result of the peculiar demands of his profession—for his age clearly saw him more as a *renga* master than as a celebrity. One ruling principle of linked verse, as well as of its practitioners, was anonymity.⁵ As the rules show so vividly, when he composed linked verse the poet entered a preconstituted world that in many ways represented a whole tradition. Thus it may be that Sōgi remains a hazy figure for the same reason that so many other linked-verse poets remain hazy figures: because those who left us his biography—and this number must include the poet himself—were less interested in the man than the poet. There was no cult of personality in fifteenth-century Japan.

Sōgi's life, therefore, appears in the chronicles as the life of a true professional. Complete with lists of appointments, publications, travels, conferences, and lectures, his biography reads like a portfolio. Few details have come down to us about his birth or early life, although we do know that as a young man he spent time as a novice at the Shōkokuji, a Zen temple situated not far from both the Emperor's residence and the larger and more imposing "Palace of Flowers" (*Hana no Gosho*) of the Ashikaga shoguns. Beyond this we can determine that he studied the art of linking under first Sōzei, then Senjun, and finally Shinkei; that he also learned about the court, its literature, and its lore at the feet of famous teachers of his time; and lastly that his education eventually led to his acceptance in both capital and provincial society as a true expert in the literary arts. For the rest, we may summarize by saying that his life followed a pattern just as surely as did his many *renga* compositions. Leaving behind him a score of critical writings as well as several volumes of verse, he spent his professional life in travel between and among the estates of the mighty, where he earned his living as a poet, critic, literary judge, and scholar. He was, in other words, the quintessential Master of Linked Verse.

Maria Corti has argued that "every genre seems to be directed toward a certain type of public, sometimes even to a specific class."[6] For linked verse that class was the middle class of Muromachi society, particularly the literate members of the warrior clans. This is not to deny that the high aristocracy also composed linked verse, of course; indeed, *Shinsen tsukuba-shū,* which as an imperial anthology of the genre provides the most complete picture of the range of poetic activity in its time, contains poems by three emperors, eight imperial princes, and around twenty ministers of state, not to mention works by other courtiers with illustrious names like Saionji, Kanroji, Nakamikado, Asukai, Reizei, Kuga, and Anegakōji. But also listed as contributors to that work are people whose names have a decidedly military ring: Ōuchi, Kitabatake, Hatakeyama, Hosokawa, Uesugi, Saitō, Ikeda, and of course Ashikaga. Dropping down in the warrior hierarchy, one can even find links by such minor barons as Yukawa Masaharu himself. These latter were the most important patrons of the traveling master in the practical sense—the most avid consumers of his critical writings and those who most often sponsored *renga* meetings and contests. Composed in a banquet atmosphere that allowed for more digressions from strict standards of etiquette than did the old *uta* form, linked verse perhaps held a natural attraction for the warrior class. It was a verse form the mastery of which bestowed some status and cultural achievement without demanding an aristocratic pedigree.[7]

Nevertheless, all we know about the conventions of the genre tells us that it was not a plebeian tradition. The link between the court and *renga,* forged in the early Kamakura period, had by the fifteenth century become an indissoluble bond. The categories of composition were the thematic categories of the *waka* anthologies, as we have seen; and the very vocabulary of the genre derived for the most part from court circles. And this meant that the *renga* master, regardless of his own background or biases, carried with him a traditionalist attitude when he traveled his poetic circuit. Even when directed toward the warrior class, in other words, the *renga* delivered a message that was in many ways aristocratic. Yoshimoto is unequivocal on the point:

> Linked verse should never deny the prevailing logic of the world. No matter how interesting a verse may be, if it runs counter to logic it is worthless . . . If the content of a verse is upright and the words subdued, then it will blend with the voices of an orderly world. This is what is meant by *renga* of courtly elegance.[8]

Once again, we see linked verse as a force for order in a disorderly world. There are no overtly political overtones in Yoshimoto's statement, but for him "the logic of the world" (*seri*) was clearly the logic of a hierarchic system that saw the emperor at the apex, followed by the court aristocracy and the military clans—with the latter group bearing the responsibility of keeping the peace. Had he chosen to do so, he could easily have traced such a view of the "natural" order of things back through court chronicles and other sources, both Chinese and Japanese; and he could also have supported his notion of literature as a force for moral order in the universe.[9] But his beliefs are clear all the same. In his age and in the later ages of the genre, linked verse was viewed as a bridge between court and country, between aristocrat and provincial warrior.

Nowhere is this view more apparent than in the example of Sōgi, whose devotion to the court and its traditions is legendary. Coming to artistic maturity just at the time of the Ōnin War and living most of his productive years surrounded by conflict, he seems to have been more sensitive even than his predecessors to the precarious situation in which court values found themselves. Etō Yasusada, drawing attention to verses like the one concluding the Komatsubara sequence, has in fact argued that it was Sōgi's belief in the moral efficacy of his art—which he seems to have inherited not only from Yoshimoto but also from other earlier medieval writings and from the *Analects*—that became one of the foundations of his conservatism.[10] Another way of putting the matter is to say that Sōgi's was a nostalgic sensibility. Kidō Saizō, for instance, notes that *Shinsen tsukubashū*, a product of Sōgi's compilation efforts, mysteriously contains only verses written after the Kakitsu Disturbance of 1441, which was the first great collapse of aristocratic government. Whether this was a conscious bias on the poet's part is beyond speculation, and perhaps the question is even beside the point. The important thing, as Kidō remarks, is that Sōgi chose to include poems that expressed an attitude of nostalgia from within a world of decline and chaos. His design was apparently to produce a lasting evocation of a vanishing world still dedicated to what Yoshimoto called courtly elegance.[11]

Many warrior barons in Sōgi's day no doubt shared his nostalgic sensibility. There is little evidence that they saw the overall message of linked verse as in any way dangerous to their own interests. The *renga* was first of all a literary pastime for the war barons who greeted Sōgi as a teacher and guest. Yet, in the end, the effect of linked verse, with its strict adherence to a classical aesthetic, was to teach standards of beauty and decorum to a class that posed a threat to the court aristocracy even in its most benign manifestations. Ultimately this teaching could do nothing to turn aside the tides of history; but it did at least succeed in holding a place for linked verse in the future order. Miyoshi Chōkei (1522–1564), Oda Nobunaga (1534–1582), Toyotomi Hideyoshi (1536–1598), and Tokugawa Ieyasu (1542–1616)—all generals of the Warring States period which followed the final Muromachi demise—were all amateur *renga* poets and patrons of the art as well. And it was linked verse, not the *uta*, that became the semi-official poetic genre of the Tokugawa shogunate.

Perhaps it was partially a sense of the cultural impact and significance of his role as a *renga* master, then, that motivated Sōgi to pursue his art with such self-effacing ardor. Leaving for his first extended journey in 1466, he lived much of his life on the road, settling down only for relatively short periods of residence in Kyoto or in the mansions of his provincial patrons; death came for him in the middle of a journey in 1502. During the intervening thirty-six years he led a career that has inspired a modern biographer to fill 352 pages with speculations about his birth and upbringing, lists of acquaintances and alliances, and a catalog of artistic accomplishments—all of which, again, serve to obscure the image of the man while creating a strong impression of professional dedication.

The months before Sōgi's trip to Komatsubara in the summer of 1492 paint a similar picture of activity. After spending the warm months of the previous year with friends of the Uesugi clan in Echigo Province, he had returned to the capital in late autumn. There he participated, as always, in *renga* sessions with disciples and noble patrons. As the retired steward of the shogun's *renga* bureau, he also found himself in demand as a teacher and critic and even as a participant in poetry meetings held at the mansions of aristocratic families such as the Konoe. These activities left little time for other projects. But we can surmise that during these months he was beginning to put together verses for his last personal anthology of *tsukeku, Shitakusa* (Undergrowth, 1493), and also preparing notes for discussions on *Genji monogatari* he was to lead at Sanetaka's mansion in the last month of the year. Finally, evidence suggests that he was already involved in the early planning of *Shinsen tsukubashū*.[12]

How long Sōgi stayed on in Komatsubara after the composition of his sequence in the early sixth month is not known. Chances are that he was on his way soon afterward, perhaps moving on to the estates of other friends in other places, perhaps returning directly to the capital.

Records show him as a participant in various literary activities back in Kyoto by early fall; and on the fifteenth of the eleventh month he was a visitor at the home of Sanetaka, where he led that young courtier and a group of students in the aforementioned discussions on *Genji monogatari*. Who recorded the 1492 sequence is not known, but a number of early copies survive in manuscript, the most important being a sixteenth-century text including a verse-by-verse commentary by Sōboku.[13]

Although he seems to have lived on into the second decade of the sixteenth century himself,[14] Yukawa Masaharu appears in the historical records of high society for the last time in an entry by a Kitano Shrine chronicler dated 3/12/1493 – not quite a full year after greeting Sōgi in Komatsubara.[15] Embroiled in regional conflicts between rival factions of the Hatakeyama clan, he ended as one of the casualties of a tumultous age. About the circumstances of his later years, when he was deemed persona non grata in the capital by virtue of his affiliations, one can only guess. The same clan records that have him serving as Sōgi's surrogate father at the time of the poet's appointment as *Renga* Steward, however, are adamant about his literary reputation. Curiously, these records say little about his military exploits but instead ask history to judge him as a master of aristocratic arts. "Yukawa Masaharu was a renowned expert in both *uta* and *renga* in his day," the scribe proclaims, "and among the well-known masters of linked verse there was not one who did not know his name."[16]

The first page of the Komatsubara sequence, as reproduced in *Yōmei sōsho*, Vol. VI, *Chusei waka shū*, p. 359, published in 1978.

CHAPTER SIX

Sōgi's Solo Sequence of 1492

Solitary the thrush,
The hermit withdrawn to himself, avoiding the settlements,
Sings by himself a song.

Walt Whitman
From "When Lilacs Last in the Dooryard Bloomed"

Prologue

Perhaps because they were written more for the consumption of would-be poets than for a general public, most medieval commentaries offer less information than is demanded by a modern reader of linked verse. Sōboku's commentary on the sequence of 1492 is a case in point. The postface to that work reads, "Transcribed just as it was spoken by Kochikusai [one of the poet's pseudonyms] during a rambling conversation one cold night"; and it is indeed a rambling discussion of Sōgi's work. Throughout its pages, Sōboku focuses on the interpretation of links between verses, paying little heed to categorization or other matters that would have posed few problems to the readers of his time. Only in its frequent attention to allusions does the commentary fulfill one of the needs of a classical reading in an explicit way.

A modern approach must attempt a more thoroughgoing analysis of the text. In the pages that follow, each verse of Sōgi's sequence is given in romanized transliteration and in translation, followed by a gloss in which I have attempted to represent the verse as it links with its predecessor. In addition, the thematic category of each verse is noted, along with a list of pertinent conventional associations, lexical categories, and allusions. Notations have been included to indicate the original division of the text into four sheets, with two sides each.

Verses that seem to fit Sōboku's Design or Ground criteria in a clear way have been identified as such. Interspersed among the verses of the sequence are short essays, which provide my own running commentary on the reading itself. Not part of that reading per se, they are intended as attempts to bring the strategies of a conventional interpretation into clear relief.

For a list of abbreviations used in the commentary and essays, see p. 189.

Solo Sequence In One-Hundred Verses Composed On the First Day of the Sixth Lunar Month, the Fourth Year of Entoku [1492]

Sheet 1, Side 1

Nanimichi   ? -path

In Place of a Title

Sōgi's sequence begins with a riddle, a reminder of the ancient *fushimono.* Essentially a "hidden topic" prescribed for the first verse of a *hyakuin,* the riddle poses a question—here, "What kind of a path (way, or road)?"—to which that verse must reply. It is the first obligation of a classical reading to solve the riddle by finding a word in the first verse of the sequence that can form a compound with the word given in the *fushimono.* The possibilities are numerous, but not unlimited, for the system is closed and allows only sanctioned responses. Following is a list of such responses found in a collection authored by Shōhaku and Sanjōnishi Sanetaka in the first decades of the sixteenth century:

> The path home, The Modern Road,[1] The Ancient Road, marketway, stone path, narrow path, path of dreams, The Western Road,[2] mossy path, the path beneath, boatway, distant path, mountain path, bay road, hidden path,[3] hunting path, night-path, wave-path, watery road, path of travel, shrine road, sky-path, cloudy way, cloud-path,[4] parting of the ways, new path, long road, middle way, station road, seaway, river path, path across the moor, cart path, The Gloomy Road,[5] coast-road, forked path,[6] The Heavenly Way, morning path, evening path, The Eastern Road,[7] tollway, hill-path, cliff-path, path in the paddies, The Capital Road, harbor-road, The Way of the Gods,[8] valley-path, the path of the eye,[9] tide-path, The Way of Love, icy path, shady path, The Imperial Way.[10]

1   Kage suzushi   It is cool in their shade,
     nao kodakakare   yet still more tall may they grow—
     komatsubara   this stand of young pines.

Summer (cool: *RGS* 891): Even now it is cool in the shade of the young pines at Komatsubara; but one hopes that they will continue to grow, providing shelter from the summer heat in coming generations.

Plants, subcategory Trees (pines: *RGS* 329)

Allusion: GSS 1373. Composed when the children of the Minister of the Left first donned adult robes,

Ōhara ya   On Mount Oshio
Oshio no yama no   above the Ōhara plain—
komatsubara   a stand of young pines.
haya kodakakare   Swiftly may they grow up tall,
chiyo no kage mimu   casting shade a thousand years.

Ki no Tsurayuki

SETTING THE SCENE

The most fundamental rule of *renga* composition is that a sequence not cohere thematically. Every *hyakuin* thus presents what can be characterized as a random train of scenes, images, and speakers. So when the first verse, the *hokku*, answers the question put by the *fushimono* (?–path = shady path) it is really only acceding to the requirements of the game. The *fushimono* is an anachronism, a superfluity which does not articulate the theme of the sequence, or even the theme of the first verse.

Among all the verses of a *hyakuin*, only the first qualifies as an example of straightforward description. As Sōseki, in a long tradition of commentators and critics, puts the matter, "When composing the *hokku*, one should treat the scenery at the time and place of writing as an obligatory topic . . . and above all else one should include a reference to the actual time of year."[11] A classical reading may therefore make certain historical assumptions based on the content of the first verse of Sōgi's sequence: first, that the work was composed at Komatsubara or at least with the Yukawa estates in mind; and second, that it took place during the summer. Although these facts are corroborated by the colophon of the text, primary evidence is also to be found in the first verse itself. Komatsubara ("stand of young pines") is mentioned by name, and the word *suzushi* ("cool"), listed by Sōgi himself in his *Shogakushō* as one of a number of words appropriate for *hokku* written in the sixth lunar month,[12] is an unambiguous reference to summer. Beyond this, the rather formal tone of the first verse indicates the kind of seriousness that was expected in a "commissioned" work.

The implication of Sōgi's allusion to Ki no Tsurayuki's poem is apparent. The pine, a classical symbol of longevity, suggests itself from the name of the Yukawa family estate: Komatsubara. The last line of the poem is thus a double entendre, with the example of Tsurayuki's poem, taken from the Felicitations chapter of the *Gosenshū* (Later collection, 951), providing an obvious precedent. Whether Sōgi's sincere intent was to pray for the prosperity of his patron's offspring may remain unclear, but that the *hokku* is in the congratulatory mode is beyond dispute. An openly dedicatory verse befitting the occasion of its composition, it sets the scene for the sequence that is to follow.

2	Kaze shizuka naru	The wind stills to a soft breeze
	yūdachi no ato	after an evening shower.

Summer (evening shower: *RGS* 891): After the passing of an evening shower through the pines, the wind dies to a soft breeze. Even now the shade of the trees provides some shelter from the rain, and one hopes that they will continue to grow, giving shelter for years to come.

Associations: evening shower—cool (*RGS* 37), wind—pines; Falling Things (evening shower: *RGS* 37)

3	Machiizuru	The awaited moon
	toyama no tsuki ni	appears over the foothills
	kumo kiete	as clouds clear away.

Autumn (moon: *RGS* 895): After the clouds of a passing evening shower clear away, the wind grows calm and the moon appears over the distant foothills.

Associations: moon—autumn evening (*RGS* 12), clouds—evening shower; Mountains (foothills: *RGS* 81); Rising Things (clouds: *S* XIII, *RGS* 26); Shining Things (moon: *S* XIII, *RGS* 12); Nocturnal Things (moon: *RGS* 906)

4	Fukaki mine sae	Even the deep mountain peaks
	aki zo shiraruru	know that the autumn has come.

Autumn: As the clouds clear away, the moon appears over the foothills, a signal to even the deep mountain recesses that autumn has come.

Associations: autumn—moon (*RGS* 895), mountains—clouds (*RGS* 26); Mountains (mountain peaks: *S* XVIII, *RGS* 902)

The Moon In Linked Verse

What *Tsurezuregusa*, the aesthetic primer of medieval Japan, says about the autumn moon holds particularly true for the *renga* tradition: "The autumn moon is incomparably beautiful. Any man who supposes the moon is always the same, regardless of the season, and is therefore unable to detect the difference in autumn, must be exceedingly insensitive."[13] The spring moon, the summer moon, and, less frequently, the winter moon all appear in *renga* sequences, but only when specifically identified as such. In all other situations the moon signifies autumn, as in the verse above, where, by the moon's symbolic power, the arrival of autumn is announced in even the most wintry mountain regions. Thus the joining of verses 3 and 4 depends entirely on the reader's competence as an interpreter of classical poetic conventions. Only a knowledge of the moon's peculiar significance in the vocabulary of the classical Japanese poetic tradition serves to link the foothills and the mountain recesses in a logical continuum. In other words, the link plays openly on the cultural code, assuming less a knowledge of nature than of the poetic perception of nature current among *renga* poets.

5	Susamajiki	A chilly current—
	nagare ya taki no	perhaps all that now remains
	sue naran	of a distant cascade.

Autumn (chilly: *RGS* 895): A chilly stream of water provides evidence that it is growing cold back in the hills, a sign that autumn has come to the distant mountain peaks. Might this be the end of a distant cascade?

Associations: cascade—mountain peaks (*RGS* 88), chilly—autumn (*RGS* 895); Mountains (cascade: *S* XVIII, *RGS* 88); Waters, subcategory Rivers (current: *S* XVIII, *RGS* 903)

6	Oto wa mumorenu	Its sound will not be suppressed:
	iwa no shitamizu	water beneath the boulders

Miscellaneous: Faint but persistent, the sound of a trickle of chilly water running under the boulders refuses to be stilled. Might it be the very end of a distant mountain cascade?

Associations: boulders—cascade (*RGS* 151); Waters, subcategory Rivers (water: *S* XVIII, *RGS* 903)

RELEASE VALVE

Although the words "boulder" and "cascade" are listed as associated words in *Renjugappekishū*, they do not belong to the same lexical category. "Boulder," in fact, is found nowhere among Shōhaku's classifications. It is one of the many words that form what might be termed the release valve of the *renga* system—the Miscellaneous category.

That boulders and mountains were strictly associated concepts in the minds of fifteenth-century poets is by no means certain. The pseudo-natural association of boulders and cascade, for one thing, would seem to vitiate such a naive view. Nonetheless, the rules make it clear that in the composition of linked verse, at least, boulders need not necessarily be conceived in the context of the Mountains category; and in a classical reading of the genre, only necessary relationships govern interpretation. So verse 6 is in the Miscellaneous category and represents a thematic move away from the autumn mountains.

If this change does not seem radical enough in a genre that champions change, it is perhaps because the natural scene of the verse can so readily be seen as an extension of what precedes it—in a word, because *free* association makes up for a lack of conventional, necessary association, making what is a subtle shift in categories seem to be a very natural continuation. This kind of "blending" of the conventions of a primary language with those of a metalanguage is perhaps a random feature of most literary genres. In linked verse, however, because it promises a temporary way out of the system, such blending is more constant—another way in which the genre draws attention to its own conventionality.

7	Furu mo mada	The snow is falling
	kōru bakari no	but still there is not enough
	yuki narade	to turn into ice.

Winter (snow: *RGS* 898): Although snow is falling, the sound of flowing water coming from beneath a boulder indicates that the stream has not yet frozen over.

Associations: snow—to be stilled (*RGS* 42), ice—boulder (*RGS* 126); Waters (ice: *S* XVIII, *RGS* 126); Falling Things (snow: *S* XIII, *RGS* 42)

PSEUDO-SCIENCE

In the world of *renga* dew falls; it does not accumulate in a process of condensation. Likewise, it is seasonal frost that colors autumn's bright leaves, eventually bringing on the withered aspect of winter. Again, it would be naive to assume that fifteenth-century poets accepted these pseudo-scientific explanations as fact. But poetic accounts of natural phenomena have a reason and force of their own. Here the reasoning is obvious: in Sōgi's perception, it is the accumulation of snow that makes ice. Temperature is irrelevant. Instead, ice is the product of the winter season, the outcome of a process of seasonal change.

| 8 | Kareha ni kakaru | Cutting through the bamboo grass, |
| | sasa wakuru michi | my path comes on withered leaves. |

Winter (fallen leaves: *RGS* 898) Travel (path: *RGS* 901): After making my way through thickets of bamboo grass, I come upon a clearing covered with fallen leaves. The snow is falling on the leaves, but not enough has accumulated to turn into ice.

Plants, subcategory Grasses (bamboo grass: *RGS* 207)

Allusion: KKS 891 (Anonymous)

Sasa no ha ni	As the snow grows deep,
furitsumu yuki no	the tips of the bamboo grass
ure o omomi	droop under its weight.
mutokudachi yuku	And I fear that I too droop,
waga sakari wa mo	with the bloom of youth now passed.

READING BY THE RULES (I)

One of the unspoken assumptions of a classical reading is that the text will not break the rules of the genre with any frequency. In medieval *renga* sessions this assumption was made concrete by the presence of a scribe-referee, the *shuhitsu*, whose duty it was to point out any infractions of the rules and make sure they were corrected. This responsibility seems to have been a heavy one. A sixteenth-century treatise on the art goes so far as to say that "the effect of the sequence, good or bad, rests with the referee."[14]

Although the attendance of a referee during the composition of the Komatsubara *dokugin* is nowhere recorded, his shadow still casts itself over a conventional reading of the 1492 sequence. The most obvious reading of verse 8, for example, displays the *shuhitsu* mentality in action. The phrase "withered leaves" (*kareha*) is not found in Shōhaku's rulebook. However, *Ubuginu* states that the word "wither" may indicate either Autumn or Winter as a thematic category.[15] A classical reading chooses the latter only in order to abide by one of the rules of the genre—that Autumn, dropped as a category only after verse 5, not be introduced again before the obligatory seven verses have passed.[16] Thus the rules move the reading in a certain direction—the direction of orthodoxy.

Sheet 1, Side 2

9	Asadateba	I set off early
	kaze wa sode fuku	as the wind billows my sleeves
	no o tōmi	toward endless fields.

Travel (setting off early: *RGS* 901): After spending a night in the hills on a blanket of withered leaves, I set off in the morning as the wind blows through my sleeves toward distant fields.

Associations: wind—leaves; fields—path; Clothing (sleeves: *RGS* 660)

| 10 | Neshi sato izuku | Where now is last night's haven? |
| | ato mo shirarenu | Not a trace of it remains. |

Travel: When I set out on my journey this morning, endless fields stretched before me. But now, as I look back, I see no trace of the village where I spent the night.

Dwellings: (*sato*, "haven": *S* XVIII)

A CALM PRELUDE

The first ten verses of Sōgi's sequence present an orthodox introduction. The first verse is noteworthy only for its lofty tone; the second verse, in traditional fashion, defers to its predecessor, adding but one simple element to an already quiet scene; and the following verses likewise offer little that is extraordinary in the way of imagery, style, or linking technique.

Numerous precedents for most of the first ten verses can be found in the imperial *waka* anthologies; some precedents are available even among Sōgi's own works. The following verses from *Shitakusa*, for instance, bear a striking resemblance to verses 2 and 3 of the 1492 work:

Samidare suguru	A summer shower passes,
ato no shizukesa	leaving all in quietude.
Kumo kiete	As clouds clear away
tsuki tachinoboru	the moon rises in the sky
yama no ha ni	on the mountain ridge.[17]

Here the temptation to accuse Sōgi of plagiarizing himself is strong. But a more likely explanation for the similarity of the verses suggests itself after reflection on the *hon'i* of the word "shower." According to Ikeda Kikan, concentration on the quiet after a storm instead of on the storm itself is a normative feature of *waka* on the subject from the Heian period on.[18] One might add that the subsequent scene of the moon appearing in a clearing sky is equally conventional as a linking technique. Far from borrowing from himself, then, Sōgi is doubtless borrowing from a long tradition of poetic treatment.

All of the verses in the introductory section are in the Seasonal, Travel, or Miscellaneous categories; none of the topics that generally make for more striking effects—Lamentation, Buddhism, Love—is represented. Even the moon is presented in a Ground verse. So the first ten verses can be said to conform in all ways to the definition of the *jo* ideal as articulated in treatises of the time: a relatively fast-paced, unchecked, and even progression of verses. Not that there are no opportunities to produce more striking effects: *ato*, in verse 2, could easily have been reinterpreted as "ruins" or even as traces left on snow or sand; and almost any of the verses could have been moved in less predictable directions by bringing into play more rare and unexpected associations. (Even an innocent word such as "cascade" boasts *yoriai* as various as "tears," "cherry blossoms," "The River of Heaven," "pillow," and "cloth bleaching.")[19] But these opportunities have been passed over in favor of links based on shared seasonal imagery, temporal or spatial progression, standard associations, and word play.

Thus, with the possible exception of the dedicatory opening verse, all the verses conform to Sōboku's description of background composition. Indeed, if they are unusual in any way, it is for what they lack—spring imagery, for instance, or more allusions. But it is a hard thing to wring sense from absence: no unusual scheme informs Sōgi's prelude.

Rather, the first verses of the sequence strike the reader as vaguely familiar—a product of the strategy of *jo* composition.

Design
11   Miru ga uchi wa   While in my dreams
      mukashi to mo naki   the past was no longer past—
      yume samete   and then I awoke.

Lamentation: (the past: *RGS* 900): While I was in my dreams, the past seemed like the present again, but when I awoke no trace was left of the place I had visited in my sleep.

Associations: dreams—trace; Nocturnal Things (dreams: *RGS* 906)

FROM REALITY TO DREAM

Verses 10 and 11 do not constitute the most arresting sort of linking found in the *renga* canon, but they do represent an example of complete reinterpretation. Verse 10 is a Travel verse when taken on its own terms, and judged in that light the phrase "last night's haven" can only refer to a country village. Looking back from the scene of verse 11, however, one must regard the haven in a new way—as the stuff of dreams, a locus of yearning for the past. The link forces an abrupt shift in context that results in a new and unexpected meaning.

The word *mukashi* ("the past") is restricted to one appearance in a *hyakuin*,[20] one sure indication that it was thought by poets of Sōgi's time to convey a powerful impression. This is perhaps one justification for identifying verse 11 as a Design verse. But *mukashi* alone does not mark the verse as a Design attempt, for such "restricted" words can also be confined in a Ground setting. *Yūdachi* ("evening shower"), the central image in the simple scene persented in verse 2, for instance, is another word in the same category. So it is treatment and conception that make the difference. Verse 2, a simple continuation of the season, imagery, and tone of the first verse, is a conventional Ground scene involving only the most ordinary associations, while verse 11 presents a contrast—a radical change in context, a reinterpretation of the previous verse that besides its technical complexity as a link also presents an intense emotional state. In this way verse 11 proceeds away from the predictability of the prelude to the experimentalism of the *ha* section of the sequence.

12   Sono hito naranu   How saddening is the visage
      omokage zo uki   of one so completely changed.

Love (visage: *RGS* 648): While I slept, my dreams took me back to my lover in the past. Now that I am awake, how saddening it is to confront a countenance so completely changed.

Associations: visage—dreams (*RGS* 648); Human Relations (*hito*, trans. "one": *S* XVIII)

13	Kinō kyō	Until yesterday
	narekite nanika	we had come to be so close—
	nikukaran	why this hatred now?

Love: Until recently we were so close; why now this animosity? How sad it is to confront a countenance so utterly changed.

| 14 | Omou amari no | Know that my resentment comes |
| | urami to o shire | from an excess of worry. |

Love (resentment: *RGS* 899): You ask why my heart has changed so from love to hatred? Know this: my resentment toward you has resulted from an excess of yearning and worry.

DIALOGUE IN LINKED VERSE

Scholars often trace the origins of linked verse back to the so-called "dialogue poems" of the earliest Japanese *waka* anthology, the *Man'yōshū*. And dialogue exchanges are a feature of the genre throughout its history, as evidenced here by a link in which two lovers confront each other, one with a question and the other with an answer.

Sōboku's commentary offers another interpretation of verses 13 and 14, seeing them together as a kind of self-analysis, a kind of interior dialogue in which the first question is directed inward ("Why have my feelings changed so radically?") and the answer is likewise a self-assessment. And since neither verse gives any indication of subject, this interpretation is as defensible as the dialogue approach. Neither of the interpretations exceeds the limits of decorum; neither contravenes the essence of Love as a topic. Thus a classical reading cannot make an unequivocal choice between the two, for when there is in the rules of a genre no obligation for thematic unity, there are correspondingly fewer overt limits on the possibilities of meaning. Conventional interpretation of any link in a *renga* sequence can tolerate a number of slightly differing readings, with some perhaps more interesting or more sensible than others but none doing damage to the integrity of the text as a whole.

	Design	
15	Yoshi ya hana	"Scatter if you will!"
	chiraba sore mo to	I proclaim to the blossoms
	uchiwabite	in my wretchedness.

Spring (blossoms: *RGS* 889): Scatter if you will, blossoms: My worry over your demise has left me with nothing but resentment toward you.

Associations: blossoms—an excess of worry (based on allusion below), wretchedness—resentment; Plants, subcategory Trees (blossoms: *RGS* 307)

Allusion: SGSS 122

Sakurabana	O cherry blossoms—
omou amari ni	in an excess of worry
chiru koto no	over your falling
uki o ba kaze ni	I have abandoned my concerns
ōsetsuru kana	to the scattering winds.
	Fujiwara no Shunzei

16　　Hitori kuraseru　　　　I pass it all alone:
　　　furusato no haru　　　spring in my native village.

Spring: Scatter if you will, blossoms: Waiting will not bring visitors to this village where I spend the spring alone.

Associations: spring—blossoms (*RGS* 889), native village—"scatter, blossoms!" (based on allusion below); Dwellings (native village: *RGS* 176); Human Relations (alone: *S* XVIII)

Allusion: KKS 74

Sakurabana	O cherry blossoms—
chiraba chiranamu	scatter, if scatter you must:
chirazu tote	were you to refrain
furusato no hito no	it still would bring no visitors
kite mo minaku ni	to my lonely native home.
	Prince Koretaka

17　　Kasumu na yo　　　　Haze, don't dim my view!
　　　yama ni nagusamu　　I take comfort from the hills
　　　mado no mae　　　　before my window.

Spring (haze: *RGS* 25): Haze, don't dim my view of the mountains outside my window. They are the only consolation I have as I spend this spring alone in my remote village.

Associations: haze—spring (*RGS* 25); Mountains (hills: *RGS* 78); Dwellings (window: *S* XVIII, *RGS* 171); Rising Things (haze: *S* XVIII, *RGS* 25)

18　　Kiyureba tsuki o　　　When the flame has died away,
　　　tomoshibi no moto　　the moon becomes a lamp.

Autumn (moon: *RGS* 895): When the flame of my taper dies away, the moon serves as my lamp. Haze, don't dim the moonlight that now illuminates the mountains before my window.

Associations: lamp—window (*RGS* 692); Shining Things (moon: *S* XIII, *RGS* 12); Nocturnal Things (lamp: *RGS* 906; moon: *RGS* 906)

Design

19	Tsuribune mo	Men on fishing boats:
	kokoro ya yadosu	even they open their hearts
	aki no umi	to the autumn sea.

Autumn: When the fires go out on their boats, the fishermen turn to the moon for their light. Surely even the hearts of the commonest of men must be purified by the sight of the moon shining on the broad autumn sea.

Associations: autumn—moon (*RGS* 12), fishing boats—lamp; Waters, sub-category Seas (boat: *S* XVIII, *RGS* 904); sea: *S* XVIII, *RGS* 904)

The Good People and the Bad

The word *ushin* has a variety of meanings, the most basic of which is "to be possessed of heart" or, in the preferred terms of the court, "to have a (cultivated) sensibility." In the classical tradition, *ushin* is an aristocratic attainment that people engaged in common pursuits—peasants, woodcutters, herdsmen, tradesmen, laborers—cannot be expected to share. Some phenomena, however, evoke a response in even the common man who has not had a poetic education. In verse 19, even the fishermen, who because of their involvement in a profession that breaks Buddhist injunctions against the shedding of blood might be judged to be particularly far from the ideal of *ushin,* are moved by the autumn sea.

The introduction of such vulgar types into an otherwise uncommon scene thus has the paradoxical effect of emphasizing the transcendant power of certain poetic symbols, in this case the moon and the sea. Shinkei draws on the same power in verses from an earlier day:

Suguru zo oshiki	How we lament their passing—
kari no hitogoe	one lone call from a wild goose.
Funabito mo	Even the fishermen
sao o wasururu	forget about their push-poles
aki no umi	on the autumn sea.[21]

In Shinkei's verse, what impresses the men on their boats is the combination of the wild goose, nearly always a forlorn figure, and the autumn sea. But in Sōgi's verse it is the moon on the sea, an even more potent image because of its Buddhist overtones. If there is a lesson in Sōgi's scene it is a simple one, stating obliquely that the moon is of sufficient power to purify even those who engage daily in the taking of life. The fishermen, after extinguishing the fires they use to attract their prey, turn to the moon—often used as a symbol of Buddhist enlightenment—for their light. But even here it is the poetic rather than the religious dimension that dominates, there being little in the verse to suggest allegory. The chief impact of the verse is to attest to the force of the moon as a quintessential symbol of poetic beauty. And again, as in verse 3, that symbolic power figures in the link between verses, for it is the moon as poetic and not as purely natural object that touches the hearts of even the most vulgar of commoners.

20   Yūnami kiyoku   Over the pure evening waves
       kari wataru sora   wild geese pass across the sky.

Autumn (wild geese: *RGS* 895): Wild geese fly across the evening sky over the clean waves of the autumn sea. Before such a sight even the fishermen must be impressed.

Associations: wild geese—autumn (*RGS* 895), wild geese—boats (*RGS* 365), sky—sea (*RGS* 1); Waters, subcategory Seas (waves: *S* XVIII, *RGS* 904); Animals, subcategory Birds (wild geese: *RGS* 365)

READING BY THE RULES (II)

At this juncture a classical reading is marked by what might be characterized as an omission. For, although the appearance of the wild geese in verse 20 can hardly be judged fortuitous after our introduction to Shinkei's similar scene—especially when we remember that Sōgi himself chose Shinkei's verse for inclusion in *Chikurinshō* (Poems by the poets of the bamboo grove, 1476)—a classical reading will nonetheless not mention the earlier work as a foundation poem. It is as if Sōgi had superimposed his teacher's idea on the already rich conception of his own verse—but all informally, without open attribution. The conventions of linked verse do not allow allusion to the *renga* canon; regardless of how clear the influence may be, Shinkei's verse may be treated only as a precedent. From the viewpoint of the rulebooks, then, Sōgi's wild geese must be said to owe their existence to the autumn sea and to a conventional association and not to a particular example from the past.

21   Harenoboru   The fall mist rises
       kiri no mura ashi   from the reeds along the shore
       kaze miete   where the wind appears.

Autumn (mist: *RGS* 895): Over the evening waves the geese pass across the sky, while along the shore the mist is lifting away, blown off by the wind among the reeds.

Associations: mist—wild geese (*RGS* 29), reeds—waves; Waters (reeds: *S* XVIII, *RGS* 905); Rising Things (mist: *S* XIII, *RGS* 29); Plants, subcategory Grasses (reeds: *RGS* 260)

Design

22	Mata kakimidare	Again it brings disarray—
	shigurete zo yuku	a passing winter shower.

Winter (shower: *RGS* 896): As the wind blows the mist off the reeds along the shore, it blows the dew into disarray, creating the effect of another passing winter shower.

Associations: showers—mist (*RGS* 29); Falling Things (showers: *RGS* 39)

Mist, Rain, Dew, and Tears

A straightforward interpretation of this link might simply see the appearance of the wind in the reeds as a signal that more showers are on their way. But Sōboku follows another line of thought: "The mists of a passing shower clear away from the reeds, leaving all covered with dew," he says, "but as the wind blows the dew into the air, the disarray resembles another shower."

No necessity dictates Sōboku's reading. But it is nevertheless based on a very natural string of associations. The word "dew" (*tsuyu*), although not mentioned in either verse 21 or verse 22, is implied in both "mist" and "showers"—since *tsuyu* may be used to refer to any sort of water droplet. And mist, rain, dew, and tears are all *yoriai*. That there is no dew explicitly mentioned in the verses is therefore a matter of little consequence. As a single scene the rain of verse 22 is true rain, a shower; but in the context of the link, the shower acts as a conceit based on the conventional association of rain and dew. Sōboku's reading is thus a truly poetic one, grasping as it does the full range of metaphoric relationships possible in the context it is given.

Thus it is only a certain attitude that favors Sōboku's reading over the simpler one: the bias for complexity and maximum "distance." And this bias also influences the way a classical reading categorizes verse 22. The rules of 1501 make it clear that the word *shigure* may imply either Autumn or Winter as a category (S VIII), but since Autumn has continued now for four verses, one seeks a change. Fortunately, there is ample support to suggest that *shigure* more often than not does denote the winter season. Kanera, in *Renjugappekishū* 894, says that the word indicates Autumn only when corroborating vocabulary is present; and Sōchō, in both *Renga sahō* (How to compose linked verse, 1489) and *Sōchō kawa* (Sōchō's talks on poetry, 1495), treats the word exclusively as a reference to Winter.[22]

Sheet 2, Side 1

23   Furisuteshi   Who can tug at them now—
      sode wa ta ga yo ni   these sleeves that have cast aside
      hikaruran   the cares of the world?

Lamentation (to cast aside the world: *RGS* 900): Again my life is thrown into disarray by a shower of tears. What is it in human society that still tugs at my sleeves after I have cast the world aside?

Human Relations (who: *S* XVIII), Clothing (sleeves: *RGS* 660)

24   Mi wa shinobu beki   For one in such a state
      inishie mo nashi   there is no past to yearn for.

Lamentation (past: *RGS* 900): Who can attract me to human society now that I have cast aside the world? For one in my position the past is forgotten; I no longer have ties with the world.

Human Relations (*mi*, trans. "such a state": *S* XVIII)

The Reluctant Recluse

The speaker of verses 23 and 24 is a recluse—one who has left the world behind. Ironically, however, one of his identifying characteristics is that he is still attracted by human society. In this respect he represents well the mask of the recluse in the linked-verse tradition. In the *renga*—as well as in medieval *uta*—to abandon the world is an ambivalent act. Seldom fully satisfying, the reclusive life, at least as it is depicted in world of medieval poetry, almost always inspires in its devotees a nostalgia for the society it has cast aside. One might even say that this is the essence (*hon'i*) of Lamentation as a thematic category: it is always the lament of someone who is haunted by reservations, someone who is not quite ready to abandon fully the cares of the world.

25   Izuku nite   Wherever I dwelled
      sumeru mo kari no   my stay was always fleeting—
      kusa no to ni   always a brush hut.

Miscellaneous: No matter where I have lived, my dwelling has always been a temporary one—always a brush hut. So now I have no past to yearn for, nothing permanent over which to reminisce.

Dwellings (*kusa no to*, trans. "bush hut": *S* XVIII, *RGS* 172)

Reading by the Rules (III)

Everything about verse 25 leads us to believe it is spoken by a recluse, especially in light of the content of verses 23 and 24. But a short comment in *Mugonshō* dictates that as a single verse, at least, it be taken somewhat differently: "Words such as 'grass hut' and 'hut under the trees' are not in the Lamentation category. They are words that refer to the rustic life."[23] Thus the brush hut of verse 25 refers to the dwelling of a rustic, but not necessarily to the hut of a recluse.

This is only a technical change, of course, worth mentioning only because it moves the sequence away from Lamentation as a strictly defined category. As it links to its predecessor, then, this statement of a man who now sees all of his past residences as temporary abodes must be read as a forlorn comment on the reclusive life. But the rules have eliminated the *necessity* of seeing the verse in those terms when read by itself. Thus it becomes a possible turning point, a door opened to new varieties of thematic development.

26	Kokoro tomaru wa	One thing alone attracts me:
	tada yama no kage	the deep shades of the mountains.

Miscellaneous: Though I have always lived in a rude brush hut far away from the world, my heart has an attachment for one thing still—the deep shades of the mountains.

Associations: attraction—brush hut (based on allusion below); Mountains (mountains: *RGS* 78)

Allusion: SZS 1135. A poem sent to the Monk Joren after the author had visited him at his hut on Mt. Koya

Tare mo mina	We are all of us
tsuyu no mi zo kashi	as transient as the dew—
to omou ni mo	this I realize.
kokoro tomarishi	But still one thing attracts me:
kusa no io kana	a brush hut in the hills.
	Sanekuni

Design

27	Tori no ne mo	A bird lifts its voice
	yūgure fukaki	as I walk in deep evening
	hana ni kite	beneath the blossoms.

Spring (blossoms: *RGS* 889): Late in the evening when I come to a grove of blossoms deep in the shade of a mountain, a bird lifts its voice in song. I too am moved by the scene before me, and I find my heart drawn by these deep mountain shades.

Associations: bird—mountains (*RGS* 78), deep shades—evening; Plants, subcategory Trees (blossoms: *RGS* 307), Animals, subcategory Birds (bird: *RGS* 335)

THE WARBLER IN THE BLOSSOMS

"Listen to the warbler singing in the blossoms and the frog in the water. Is there any living thing that does not compose poetry?"[24] Thus the preface to Japan's first imperial anthology of *waka* gives to birds the sensibility so often denied to peasants and fishermen. That gift is apparent in verse 27, where the singing bird, no less so than the speaker, is impressed by the blossoms in evening light.

As the following two examples from Sōgi's critical work *Oi no susami* make abundantly clear, blossoms in late evening light seem to have had a special status in the aesthetics of fifteenth-century *renga* masters.

Onowanu iro o	Within my heart it appears:
kokoro ni zo miru	an unexpected color.
Yūmagure	Late in the evening
tomo no mare naru	companions are few
hana ni kite	beneath the blossoms.
	Senjun
Omou to mo	Well may one wish—
wakareshi hito wa	but will those who have parted
kaerame ya	return once again?
Yūgure fukashi	Late into the evening
sakura chiru yama	blossoms fall on the mountain.[25]
	Shinkei

Not all blossom verses are Design verses. These, however, are exceptional by any standards, and Sōgi's verse deserves to be ranked among them. For even if his conception of the blossom scene is somewhat less than unique, as a link his verses present the kind of simple, subtle beauty for which Sōgi is justly famous. Blossoms seen in the evening light are captivating; but blossoms rendered nearly colorless by the dusky twilight of the mountain shadows take on an almost metaphysical aura of mystery and depth. And in this context the bird's call also takes on a new dimension: it is an unseen song in the shadows, not a sight but a sound. Sōgi's verse, then, has about it a certain quality of intangibility, presenting an effect rather than a spectacle.

Design

28	Kasumu o mireba	As I watch the haze spread out,
	tsuki zo honomeku	the moon lights the horizon.

Spring (haze: *RGS* 25): As I stand beneath the trees, enchanted by the sight of haze spreading through the grove in late evening, a bird sings from among the blossoms and I raise my eyes to see the moonlight glimmering on the horizon.

Associations: haze–evening, deep (*RGS* 25), moon–deep evening; Rising Things (haze: *S* XIII, *RGS* 25); Shining Things (moon: *S* XIII, *RGS* 12); Nocturnal Things (moon: *RGS* 906)

29	Haru no yo o	It seems I await
	omowanu hito ya	one who is left unimpressed
	mataruran	by the spring night.

Spring Love (to wait: *RGS* 899): As I watch the spring haze spreading, the moon glimmers on the horizon, about to appear. But still there is no sign of my lover. Can it be that I await one left unimpressed by the spring night?

Associations: spring–haze (*RGS* 25), night–moon; Nocturnal Things (night); Human Relations (*hito*, trans. "one": *S* XVIII)

THE WAITING LADY

Sōgi's *Wakuraba* (Old leaves, 1485) contains the following verse:

Kasumi no komoru	Almost engulfed by the haze,
yama no harukesa	mountains loom in the distance.
Haru no yo o	It seems I await
omowanu tsuki ya	a moon left unimpressed
mataruran	by the spring night.[26]

The precedent is clear. In verse 29, however, the awaited moon becomes a tardy lover. In linked verse, as in *waka*, it is the woman who waits, and typically she waits in vain. Frustration is the essence of Love. Here the lady is seeking a reason for her lover's delay: "Could it be that I await a man who is not impressed by the moon on this spring night?" One cannot help but remark on how typical it is of the classical conception of love that her doubts should center as much on her partner's reaction to the beauty of the spring night as on his romantic ardor. In the classical consciousness, lovemaking and the appreciation of natural beauty were nearly synonymous. Again, a passage from *Tsurezuregusa* comes to mind: "The man who has never hesitated under a cloudy moon on a night fragrant with plum blossoms, or has no memories of the dawn moon in the sky as he started to walk through the dewy gardens inside the palace gate, had better have nothing to do with love."[27]

30	Tomo ni awaremu	To enjoy ourselves together—
	chigiri naraba ya	how I long for such a pledge!

Love (pledge: *RGS* 899): It seems that I wait for one who is unimpressed by the spring night. How I long for a pledge to enjoy nights like this together, instead of waiting alone.

Associations: friend (untranslated)—moon (*RGS* 532), to enjoy time together—spring night (based on allusion below); Human Relations (friend, untranslated: *S* XVIII, *RGS* 532)
Allusion: WRS 27

> Turning the lamp to the wall,
>> we enjoy together the moon on a spring night;
> Treading the fallen flowers,
>> we lament alike the passing of spring and youth.

Po Chü-i

Design

31	Wasuru tote	She vows to forget:
	sore ni narawan	but to follow her in this
	koto mo ushi	would mean only grief.

Love (to be forgotten: *RGS* 899): She says she wants to forget me, but for me to follow her example in this would mean only pain. Would that we had a pledge to enjoy each other instead!

THE ESSENCE OF LOVE

The joys of love are almost unknown in linked verse. The essence of poetic love is rather to suffer, to waste away, to wait. In *Renjugappekishū* 899, the following are among the words given as expressing the "heart" of Love as a topic: waiting, parting, lies, resentment, sleeping alone, to be forgotten, to meet in dreams, River of Tears, to weep, wet sleeves, grief, to yearn for.

Verse 31 is unusual because it constitutes a minor departure from precedent. To lament over being cast aside and forgotten is after all the essence of Love, and to persist against this knowledge would seem to be futile. But this is not to say that the verse is more than slightly unconventional, because there is no confidence in the speaker's hope for a lasting pledge. His statement is tentative in tone and maintains the "proper" attitude toward love—hopelessness.

32	Urami no hodo wa	The depths of this resentment
	shirare koso seme	should already be known.

Love (resentment: *RGS* 899): She wants to forget, but I cannot follow her example. Surely she must know that my resentment will not easily die.

33	Ōyodo ya	Waves at Ōyodo—
	matsu ni yoru nami	you need not break so noisily
	sawagu na yo	on the pinebound shore.

Miscellaneous: The waves of Ōyodo need not break so violently along the pinebound shore. The pines already know full well the depths of the resentment the waves express.

Associations: Ōyodo—resentment (based on allusion below); Waters, subcategory Seas (waves: *S* XVIII, *RGS* 904); Plants (pines: *RGS* 329); Famous Places (Ōyodo)

Allusion: SKKS 1433 (Anonymous)

Ōyodo no	The Ōyodo pines
matsu wa tsuraku mo	show no sign of unkindness
aranaku ni	toward the waves—
uramite nomi mo	but still they draw back at bay,
kaeru nami kana	as if to voice resentment.

34 Miru me mo kurushi   Just to watch it is painful:
kaze ni yuku fune   a boat blown by gusty winds.

Travel (boat: *RGS* 901): It is painful just to watch the boats in the bay being tossed about by the wind. Waves breaking on the Ōyodo shore, you need not storm so violently!

Associations: mirume—Ōyodo (*RGS* 280, and see "Word Games" below); Waters (*mirume: S* XVIII, *RGS* 905); boat [subcategory Seas]: *S* XVIII, *RGS* 904); Plants, subcategory Grasses (*mirume: RGS* 280)

WORD GAMES

Verses 33 and 34 are linked by seashore imagery and sense. But they are also joined by a word game in which the name *mirume,* literally "watching eyes" when verse 34 is read alone, becomes a pivot-word referring also to the sea plant *Codium fragile* in the context of the link. Since the plant and Ōyodo are listed in *Renjugappekishū* 280 as *yoriai,* the word play links the verses beneath the thematic surface.

Links based on such word play, although more common in *haikai* than in orthodox linked verse, figure in almost any *renga* sequence. Demanding virtuosity of the poet and a store of what would otherwise be inconsequential "knowledge" of readers, word play is a method of "hidden" linking that may have little to do with meaning. The games are simply that, games; they contribute a sense of poetic play to the verses in which they appear. In some cases, however, the play of words may be more pertinent to the semantic essence of the link than in others. In verses 32 and 33, for instance, the words joined together in *urami* (a double entendre meaning both "to see the bay" and "resentment") are of some significance in the interpretation of the link. But even without this sub-link the verses would remain joined by other factors. Word play is generally a reinforcement of meaning and not the source of meaning itself.

35	Koegataki	On a rugged path
	aki no yamaji ni	passing through the autumn hills,
	yasuraite	I pause for a rest.

Autumn Travel (crossing the hills: *RGS* 901): As I pause to rest beside a rugged path in the autumn hills, I spy a boat in the distance that seems to be having an easier time of it; but when I see the gusty winds, I realize that travel is easy for no one.

Mountains (hills: *RGS* 78)

Ground

| 36 | Karine no tamoto | The sleeves I spread out in sleep |
| | tsuki zo shioruru | are dampened in the moonlight. |

Autumn (moon: *RGS* 895) Travel (*karine*, trans. "sleep": *RGS* 901): Beside a path in the autumn hills I pause for a night's rest. Beads of dew, reflecting the image of the moon, gather on my sleeves.

Associations: moon—autumn (*RGS* 895), sleep—rest; Shining Things (moon: *S* XIII, *RGS* 12); Nocturnal Things (moon: *RGS* 906)

Sheet 2, Side 2

Ground

37	Io chikaku	Close by my brush hut
	mushi mo wabitsutsu	the insects too seem forlorn
	akasu yo ni	as I await dawn.

Autumn (insects: *RGS* 895): Nearby my brush hut, bugs chirp mournfully as I await the dawn. Tears, reflecting the image of the moon, wet the sleeves of my robe.

Association: awaiting dawn—moon; Dwellings (brush hut: *S* XVIII, *RGS* 194); Animals, subcategory Insects (insects: *RGS* 437)

TEARS, DEW, AND MOONLIGHT

How can sleeves be dampened in the moonlight? By dew, according to the logic that associates beads of water with the round moon. The same logic associates tears with dew and the moon, linking these two verses in the mind of any reader who has been schooled in the conventions of the system. The insect is not alone in crying before dawn. The speaker too weeps, the tears on his sleeves glistening in the moonlight.

| 38 | Yume ni nasareba | If I made it all a dream, |
| | omoi narame ya | what would become of my thoughts? |

Love (thoughts: *RGS* 899): A bug chirps forlornly as I come to the end of a sleepless night spent in yearning for my lover. I could drift off into sleep—but what would then become of my poignant thoughts?

Associations: dream—an insect near my hut (based on allusion below); Nocturnal Things (dream: *RGS* 906)

Allusion: SKKS 1388

Yuka chikashi	Close by my bed
anagama yowa no	he drones on into the night—
kirigirisu	that noisy cricket.
yume ni mo hito no	I had hoped to see my love,
mie no koso sure	if only in my dreams.

Fujiwara no Mototoshi

THE USES OF ALLUSION (I)

More often than not, reference to a foundation poem in linked verse serves primarily to provide a sense of depth and resonance. By nature a very brief form, the *renga* stanza leaves little room for more creative use of allusion—for parody, contrast, or other types of variation. In the link between verses 37 and 38, however, we have an exception. Mototoshi in his famous poem laments the noisy drone of the cricket, wishing that he could be allowed to drift off into the dream world where his lover supposedly awaits. Sōgi's verses make use of this context, but only in such a way as to refute Mototoshi's sentiments. For the speaker of Sōgi's verse seems to value the loneliness of the night itself more than the world of dreams. Thus we see a subtle contradiction of the desire expressed in the foundation poem: a request to stay instead in the lonely midnight world relishing the forlorn cry of the insect and the poignant feelings that cry evokes. The dream world of sleep might bring peace, the speaker says, but it would also bring an end to the forlorn sadness that is the very essence of the experience of love.

39	Ukare tada	Be trying, if you must!
	sarazuwa ii mo	For all converse would soon end
	taetsu beshi	if you were not so.

Love (trying: *RGS* 899): I could drift off into dreams, but then what would become of poignant thoughts? Be as trying as you wish, my love! Better to suffer the pain of your rejections than to see all our contact come to an end.

Associations: trying—thoughts

Poetic Love

Etō Yasusada has written at some length on the usage of the word *ukare* ("unsettling" or "trying") in Sōgi's poetry. His conclusion is that Sōgi extends the range of the word's meaning from anxiety over love to worry over the spring blossoms or excitement over the sight of the autumn moon.[28] In verse 39, however, it seems clear that the speaker is troubled over love. In *Sōgi sode no shita* the master says that it is not right to drop Love after only one verse.[29] And Yoshimoto in *Renri hishō* states, "When it is difficult to decide whether a verse should be Love or Miscellaneous, one should follow the category of the previous verse."[30] This statement is repeated almost verbatim in Kanera's *Renga shogakushō* (Notes for *renga* beginners, 1456), no doubt reflecting the practice of contemporary referees.[31]

After the example of its predecessor, then, verse 39 is best seen as a statement about the nature of Love. In Sōboku's apt words, "This is a forceful expression of the essence [*hon'i*] of love." Anxiety and heartache elevate love from the mundane world to the arena of poetic sentiment; and without the pain, as Sōgi suggests, what attractions would Love hold?

Design

40	Sumaji miyako no	One must leave the capital
	oi no aramashi	before the spectre of old age.

Lamentation (old age: *RGS* 900): When one thinks of old age one must admit that the capital is too unsettled and lively a place to spend one's last years. But for now, be as trying as you wish, great city! If you were not so, people would have little need to maintain contact with each other.

Design

41	Tsurenaku ya	A pitiful sight
	hito goto ni miru	to all whom it now confronts:
	waga inochi	this life of mine.

Lamentation (life: *RGS* 900): My life has become a pitiful sight to all I meet, and so I must leave the capital and live out my days in solitude.

Associations: life–old age (*RGS* 568); Human Relations (*hito*, trans. "whom": S XVIII)

42	Oshimi kanashimu	They bring us regret and grief—
	haru aki no sora	the skies of spring and autumn.

Miscellaneous: My life is a pitiful sight to all it confronts, and the passing seasons now bring only regret and pain.

Associations: regret, grief–pitiful

Allusion: San t'i shi

Day by day I watch from the bank
    as the waters flow by;
Before spring's regret has passed,
    the grief of autumn is upon us.
In the hills, the old house
    is now without inhabitants;
Roaming in the world's dusty ways,
    we have both gone grey.[32]

Tai Shu-lun

THE SOURCES OF ALLUSION (I)

According to the rules of the genre, allusion in linked verse is limited to poems by authors writing before the *Shoku gosenshū* of 1251. Other allusions come from Heian prose classics, particularly from *Genji monogatari* and from poem-tales such as *Ise monogatari* and *Yamato monogatari* (Tales of Yamato, 951). But allusion was not entirely restricted to sources from the native tradition. Chinese poetry and prose were also admissible sources of allusion, and many of Sōgi's sequences contain references to, for instance, the Confucian *Analects*. Most other allusions to Chinese sources, however, are to a small group of works popular in Japan during the Muromachi period. *San t'i shi*, a southern Sung collection of mostly T'ang-dynasty poems, is perhaps chief among them; allusions to it are second in number only to the Sino-Japanese anthology, *Wakan rōeishū* (Collection of songs in Chinese and Japanese, 1013).

The guiding principles behind these limitations seem to have been two: antiquity and recognizability. The esoteric was not admitted into the canon, nor was the contemporary or the common. Thus at times *renga* poets alluded to classical *saibara*, the folk songs of the Heian court, but never to Nō librettos, Muromachi tales, or the famous works of the *renga* tradition itself. To admit such common elements into the genre would have been, in the minds of fifteenth-century masters in particular, to sully a pure world. And although in reality some sullying was inevitable, since the vocabulary of linked verse was not totally synonymous with *waka* vocabulary, the restriction of allusion to temporally remote sources did have a profound effect on the genre.[33] For one thing, it meant that men such as Sōgi kept company with Ariwara no Narihira (825–880), Ono no Komachi (fl. ca. 850), Ki no Tsurayuki (884–946), and the redoubtable Prince Genji, while contemporaries of note—Zeami (1363–1444), Ikkyū (1394–1481), Shōtetsu (1381–1459), and so on—remained forever strangers to the *renga* world.

43	Yamazato ni fureba kusaki o kokoro nite	As time passes on my heart grows with the greenery of my mountain home.

Miscellaneous: As time passes by in my mountain village, I become one with the greenery around my home that regrets spring's end and grows sad with the onset of autumn.

Mountains (mountain: *RGS* 78); Dwellings (mountain home: *S* XVIII); Plants, subcategory Trees (greenery: *RGS* 298)

> *Ground*

44	Omou koto naki mi zo shizuka naru	Empty of disturbing thoughts, my soul grows ever more still.

Miscellaneous: As I settle into life in my mountain home, my heart grows as calm as the plants around me.

Associations: thoughts—heart; Human Relations (*mi,* trans. "my soul": *S* XVIII)

45	Midareshi mo mata osamareru kimi ga yo ni	A chaotic world is again restored to peace in our sovereign's reign.

Miscellaneous: In our sovereign's reign the chaotic world is once again restored to order, allowing my soul to attain peace.

Associations: peace—still

THE MASK OF THE MASTER

The Komatsubara sequence is a dedicatory *hyakuin,* a work that was essentially requested by Yukawa Masaharu as a prayer for the prosperity of his house. And thus Sōgi is in a way obligated to consider the place of his patron as he composes verses for the sequence. In other words, he is obliged to wear the mask of the true Renga Master: the poetic mendicant whose task it is to answer the requests of warrior patrons.

This does not mean that the few congratulatory verses of the sequence are necessarily insincere; it does mean, on the other hand, that those verses follow conventional lines of thought and expression. They are spoken by the *rengashi,* another of the genre's masks. This role is adopted for certain purposes. Here these are obvious: the verse is one of several in the sequence designed to acknowledge the position of the military in restoring peace to the realm. Thus it is that the meaning of the verse centers around its role in the sequence rather than around the false vision of order it presents. Despite the end of the Ōnin War in the late 1470s, the world of Sōgi and his counterparts was anything but peaceful in 1492; and what verse 45 expresses is thus little more than a hopeful sentiment, the origins of which must be sought in precedents from the poetic tradition and not in the war-filled world of late Muromachi politics.

46   Ima yori michi no   From now until journey's end
          sue tadashikare   may our way continue straight.

Miscellaneous: Until now the world has been in war and chaos, but in our sovereign's reign peace has been restored. May the future, too, bring order and uprightness.

Associations: sovereign—way

47   Machimachishi   So long awaited,
          hiyori o kyō no   today it appears off the bow:
          fune ni mite   fair sailing weather.

Travel (fune, trans. "bow": *RGS* 901): The good weather we have been waiting for has finally appeared off the bow today. May our journey from now on continue untroubled and without incident.

Associations: boat—way; Waters, subcategory Seas (boat: *S* XVIII, *RGS* 904)

48   Naminarekoromo   In a moment of respite
          hakanaku zo hosu   I dry my wave-drenched robes.

Travel (traveling robes: *RGS* 901): The good weather I have so long awaited finally appears over the bow today. Now I have a brief moment of respite from the storms to dry my wave-drenched robes.

Associations: waves—boat; Waters, subcategory Seas (waves: *RGS* 904); Clothing (robes: *RGS* 657)

49   Koi wa fuchi   Love is in the pools:
          kari no ōse o   don't put trust in shallow trysts
          tanomu na yo   among the rapids.

Love (pool: *RGS* 639): True love is like a deep pool. Shallow trysts that allow one time to dry one's tear-drenched sleeves cannot be trusted.

Associations: rapids—waves, shallow—moment; Waters (pools: *RGS* 115; rapids: *RGS* 116)

50   Ukihito kokoro   A heart astir with passion:
          nani ka tsune naru   what in it can be constant?

Love (ukihito, trans. "a heart astir . . ": *RGS* 899): What is there in the heart of one moved by passion that can be called constant? Love is in the pools, but the lover is drawn irresistibly toward the shallows.

Associations: What in it can be constant?—pools, rapids (based on allusion below); Human Relations (*hito,* untranslated: *S* XVIII)

Allusion: *KKS* 933 (Anonymous).

Yo no naka wa	In this world of ours
nani ka tsune naru	what is there that is constant?
Asukagawa	In the Asuka River
kinō no fuchi zo	where yesterday there were pools
kyō wa se ni naru	today there are only shallows.

Breaking Away (I)

The prelude of the Komatsubara sequence was dominated by the four seasons. In the back side of the second sheet (37–50), however, there is only one seasonal verse; the rest fall into the categories Love, Lamentation, Travel, and Miscellaneous. This alone is enough to clarify the differences between the principles that govern development in the *jo* and *ha* sections of the fifteenth century *hyakuin*.

But the contrasts go further, for as Kensai says in *Wakakusa-yama* (Mountain of new grass, 1497), the *jo* and *ha* sections should be distinguished by more than differences in subject matter: the prelude should "proceed smoothly, without arresting vocabulary," whereas the following sections of a sequence should be "now pale, now deep in hue, a mixture of Design and Ground."[34] Sōgi's sequence shows just such a pattern, with the unbroken background of the prelude contrasted to the variety of scenes, styles, and techniques of the "breakaway" middle section. Verses 11, 15, 19, 22, 27, 28, 31, and 41 are particularly striking by Muromachi standards; and they are complemented in this latter section by the noteworthy Ground scenes presented in 35–37 and 44. Likewise, linking technique in the development section exhibits great variety. There are links based on allusion (14 and 15, 15 and 16, 25 and 26, 29 and 30, 32 and 33, 37 and 38, 49 and 50), links founded at least partly in word play (32 and 33, 33 and 34), links of natural description (20 and 21, 21 and 22), 27 and 28), links that involve the total reinterpretation of one verse by another (10 and 11, 22 and 23, 32 and 33, 46 and 47), and even a dialgoue link (13 and 14). Most of the verses are joined by related words and imagery, but a few qualify as *kokorozuke*, or links that hinge more on creative interpretation than on conventional association. Verses 38 and 39, for example, share a context only by virtue of the reader's willingness to interpret them together as a statement about poetic love.

The court sensibility informs the verses of the development section, just as it did in the prelude. But new categories produce new masks: the lover dreaming of the past, the recluse, the waiting lady, the lover rebelling against his fate, the old man preparing to leave the busy life of the capital, the weary traveler, and, of course, the mask of the Master of the Art, whose voice is heard once, as if to affirm the occasional nature of the sequence.

The verses following upon the prelude are thus characterized by variety in content, context, texture, and pace, as well as by thematic diversity. But what animates the reader's mind while reading through these verses is not so much the scenes themselves as a sense of anticipation, for reading by the rules means active participation in the process of composition. An allusion can be exploited or abandoned, an ambiguous word taken in one direction or another, a category continued or dropped, a verse taken in a new light, given a new subject, or literally cast aside in favor of a new context. Thus the informed reader's mind must be occupied with the constant questioning imposed by the rules of the game: Will the moon appear now, in Autumn, or will it wait for a Spring night? After three Autumn verses, an equal number of Spring verses, and a Love verse, the options of the sequence are limited—will it move into Travel, Lamentation, Miscellaneous? The classical reader is a consumer in the sense that he is led by the text; but the text's leads are many times ambiguous, and sometimes even false. And, again because of the absence of a governing thematic in the tradition of *renga* interpretation, the reading of any sequence must "explode" its text, drawing attention to fissures, to unexploited possibilities of meaning. One cannot read linked verse without writing in the margins.

Sheet 3, Side 1

51   Itazura no   Among these words
       koto no ha ōki   so many do not hold true—
       fude no ato   vain strokes of the brush.

Love: What is written in these letters but false promises and senseless talk? The heart of one moved by passion cannot be trusted.
Associations: itazura, trans. "vain"—a heart astir with passion

       Design
52   Tsutawarikureba   In transmission it was lost:
       sono nori mo nashi   the Law is not what it was.

Buddhism (the Law: *RGS* 576): As it was passed down through the generations, the Law has been corrupted. Among the words of the sutras, so many seem useless in this world of troubles!
Associations: the Law, transmission—strokes of the brush

The End of the Law

In an earlier age, the *renga* master Ryōa, a rather obscure contemporary of Gusai, responded to a verse similar to verse 51, but in a very different way:

    Itsuwari ōki   So many of them are lies—
    fude no ato kana   these strokes left by the brush.

E ni kakeba	Put in a picture,
hana mo momiji mo	the blossoms and autumn leaves
tokiwa nite	become evergreens.[35]

Both verses, again so similar as to argue for direct influence, may be taken as Love poems lamenting the nature of love letters when taken as individual statements. In the context of the link, however, each takes on a new meaning—a rather playful one in the hands of Ryōa, and a more serious one in the hands of Sōgi.

The destructiveness of the many wars of the fifteenth century was sufficient evidence to convince many that the world had truly entered the period of the End of the Law (*mappō*), when the teachings of the Buddha would cease, of themselves, to have their saving effect. And it was under the influence of this kind of thinking that even some among the high court nobility forsook the older Buddhist establishments and turned to the faith sects which had grown up in the late Heian and early Kamakura periods. Even Zen, the sect of the military aristocracy, saw itself as a tradition outside the scriptures.

Sōgi, a Zen monk by devotion, is therefore not expressing a personal sentiment when he laments the decline of the Law, but rather a widely held belief. For even the most devout of medieval Buddhists—indeed, particularly for them—the state of the world was seen as in a long decline during which even the sutras could not be relied upon as a guide to salvation. One could even go so far as to put this seeming heresy in the mouth of a monk, for whom the vanity of conventional devotion would be most apparent in an age of war and degradation.

53	Kiku ya tare	Who will hear it?
	tōyamadera no	The temple bell from the hills
	kane no oto	off in the distance.

Buddhism (temple: *RGS* 574): In the centuries of its transmission the Law has lost its power. Who now will hear the temple bell from the hills in the distance?

Associations: bell—Law (*RGY* 278), hear—transmission; Mountains (hills: *RGS* 78), Human Relations (who: *S* XVIII)

Ground

54	Akatsuki tsuki wa	The moon before break of day—
	ware nomi zo mishi	I gazed upon it alone.

Autumn (moon: *RGS* 895): I was alone when I gazed at the moon before daybreak. Who else, then, will hear the morning bell from the temple off in the distance?

Associations: daybreak—bell (*RGS* 66); Shining Things (moon: *S* XIII, *RGS* 12); Nocturnal Things (moon: *RGS* 906); Human Relations (I: *S* XVIII)

THE "ESSENCE" OF LINKED VERSE

In *Oi no susami*, Sōgi makes a declaration that breaks some-what with the tradition of his art: "To compose in response to Ground verses, this is the most essential facet of *renga* art."[36] Many earlier poets had concentrated on the composition of Design verses, but Sōgi's approach to the art was to first master the simple, inconspicuous scene and then to go on to the more complex. Hence, for late Muromachi poets, the idea of Ground composition took on a positive value of its own. In the time of Bashō, the great Edo practitioner of *haikai no renga*, Ground scenes were in fact to become the main focus of attention in the art.

The process by which *mumon* (Ground) replaced *umon* (Design) as a primary value in the *renga* began in Sōgi's own time, and in Sōgi's own aesthetic. And verse 54 presents a good example of the effect of Ground composition on a *hyakuin*. By Sōboku's standards the verse is in all respects a background attempt: it continues the general scene of its predecessor, introduces no reinterpretation, and contains no unusual vocabulary or reasoning. In a word, it is a simple, unpretentious *extension* of the verse to which it responds. But by its very simplicity and its easy and natural reply to the demands set by its predecessor (the verse subtly adds a speaker and a time context to the previous landscape), the verse has an impressiveness all its own. However unobtrusive, such verses form a "pattern" as recognizable as that formed by the Design.

Ground
55   Ayaniku no   Why must it be now
       aki no sora nado   that rain clouds start to gather
       shigururan   in the autumn sky?

Autumn: I gazed upon the pre-dawn moon by myself, wishing that I could share my experience with a friend. Why must the autumn sky choose now to cloud up and threaten rain?

Associations: autumn—moon (*RGS* 895), rain clouds—moon (based on allusion below); Falling Things (*shigure*, trans. "rain clouds": *RGS* 39)

Allusion: SKS 324

       Kaminazuki   In the Godless Month
       ariake no sora no   the rain clouds start to gather
       shigururu o   in the pre-dawn sky.
       mata ware naranu   Who else besides myself
       hito ya miruramu   will be up to see this moon?

                            Akazome Emon

Ground
56   Tsuyukeku wakuru   My way ahead uncertain,
       nobe no yukusue   I cut through dewy fields.

Autumn (dewy: *RGS* 895) Travel (to cross fields: *RGS* 901): As I make my way across the dewy fields, I look ahead and see the autumn sky clouding up. Why must it choose now to threaten rain?
Associations: dew—rain (*RGS* 38), dewy—autumn (*RGS* 895); Falling Things (dew: *S* XIII, *RGS* 38)

TRAVEL IN THE FIELDS OF POETRY

In the world of linked verse, the word "fields" is synonymous with the idea of Travel, and Travel is a lonely experience. The *renga* traveler is nearly always alone; the fields he crosses are a kind of unfamiliar space, desolate and forbidding.

To an extent this impression of travel was probably the product of the experience of *renga* masters making their rounds among the provinces. Sōgi's own *Shirakawa kikō* (Journey to Shirakawa, 1468), his record of a journey to the eastern frontier during his early days as a professional poet, gives an account of his bewilderment in crossing the moors on his way to the Shirakawa Barrier.[37] Fear of bandits or of losing one's way in the tall grasses was no doubt a very real thing for itinerant poets. But even in Sōgi's travel diaries, which recount actual journeys in great detail, there is much that smacks of conventional decoration. The idea of travel away from the capital as a melancholy experience figures in court poetry as early as the *Man'yōshū*, after all, and Bashō, Japan's most famous traveler, looks back not only to Sōgi but to Saigyō (1118–1190) and Nōin (998–1050) as the sources of his own sober view of the sojourner's lot. Perhaps one could even trace the *hon'i* of literary travel back further—to folk poems and the songs of eastern border guards. What is important, however, is that Sōgi's traveler be seen for what in the larger sense he is: a type, a poetic traveler with predictable responses to his environment.

57	Furusato mo	If my native home
	kakaraba yoshi ya	is like the rest, so be it!
	tabi no kure	Evening on the road.

Travel: If even my native village is covered with dew, then so be it! I will continue out across the fields, accepting the sadness that is part of the traveler's life.
Associations: travel—crossing fields (*RGS* 901), *kakaru,* "to rest upon" (untranslated)—dew; Dwellings (native home: *RGS* 176)

| 58 | Ta ga tsurasa to ka | Who is the cause of my pain? |
| | mi no usa o shiru | Now I know my own sad state. |

Love (pain: *RGS* 899): Who is the cause of my pain if not myself? It was I who chose the traveler's life; and if even my native village now seems a sad place, then so be it! I will spend my nights on the road.
Human Relations (who: *S* XVIII)

59   Saki no yo ya   In that former world—
       hito ni omoi o   it was then that these thoughts
       tsuketsuran   first seized our hearts.

Love (thoughts: *RGS* 899): Might it be that my bonds of love were forged in a previous existence? If so, then I have no one but myself to blame for my sad state.

Human Relations (*hito*, untranslated: *S* XVIII)

Design

60   Hana no miyako no   A capital once in bloom—
       ato no matsukaze   now only the wind in the pines.

Spring (*hana*, trans. ". . in bloom": *RGS* 899): The wind in the pines now blows harmlessly through the bare trees of the former capital. But when the city was in full bloom, how that wind must have worried those admiring the blossoms.

Associations: ato, trans. "once"–former world; Plants, subcategory Trees (hana: *RGS* 307)

MISINTERPRETATION

Under normal circumstances, the phrase "that former world" would function as an unambiguous reference to a previous existence in the Buddhist chain of reincarnations. So the link between verses 59 and 60, which takes the phrase to mean literally "the world in the past," is based on a deliberate misinterpretation. The link amounts to an insistence on the power of the pun.

Exhibiting the high degree of rhetorical complexity that is one of the hallmarks of Sōboku's Design category, verse 60 is impressive in its own right. The phrase *hana no miyako*, to begin with, means at least two things: "the splendid capital" and "the capital during blossom time." Both meanings are implied here, and the richness they bring to the verse is compounded by the anticipation they create as to which will be taken up in the next link. And the word *ato* performs the same kind of function. Its three or four meanings, "after" and "ruins" being chief among them, are all poised in the reader's mind for use in the interpretation of the following verse.

The combination of these ambiguities makes this one of the most striking verses of the sequence. But it is as part of a link that the verse achieves status as a Design verse, joining with verse 59 to create a delicate statement about the past. Despite the fact that the blossoms are mentioned only as an absence, the rules must judge the verse a blossom verse.[38] As in the case of Teika's famous poem about a landscape with "neither cherry blossoms nor crimson leaves" (*SKKS* 363), the color implied in the scene cannot be fully negated by grammar. Kenkō puts the matter best in *Tsurezuregusa:* "Are we to look at cherry blossoms only in full bloom, the moon only when it is cloudless? To long for the moon while looking on the rain, to lower the blinds and be unaware of the passing of spring—these are even more deeply moving."[39] That the blossoms of Sōgi's verse remain only as a memory simply adds to the sense of evanescent beauty they represent.

61	Haru fukaki	A bleak sight indeed—
	Shiga no yamamoto	the bay below Shiga's peak
	urasabite	late in the spring.

Spring: How forlorn and desolate is the ancient capital at Shiga in late spring. Over the ruins of the once blossoming capital the pine wind now blows.

Associations: spring—blossoms (*RGS* 899), Shiga—the capital (*RGS* 162); Mountains (*yama*, trans. "peak": *RGS* 78); Famous Places (Shiga)

THE POET'S GAZETTEER

Shiga, a city on the southern shore of Lake Biwa, was the site of the imperial capital during the reign of Emperor Tenji (r. 668–671). As such it became one of the Famous Places (*nadokoro*) of the medieval tradition, another of the vague rubrics of the *waka* anthologies that came to form a distinct category in the writings of *renga* poets. Sōgi dedicated fully half of one of his last critical works to listing the more well-known Famous Places by province, along with instructive comments as to how they should be treated in poetry.[40] And this concern for a proper knowledge of poetic geography is also apparent in Sōzei, who is mentioned in *Azuma mondō* (East Country queries, 1470) as being particularly given to the use of *nadokoro* in composition,[41] and in Shōtetsu, who includes a very revealing comment on the use of Famous Places in the longest and most detailed of his treatises: "If someone asks you in which of the provinces Yoshino may be found, you should answer this way: When I write my poems I simply remember that for blossoms one goes to Yoshino, for red leaves to Tatsuta. Whether those places are in Ise or wherever is not my concern."[42]

As Shōtetsu's words illustrate, the essence (*hon'i*) of any Famous Place is defined in terms of a history of poetic treatment; such places occupy poetic rather than physical space. Hence, in his lists of *nadokoro*, Sōgi gives no attention to the details of the landscapes he has seen in his travels, but instead gives precedents. Shiga was famous for its cherry blossoms in the earliest days of Japanese poetry, and it remained so in the fifteenth century. Among other things, this meant once again that knowledge of the past was of greater importance than knowledge of the present; it was not necessary for a poet of Sōgi's day to visit the Famous Places about which he wrote, for his time might be better spent in perusing the pages of the imperial anthologies. Uji and cormorant boats, Fukakusa and quails, Musashino and the autumn wind—these were the conventional associations that provided a guide to the "meaning" of Famous Places in linked verse. Thus one can come closer to a Muromachi perception of any place through *Renjugappekishū* than through any excursion. In the *renga*, a place name is little more than an index to a set of traditional descriptions, a listing in one of the era's dictionaries or literary gazetteers.

62	Kasumi no izuku	To where is the boat destined
	watari suru fune	as it sails into the haze?

Spring (haze: *RGS* 25) Travel (boat: *RGS* 901): Where does the boat head as it cuts through the haze on the bay below Shiga's peak in late spring?

Associations: haze—bay, spring (*RGS* 25); Waters, subcategory Seas (boat: *S* XVIII, *RGS* 904); Rising Things (haze: *S* XIII, *RGS* 25)

63	Okiizuru	From far villages
	tō no satozato	come voices in the morning
	koe sunari	as people arise.

Travel: As I watch a boat leave shore, heading for some unknown destination, I hear through the morning haze the voices of people getting up and setting about their business.

Associations: oki ("offing," untranslated)—boat; Dwellings (village: *S* XVIII); Waters, subcategory Seas (*oki*, untranslated: *S* XVIII, *RGS* 904)[43]

64	Mi wa yomogiu ni	Awaiting dawn in the weeds:
	akasu yo zo uki	a lament in loneliness.

Lamentation: (uki, trans. "loneliness": *RGS* 900): As I await dawn after a sleepless night in the weeds, I hear the voices of people arising in a far-off village and feel more intensely my own loneliness.

Associations: awaiting dawn—morning; Plants, subcategory Grasses (weeds: *S* XVI, *RGS* 253), Human Relations (*mi*, untranslated: *S* XVIII)

Sheet 3, Side 2

65	Waga kokoro	Does it know my heart—
	tsuki wa shiru ya	this moon that is sending forth
	kage sabite	such mellow rays?

Autumn (moon: *RGS* 895): Can it be that the moon knows the thoughts of my heart as I lament my loneliness here among the weeds?

Associations: my heart—in the weeds (based on allusion below); Shining Things (moon: *S* XIII, *RGS* 12); Nocturnal Things (moon: *RGS* 906); Human Relations (my: *S* XVIII)

Allusion: KKS 878 and *Yamato monogatari* (anonymous)

Waga kokoro	Ah, my troubled heart—
nagusamekanetsu	how can it find any peace
Sarashina ya	in the moonlight
Obasuteyama ni	shining at Sarashina
teru tsuki o mte	on Castaway Mountain?

FOLK LEGENDS IN LINKED VERSE

Although Japanese mythology and the gods of the Shinto pantheon are seldom alluded to in linked verse, certain folk tales are referred to with frequency. One such tale concerns Obasute Mountain— literally, "the mountain where Auntie is cast away." The tale probably existed in numerous versions during the Muromachi period, but the most commonly known one is recorded in the early Heian poem-tale *Yamato monogatari*. The scene is a mountain in Sarashina, Shinano province, and the gist of the story concerns a young man who is prodded by his new wife into leaving to die on the mountainside the aunt who had raised him. The poem in the tale is attributed to the man and is a lament written as he gazes at the moon after his heartless act.[44]

Sōgi's allusion is primarily to the poem, and this is entirely typical of *renga* poets, for whom the prose section of any tale was of only secondary importance. Thus for Kanera, even the reading of a great work like *Genji monogatari* is justified largely in terms of that work's value as a poetic primer: "In general, the reason one reads through books like *Genji monogatari* is so that one can use them for allusions in one's *uta*."[45] If tales and legends were important, then, it was often less for their own intrinsic literary value than for the contexts they provided great poems.

66	Kaze hiyayaka ni	There is a bite in the wind
	aki fukuru koro	as autumn begins to deepen.

Autumn: As autumn deepens there is a chill in the wind, and the moon shines with a lonely light. Everything around me reinforces the sadness that fills my heart.

Associations: autumn—moon (*RGS* 895)

67	Ojika naku	From the mountains
	yama wa yūbe no	comes the call of a stag:
	ikabakari	how forlorn an evening!

Autumn (stag: *RGS* 895): A chilly wind blows as I listen to the call of a stag from the mountains at evening. Autumn is growing deeper.

Associations: stag–autumn (*RGS* 895); Mountains (mountains: *RGS* 78); Animals, subcategory Beasts (stag: *RGS* 414)

68	Omoiiru beki	There is no place for escape
	yo no hoka ya naki	outside of the world itself.

Lamentation (outside of the world: *RGS* 900): There is no path out of this world of sadness, for even in the mountains where I have come to flee society, a stag calls forlornly.

Associations: the world, to escape–the call of a stag (based on allusion below)

Allusion: SZS 1151

Yo no naka ya	From this world of ours
michi koso nakere	there is simply no escape:
omoi iru	even in the hills
yama no oku ni mo	where I go to flee my cares
shika zo naku naru	I hear the call of a stag.

Fujiwara no Shunzei

THE USES OF ALLUSION (II)

As many examples in Sōgi's sequence show, the primary effect of allusion in linked verse is to provide the genre with a classical underpinning. But references to foundation poems and tales also serve more practical ends. We have already seen how the reference to Tsurayuki's congratulatory poem in the first verse of the sequence added depth and credence—as well as a key to interpretation—to Sōgi's own dedication to the Yukawa house. The terseness of the linked-verse form made this sort of appeal to precedent through allusion a necessity of the genre's existence.

Another function of allusion was to justify *yoriai*. Indeed, a book like *Renshōshū*, the first "dictionary" of conventional associations, is no more than a compendium of *waka* showing associations that had by the Kamakura period become basic to the tradition of "linking" verses. And many of the allusions noted by *renga* commentators of the fifteenth and sixteenth centuries are of precisely this nature: they do not link verses so much as provide authority for linking. Sōboku's reference to *KKS* 891 in verse 8 is such a case. It does not indicate a true echoing of the poem but merely serves as a precedent for the idea of linking together "snow" and "bamboo grass."

The most common use of allusion in linked verse, however, is as a linking technique in which a foundation poem, an incident from *Genji monogatari*, or perhaps a Chinese legend, will form a "hidden" bridge between two verses. The link between verses 67 and 68, for instance, is based on a clear allusion to Shunzei's poem, which acts not only as a precedent for the *yoriai* but also as the entire unifying context of the verses. Taken as a complete statement, then, the two verses simply reiterate what Shunzei had said some three centuries earlier. And it is in this kind of reiteration that the work of allusion is most transparent, for Sōgi's reference literally brings a great poem of the past into the play of verses in his own sequence.

Design

69	Uki mo tada	The suffering too
	yume no yadori mo	takes place in this house of dreams—
	nageku na yo	no cause for despair.

Lamentation (*uki*, trans. "suffering": *RGS* 900): One cannot hope to escape the world and its cares. But this dreamlike existence, with its joys and sorrows, will pass quickly: there is no cause for despair.

Associations: dream—world

READING BY THE RULES (IV)

Mugonshō is explicit about something that other rulebooks only imply: that the word *yume* ("dream") signifies Love unless otherwise qualified,[46] a fitting identification, since Love in linked verse is nearly always cast in the realm of dreams. But the use of "dream" in verse 69 seems to demand another interpretation, for the phrase *yume no yadori* ("a house of dreams") is a figurative expression connoting the fleeting nature of life. The rules give us a clear guide about how such nonliteral expressions should be categorized when they insist that "snowfall of blossoms" does not clash with true "snow" because of the former's metaphorical nature.[47] And another example from the rules is even more apt: *yume no yo* (this world of dreams) is deleted from the category of Nocturnal Things, presumably because the dream it represents has nothing to do with dreams of the night. The rules thus seem to exclude open metaphors from the categorization their vocabularies would otherwise require. Since the dream it includes is not a Nocturnal Thing, then, the dream of verse 69 implies no romance, functioning only as a symbol of ephemerality.

70	Sanagara sode mo	The rain has drenched my sleeves
	ame no ko no moto	even here beneath this tree.

Miscellaneous: I sought shelter from the rain beneath the trees, and still my sleeves were drenched through. But that is the way of the world—no cause for despair.

Associations: in the trees—suffering (based on allusion below); Falling

Things (rain: *S* XIII, *RGS* 34); Plants, subcategory Trees (tree); Clothing
(sleeves: *RGS* 660)
Allusion: KKS 292

<table>
<tr><td>Wabibito no</td><td>Underneath this tree</td></tr>
<tr><td>wakite tachiyoru</td><td>one weary of the world</td></tr>
<tr><td>ko no moto wa</td><td>sought a brief refuge.</td></tr>
<tr><td>tanomu kage naku</td><td>But now no shelter remains:</td></tr>
<tr><td>momiji chirikeri</td><td>the leaves have fallen away!</td></tr>
</table>

Archbishop Henjō

71	Ume no hana	Who has broken off
	ta ga taoraba ya	a bough of blossoming plum
	shioruran	and left a blighted tree?

Spring (plum: *RGS* 899): Who has broken off a branch of flowering plum
and left this blighted spot on the tree? I sought shelter from the rain under
these boughs only to have my sleeves further dampened by rain.

Associations: blossoming plum—tree; Plants, subcategory Trees (plum
blossoms: *RGS* 300); Human Relations (who: *S* XVIII)

A Touch of Humor

"Comic linked verse," the usual translation for *haikai no
renga*, is a misleading term for two reasons: first, because the *haikai* tradition of medieval Japan was often characterized less by humor than by
looser restrictions on vocabulary and content—in other words by unortho-
doxy; and second, because there is humor of a sort in orthodox *renga* as
well. Usually the latter is restricted to linguistic humor of the sort involving punning and word-play; but occasionally a "serious" sequence will
present a semi-comic situation, as in verse 71, where a man seeking shelter
under a plum tree is frustrated to find that someone has carried off the
branch over his head.

This is restrained humor, to be sure—humor with a touch
of pathos. But even if it is a far cry from the earthiness of *Chikuba kyōginshū* (Crazy verses on bamboo stilts, 1499),[48] the earliest medieval *haikai*
anthology, it does show that linked verse was a game played with all the
pieces of the court heritage. That more serious styles prevailed in all *renga*
sequences is beyond dispute, then; but the wittiness of the earlier Heian
uta anthologies—as represented by Henjō's poem and Sōgi's allusive variation upon it—was also part of the *renga* system.

72	Kaeru o uramu	The sad cry of the warbler
	haru no uguisu	resents the passing of spring.

Spring: The sad cry of the bush warbler voices resentment toward the one who has carried away a branch of blossoming plum and left behind a blighted tree.

Associations: bush warbler–plum (*RGS* 300), spring–plum (*RGS* 899); Animals, subcategory Birds (wood thrush: *RGS* 363)

Design

73	Kasumi ni mo	In the spreading haze
	ima wa to kari no	the geese cry, "The time has come!"
	yasuraite	—and yet hesitate.

Spring (haze: *RGS* 25): Before leaving for the north, the wild geese hesitate for a moment in the spreading spring haze. Perhaps they hear the forlorn cry of the bush warbler, who resents being left behind.

Associations: haze–spring (*RGS* 25); Rising Things (haze: *S* XIII, *RGS* 25); Animals, subcategory Birds (geese: *RGS* 365)

74	Sue ni ika naru	What peaks remain to be crossed
	yama o koenan	before this journey is done?

Travel (crossing mountains: *RGS* 901): Before setting out for the north, the wild geese pause for a moment to ponder the long journey before them. What peaks will they cross before their journey is done?

Associations: mountains–wild geese (*RGS* 78); Mountains (mountains: *RGS* 78)

Ground

75	Saemukau	Astray on the fields,
	arashi o wabite	I lament the cold approach
	mayou no ni	of a rising storm.

Travel: As I wander lost in the fields, I lament the approach of a cold storm ahead of me. What hostile peaks will I cross before my journey is done?

Associations: storm–mountains

Ground

76	Higure ni kakaru	How lonely is the pathway
	michi no monousa	when day comes to an end.

Travel (pathway: *RGS* 901): As I wander lost in the fields at the end of day, a storm mounts ahead of me. How forlorn is the traveler's path at sundown.

Associations: pathway–fields.

77	Magiru ya to	I sought diversion—
	tanomu hitome mo	but the one who could give it
	kage taete	had disappeared.

Love (*tanomu*, untranslated: *RGS* 899): I sought diversion and solace from a friend, but the friend had disappeared without a trace. How lonely it is to be alone on the road as the sun goes down.

| 78 | Koishiki koto o | Now who will help me forget |
| | tare ni wasuren | the affection I still feel? |

Love (affection: *RGS* 899): I sought diversion from a friend, but the friend had gone without leaving a trace. Now who will help me forget the love I have lost?
Human Relations (who: S XVIII)

Sheet 4, Side 1

79	Tsurashi tote	It is painful, yes—
	mata itsukata ni	but now to what direction
	utsuramashi	am I left to turn?

Love (painful: *RGS* 899): Now that my love is gone, who will help me forget? I am in pain, yes, but it will be no easy matter to find someone to replace the one I have lost.
Association: based on allusion to the "Trefoil Knots" chapter of *Genji monogatari* (see "The Sources of Allusion" below)

The Sources of Allusion (II)

Among the many sources that provided a foundation for the neoclassical revival of the fifteenth century, none was so prominent as *Genji monogatari*. Ichijō Kanera and Shōtetsu, two of the major participants in the revival, were both scholars of the Heian classic, and the major *renga* poets of the century—Sōzei, Shinkei, Chiun (d. 1448), Sōgi, Shōhaku—were their students. As a result, it was to the story of the Shining Prince and his heirs more than to any other single source that Muromachi artists looked for inspiration in their attempt to reconstruct the past. Almost every *hyakuin* of Sōgi's day contained at least one allusion to the tale, which acted as a symbol of court culture.

As with allusion to other tales and legends, Murasaki Shikibu's work was treated in its parts rather than as a whole. It was a source of poems and anecdotes—an encyclopedia of sorts. Only seldom was it dealt with even by more sophisticated readers as a complete tale—as fiction rather than chronicle. Literary competence required only the ability to quote from the book and recognize allusions, such as the one involved in the link between verses 78 and 79. Here the story of the rejected Kaoru, who cannot seem to relinquish his affection for Oigimi, forms a prototype for the more fleeting suggestion of unrequited love found in Sōgi's sequence. The allusion is a fairly general one, meant to conjure up the whole tragic affair between Kaoru and the two daughters of the Eighth Prince, but one quotation serves well as a dramatic context for the link. In the previous scene Oigimi, the older of the two sisters, has gone to her grave, a victim of the one of the tale's unexplained maladies.

> ... Kaoru's mind was in a turmoil. Perhaps it would have been better if he had done as Oigimi suggested, taken her sister in her place. Try though he might to think of them as one, he had not been able to transfer his affections. Rather than invite the despair into which he now was plunged, might he not better have taken Nakanokimi, and sought in his visits to Uji consolation for unrequited love?[49]

Sōgi's verses borrow rather directly from Kaoru's sentiments, evoking the sad image of a lover bereft of the object of his affections. But it must also be said that Kaoru's predicament is not an uncommon one in the annals of court love. And the *renga* image is perforce more abstract than its referent; it seems to make a more universal statement about Love, using the world of the famous tale only as another kind of precedent.

| 80 | Narekoshi iori | I am well used to my hut— |
| | matsukaze mo fuke | so blow on, wind in the pines! |

Miscellaneous: I am accustomed to life in my lonely hut, so blow on, wind in the pines! My life here is painful, but I have nowhere else to go.
Dwellings (hut: *S* XVIII, *RGS* 194)

Design

81	Kokoro koso	Beneath such a moon
	naku to mo tsuki ni	could even the unfeeling
	yume ya min	drift off into dreams?

Autumn (moon: *RGS* 895): Could even one who has no more feelings for the world sleep on such a night as this? Blow on, wind in the pines—you can only add to the effect of the autumn moon shining over my hut.
Shining Things (moon: *S* XIII, *RGS* 12); Nocturnal Things (dream, moon: *RGS* 906)

DISTANT ECHOES

In his rulebook Shōhaku adopts a rather liberal attitude toward what his tradition referred to as *tōrinne,* or "remote recurrence"—the practice of using two very similar links in the same *hyakuin,* although widely separated.[50] And, judging from verse 81, one would have to conclude that Sōgi too saw no harm in the same kind of repetition not explicitly prohibited by the rules of intermission or seriation. Here the repetition is less of a link than of an idea already presented in the Komatsubara sequence: that even those "without feeling" are attracted by the beauty and symbolic power of the moon (see verse 19).

Thus, in this one instance at least, Sōgi's sequence repeats itself. More important, however, it can be said to reiterate a major theme of the medieval poetic and religious psyche—that there is no final means of eluding the attachments that are the essence of human experience, or, to refer back to another statement of the same idea in this very sequence, "no place for escape / outside of the world itself" (verse 68). In verse 19 it was the fishermen, Buddhist sinners by virtue of their sanguineous occupation, who were moved despite themselves by the sight of the moon shining on the autumn sea; now it is one who has turned his back on the world (*kokoro naki mono*) who finds himself similarly swayed. Although at opposite ends of the religious spectrum, both are alike in being ineluctably drawn by a symbol of poetic power.

Inevitably so powerful and pervasive a theme calls to mind earlier formulations. The most famous is Saigyō's.

Kokoro naki	Even one who claims
mi ni mo aware wa	to no longer have a heart
shirarekeri	feels this sad beauty:
shigi tatsu sawa no	a snipe flying up from a marsh
aki no yūgure	on an autumn evening.[51]

Another allusion? Perhaps not. But certainly Saigyō's poem can be called a past declaration of which Sōgi's verses are distant echoes.

So verse 81 is nothing new. Yet it is a Design effort all the same—partly because of its enunciation of an old theme, but also because of the way it adds to its predecessor. By itself, verse 80 is simply a statement of a hermit's defiance. But verse 81 gives that defiance justification as not mere stubborn will, but aesthetic and religious sensitivity.

82	Obasuteyama no	A fleeting fall night passes
	aki no karifushi	at Obasute Mountain.

Autumn Travel: I lie down for a night's rest at the foot of Obasute Mountain. But, recalling the legends associated with this place, could even one without strong feelings drift off into dreams beneath the haunting moon?

Associations: autumn—moon (*RGS* 895), Obasute—moon (based on allusion to the Obasute legend alluded to in verse 65); Mountains (mountains: *RGS* 78)

83	Koromo utsu	Robe on fulling block:
	oto sae tabi no	resentment toward travel
	urami nite	echoes in its sound.

Autumn (fulling block: *RGS* 895) Travel: As I rest for the night at Obasute Mountain, even the sound of the fulling block in the distance reminds me of my home and fills me with resentment toward the traveler's fate.

Associations: fulling block—autumn (*RGS* 895), travel—fleeting night (*RGS* 901); Clothing (robe: *RGS* 657)

| 84 | Tōzakarikinu | Does my wife still wait for me |
| | imo mo matsuran | though I leave her far behind? |

Travel and Love (to wait, "distant" wife: *RGS* 899): Is my wife, now so far away, still waiting for me? The sound of the fulling block reminds me of her as it echoes the resentment she must feel toward my travels.

Associations: to wait—fulling block (*RGY* 191); Human Relations (wife: *RGS* 524)

THE WAITING WIFE

The speaker of verse 84 is a traveler, but he refers to another of the masks of the genre: the waiting wife. Patient and long suffering, the waiting wife is a paragon of fidelity, yet she suffers greatly in her long wait for a mate away from home. The emphasis in her depiction is therefore not on fondness but resentment. Travel is seldom a positive experience even for the wayfarer himself, and much less so for the wife he has left behind.

It is rare to find the waiting wife outside of the Travel context. The so-called "wife for a night" and the prostitute both imply Love as a category, while the true wife is generally noted as an absence. A figure in the distance, she is brought back to memory by the heavy sound of mallet on fulling block.

85	Kawaraji to	"I will never change"—
	iishi o ima mo	to this day I still rely
	tanomu yo ni	on that pledge of love.

Love (to rely: *RGS* 899): I still rely on the promise my wife made to me that her feelings would never change. Is she still waiting for me now that I am so far away?

| 86 | Shiishiba soyogu | Rustling in the beech branches, |
| | kogarashi no kaze | a withering winter wind. |

Winter (withering wind: *RGS* 898): When I hear the sound of the withering wind in the beech branches, I remember your promise never to change toward me.

Associations: to never change—beech (based on allusion below); Plants, subcategory Trees (beech: *RGS* 328)

Allusion: *SIS* 1230 (Anonymous)

Hashitaka no	On Mount Togaeru
Togaeru yama no	the beeches may change their hues
shiishiba no	like a molting hawk.
Hagae wa su tomo	But of this I am certain:
kimi wa kaeseji	you will not change toward me.

READING BY THE RULES (V)

Just as Love and Travel are idealistic categories, the seasonal categories of linked verse too abide by predictable patterns of reference. Thus Summer is marked by images of refreshing coolness rather than heat: mountain-spring, fan, trout, evening showers, and so on. Even mosquitoes, the minions of summer in Edo *haikai*, bother the *renga* poet only rarely. The experience of Summer is concentrated around the edges of the season, where hot days give way to nights full of fireflies, cormorant boats, and cool breezes. And Winter likewise appears in linked verse in attenuated aspect: a frosty morning, a windy and withered garden, a day of wintry showers. The more extreme weather of the winter months—the heavy snowfalls and great storms—are almost absent from the season as it presents itself in *renga* imagery.

Summer and Winter are the minority seasons of the *hya-kuin*. Either may be abandoned after only one verse according to the rules, and together they seldom account for more than six or seven verses in a sequence. Hence it is that the dominant seasons in linked verse, as in most medieval poetic genres, are Spring and Autumn. In these seasons there is more variety in treatment. But still they are poetic seasons that express a *hon'i* of their own. Haze and blossoms are the quintessential symbols of Spring, and the moon that of Autumn. Most series involving either season tend to cluster around these central images. What this means for a classical reading is once more that a literary knowledge of natural phenomena must take precedence over more scientific knowledge. Snow, hail, showers, wind, mist, and so on, as they appear in the *hyakuin* are indices to poetic conceptions of the seasons rather than to weather. Returning again to Jōha's words, "It may be that there are long rains in winter, but the essence of the season demands intermittent showers."[52] By the same token, it may be that in life cold winds occasionally blow in autumn, but the rulebooks state that the word *kogarashi* ("withering wind") signifies a later season. Autumn is the time for falling leaves and chilly nights, but withering is left to the Winter wind.

87	Hatsushimo no	On winter's first frost
	sono no kashidori	they flit about the garden:
	asari shite	jays on the hunt.

Winter (first frost: *RGS* 898): In the garden, where winter's first frost covers all, the jays forage as the wind blows through the trees.

Associations: first frost—withering wind; jays on the hunt—beeches (based on allusion below); Dwellings (garden: *RGS* 199); Falling Things (frost: *S* XIII, *RGS* 40); Animals (*kashidori*, trans. "jays")

Allusion: Eikyū hyakushu (Hundred-poem sequence of the Eikyū era)[53]

Natsuso biku	Among the beech trees
Unakamiyama no	of Unakami Mountain
shiishiba ni	—famed for its summer flax—
kashidori nakitsu	cawing jays flit through the branches
yūasari shite	intent on their evening hunt.
	Minamoto no Toshiyori

Ground

88 Miyamazutai no   Beside a range of mountains—
    katawara no sato   a little country village.

Miscellaneous: In a country village, beside a range of mountains, jays forage in the garden on winter's first frost.

Associations: mountains—birds (*RGS* 78), village—garden; Mountains (mountains: *RGS* 78); Dwellings (village: *S* XVIII)

Ground

89 Noki chikaku   A fall of water:
    kakehi bakari no   so close it could be from a pipe
    mizu ochite   out under the eaves.

Miscellaneous: Running near the village along the mountain range is a small stream. The water falling over the rocks near my eaves sounds so close it could be taken for the trickle of the bamboo pipe.

Associations: pipe—mountain village (*RGS* 129), eaves village; Dwellings (eaves: *S* XVIII); Waters (water: *S* XVIII; bamboo pipe: *S* XVI, *RGS* 129)

Ground

90 Take no ha midare   Bamboo leaves in disarray—
    ame suguru oto   the sound of passing rain.

Miscellaneous: A rain shower passes by, disturbing the bamboo leaves. The sound of the rain striking the leaves is like the sound of the water falling from the bamboo pipe out under the eaves.

Associations: bamboo—pipe (*RGS* 129), rain—water; Falling Things (rain: *S* XIII, *RGS* 34); Plants, subcategory Grasses (bamboo: *RGS* 204)

Breaking Away (II)

The characteristics of any development section are paradoxically constant. Displaying in concrete terms the law of obligatory change that rules the genre, the breaking pattern is one of smooth transitions punctuated with abrupt shifts in theme and imagery, of Design mixed with Ground, and of links that exhibit a variety of approaches to the art of joining verses. If there is anything unusual about the latter half of Sōgi's sequence it is that it presents only five unequivocal Design verses (52, 60, 69, 73, and 81). In all other respects, however, it follows the breaking ethic with studied precision, offering a whole range of linking techniques (allusion, dialogue, reinterpretation, misinterpretation, word play, and so on) and a number of finely conceived Ground series (54–56, 75–76, and 88–90). As the canons of the genre dictate, the development section is fast-paced and follows an uninhibited line of organization. It is perhaps for this reason that fewer than half of the verses from 50 on end up in the seasonal categories. The last ten verses show a particularly striking tendency toward non-seasonal themes as well as a penchant for rapid contextual changes:

79 Love				
80	Miscellaneous			
81		Autumn		
82		Autumn Travel		
83		Autumn Travel		
84			Travel and Love	
85			Love	
86				Winter
87				Winter
88					Miscellaneous
89					Miscellaneous
90					Miscellaneous

Here even Autumn, the most dominant of the seasons, must share its place with Travel; and it is dropped after only three verses, the minimum Autumn series according to Shōhaku's rules. Thus the changes from category in the last part of the development section are rapid and complex, serving as a kind of literary exercise in preparation for the approaching climax of the sequence.

91	Mezamashite	Suddenly awake,
	tsuyu harō yo ya	I brush dew from my sleeves
	fukenuran	in the depths of night.

Autumn (dew: *RGS* 895): The sound of rain striking the bamboo leaves wakes me in the night, and I brush the droplets from my sleeves.

Associations: dew–rain (*RGS* 38), night–bamboo (*RGS* 204); Falling Things (dew: *S* XIII, *RGS* 38); Nocturnal Things (night)

92   Nishi fuku kaze ni   The west wind clears the sky
      tsuki hosoki sora   to reveal a crescent moon.

Autumn (moon: *RGS* 895): I wake in the night to find that the west wind has blown away the storm that left these droplets on my sleeves, revealing a crescent moon in the sky above.

Associations: moon–night (*RGS* 12); Shining Things (moon: *S* XIII, *RGS* 12); Nocturnal Things (moon: *RGS* 906)

Sheet 4, Side 2

93   Aki kinu to   The autumn has come—
      omoeba yūbe   and before I fully know it,
      mi ni shimite   evening strikes my soul.

Autumn: As I see the crescent moon in a clear sky, I realize that autumn has come. And then, before I know it, the proverbial melancholy of evening in autumn strikes deep into my soul.

Associations: autumn–moon (*RGS* 895), pierce the soul–wind (*RGS* 895); Human Relations (*mi*, trans. "soul": *S* XVIII)

FULL CIRCLE

Again, as in the earliest scenes of the sequence, the moon announces autumn. But, even without the moon, the season's arrival would be apparent—and this is the burden of verse 93—in the word "evening." As Sei Shōnagon said in her pillow book, autumn is the time for evening.[54] Sōgi's restatement of this common wisdom seems to signal that his sequence has entered the final stage of its genesis, the presto section, in which the pace is to be smooth and the progress relatively unchecked by arresting scenes or linking techniques.

94   Suzuro ni kokoro   Why should my heart be stirred
      nani ukaruran   in such a senseless way?

Miscellaneous: Why is it that suddenly my heart is unsettled? No sooner do I realize that autumn has come than the proverbial autumn evening strikes deep into my soul.

95   Tōku mite   I look from afar:
      hana ya sore to mo   are those spring trees in blossom
      shirakumo ni   or white banks of cloud?

Spring (blossoms: *RGS* 889): From afar I cannot tell whether what I see is blossoms or clouds, and this uncertainty stirs my heart in an unexplicable way.

Associations: clouds—to be stirred (*RGS* 26), blossoms—heart (*RGS* 307); Rising Things (clouds: *S* XIII, *RGS* 26); Plants, subcategory Trees (blossoms: *RGS* 307)

Ground

96	Muramura kasumu	Here and there the haze gathers
	yama no tokiwagi	in the mountain evergreens.

Spring (haze: *RGS* 25): The evergreens on the mountainside are dotted with clumps of haze. Seen from afar the shapes are unclear—are those spring trees in blossom, or perhaps white banks of cloud?

Associations: mountain—clouds (*RGS* 26); Mountains (mountains: *RGS* 78); Rising Things (haze: *S* XIII, *RGS* 25); Plants, subcategory Trees (evergreens: *RGS* 297)

Ground

97	Kage takaki	The Shrine of the Gods
	kami no miyadachi	has cast its lofty shadow
	haru o hete	over many springs.

Spring and Shinto (gods: *RGS* 610): The Shrine of the Gods has passed through many springs, and now again the spring haze gathers in the evergreens around the sacred precincts.

Associations: spring—haze (*RGS* 25), Shrine of the Gods—evergreens

READING BY THE RULES (VI)

Pillar, wall, hut, garden, rooftile, fence, door, gate—all of these are in the Dwellings category. But the word *miya* (shrine), according to Shōhaku (*S* XVIII), is not. If it is a dwelling at all, a shrine is a dwelling of the gods, who fall outside the rules.

Although a Zen monk by affiliation, in his travels Sōgi showed the eclecticism that is so characteristic of the medieval religious milieu. *Tsukushi no michi no ki* (On the road in Tsukushi), his record of a trip through Suō and Dazaifu in 1480, notes visits to both shrines and temples. But the unifying factor in his religious habits seems not to have been dogma. Instead, his religious understanding appears inseparable from the poetic tradition. To Sōgi, in other words, shrines and temples were also Famous Places, whether legendary or mythical, Shinto or Buddhist. Their importance was bound up in their long history within the court tradition, in a string of poetic associations rather than a chronicle of ecclesiastical vicissitudes.

Thus, the Way of the Gods implies simply the Imperial Family and the creation myths that supported that family's claims to power. This Shinto Way can be easily contrasted with Buddhism, although in aesthetic rather than philosophical terms. Venerable, lofty, bright, and unsullied by the sordid aspects of the world, the Way of the Gods stands in aloof opposition to the dark and sometimes despairing precincts of the Buddhist establishment. And to join the Shinto Way to Spring, the brightest of seasons, is to adhere to the essence of both categories. Shrines are by nature surrounded by haze, providing a fitting contrast to the autumnal mistiness of the Buddhist temple.

98	Minami matsuri o ōganu wa nashi	All bow in veneration at the Southern Festival.

Spring and Shinto (festival: *RGS* 610): Through the many springs since the Southern Festival was first held at the Iwashimizu Hachiman Shrine, all have bowed in veneration toward the warrior god of the Minamoto clan.

DENOUEMENT

Unless one accepts certain general topics (the court tradition of aesthetics, the primacy of interpretation) as themes, there is no thematic unity in any *renga* sequence. And it follows that a true "climax," at least in the usual sense of that term, is therefore impossible. But the beginning and end of Sōgi's Komatsubara sequence are nevertheless united in tone. The Iwashimizu Hachiman Shrine, site of the yearly Southern Festival each spring, was the hereditary shrine of the Minamoto clan, of which Yukawa Masaharu was a descendant. Dedicated to the war god Hachiman, the shrine is a symbol, then, of another Way: the Way of battle. And its appearance at this point in the *hyakuin* is another sign of the eclecticism of Sōgi and his tradition: a Shinto shrine to a Buddhist bodhisattva whose vow to save his people becomes a pledge of divine assistance in war.

99	Waga hito to wakete chikai no suehisa ni	In the distant past I parted from my people with a solemn vow.

Miscellaneous: In the distant past, I, Hachiman, made a vow to save my people, and because that vow is still in effect there is no one who does not venerate my name at the Southern Festival.

Human Relations (my: *S* XVIII)

100	Yumi toru michi zo moto o tsutomuru	This is the way of the bow: to work at the foundation.

Miscellaneous: The vow of Hachiman was to save his people, and the way of the warrior who takes Hachiman as his god must be to work at the foundation, in service to the nation.

Allusion: The Analects

Those who in private life behave well toward their parents and elder brothers, in public life seldom show a disposition to resist the authority of their superiors. And as for such men ever starting a revolution, no instance of it has ever occurred. It is upon the trunk that a gentleman works. When that is firmly set up, the Way grows. And surely proper behavior toward parents and elder brothers is the trunk of Goodness?[55]

Closing the Reading

The final verse of a full hundred-verse sequence is called the *ageku*, a term suggesting finality—the "offering up" of a work that is semi-devotional in character. And yet the *ageku*, a final word, is clearly not a conclusion in the usual sense of that word. Carrying no more weight than its predecessors, the final verse offers only a dubious sense of conclusion— the authority of a purely temporal ending, and no more.

There can be no true summing up of Sōgi's sequence. Any review must be simply that, a rereading. But a chart can rehearse the work of the rules by showing the balance of words and categories.

Representation of Thematic Categories

Spring (16), Summer (2), Autumn (22), Winter (5), Travel (18), Miscellaneous (17), Love (19), Lamentation (8), Buddhism (2), Shinto (2).

KEY TO CHART

S	Spring	Sh	Shinto	r	Rising Things
Su	Summer	O	Moon	f	Falling Things
A	Autumn	*	Blossoms	s	Shining Things
W	Winter	D	Design	n	Nocturnal Things
T	Travel	G	Ground	p	Plants
M	Miscellaneous	m	Mountains	a	Animals
L	Love	W	Waters	h	Human Relations
La	Lamentation	d	Dwellings	c	Clothing
B	Buddhism	fp	Famous Places		

	1	2	3	4	5	6	7	8	9	10	11	12	13	14	15	16	17	18	19	20	21	22
Seasons	Su	Su	A	A	A	W	W	W							S	S	S	A	A	A	A	W
Travel / Miscellaneous						M		T	T	T												
Love / Lamentation								T	T		La	L	L	L								
Buddhism / Shinto																						
The Moon / Blossoms			O												*			O				
Design / Ground											D				D				D			D
Mountains / Waters			m	m	m/w	w	w										m		w	w	w	
Dwellings / Famous Places										d						d	d					
Rising Things / Falling Things		f	r				f										r				r	f
Shining Things / Nocturnal Things			s/n								n							s/n				
Plants / Animals	p							p							p					a	p	
Human Relations / Clothing									c			h				h						

Table (rows = topical categories; columns = numbered books/sections 23–50). A downward arrow (↓) is marked above columns 36/37 in the original.

	23	24	25	26	27	28	29	30	31	32	33	34	35	36	37	38	39	40	41	42	43	44	45	46	47	48	49	50
Seasons					S	S	S						A	A	A													
Travel			M									T	T	T						M	M	M	M	M	T	T		
Miscellaneous			M	M							M									M	M							
Love		La					L	L	L	L						L	L	La	La								L	L
Lamentation	La							L	L							L	L	La										
Buddhism																												
Shinto																												
The Moon					*	O								O														
Blossoms																												
Design					D	D			D									D	D									
Ground														G	G			D				G						
Mountains				m									m								m							
Waters											w	w													w	w	w	
Dwellings			d												d						d							
Famous Places											fp																	
Rising Things						r																						
Falling Things																												
Shining Things						s/n								s/n														
Nocturnal Things							n									n												
Plants					p/a						P	P									P							
Animals															a													
Human Relations	h/c	h					h	h											h			h						h
Clothing																										c		

No.	Seasons	Travel / Miscellaneous	Love / Lamentation	Buddhism / Shinto	The Moon / Blossoms	Design / Ground	Mountains / Waters	Dwellings / Famous Places	Rising Things / Falling Things	Shining Things / Nocturnal Things	Plants / Animals	Human Relations / Clothing
51			L									
52				B B		D						
53				B			m					h h
54	A				O	G				s/n		h h
55	A					G			f			
56	A	T				G			f			
57		T						d				
58			L L									h h
59			L									h
60	S				*	D					P	
61	S						m	fp				
62	S	T					w		r			
63		T					w	d				
→ 64			La								P	h
65	A				O					s/n		h
66	A											
67	A						m				a	
68			La La									
69			La			D						
70		M							f		P P	c
71	S										P	h
72	S										a	
73	S					D			r		a	
74		T T					m					
75		T T				G G						
76		T				G						
77			L									
78			L									h

	Seasons	Travel / Miscellaneous	Love / Lamentation	Buddhism / Shinto	The Moon / Blossoms	Design / Ground	Mountains / Waters	Dwellings / Famous Places	Rising Things / Falling Things	Shining Things / Nocturnal Things	Plants / Animals	Human Relations / Clothing
79			L									
80		M						d				
81	A				O	D				s/n		
82	A	T					m					
83	A	T										c
84		T	L									h
85			L									
86	W										P	
87	W							d	f		a	
88		M				G	m	d				
89		M				G	w	d				
90		M				G			f		P	
91	A								f	n		
92	A				O					s/n		
93	A										h	
94		M										
95	S				*				r		P	
96	S					G	m		r		P	
97	S			Sh		G						
98	S			Sh								
99		M										h
100		M										

CHAPTER SEVEN

A Final Word

And as you read
the sea is turning its dark pages
turning
its dark pages.

Denise Levertov
From "To the Reader"

Aɴʏ ʀᴇᴀᴅɪɴɢ involves a reduction of its text according to patterns of special attention and emphasis. And because it confines itself so totally to prescribed conventions and codes, one may argue that a rule-based reading of the *hyakuin* is particularly constricting in its effect on the interpretive process. In other words, a rule-based reading, although first seeming to involve the reader as an active participant in the production of meaning, can be seen in the end to give dictatorial authority to the text itself. Thus one may say of linked verse read by the rules what one may say of many other so-called "open" texts: "You cannot use the text as you want but only as the text wants you to use it."[1]

Yet, for all its limitations, a rule-based approach to reading linked verse also has its virtues. First, since it captures within itself the traces of an entire poetic tradition, it can claim an allusive power that is rare even in poetry—a power to make the reader aware of the wealth of poetic experience behind every image and every link in every sequence. And equally alluring for a modern critic is the sense of artificiality that is so much a part of reading by the rules. Unlike most reading strategies, a rule-based reading of linked verse announces itself as conventional and provisional from the outset. Its vocabulary restrictions, its disavowal of all but classical sources for allusion, its strictly enforced ideal of constant thematic and lexical change—all of these features amount to an admission that the interpretation of this genre is, after all, a highly motivated activity.

Stanley Fish suggests that in literary criticism the choice "is never between objectivity and interpretation but between an interpretation that is unacknowledged as such and an interpretation that is at least aware of itself."[2] We may claim that the *renga* tradition, as represented in the rulebooks and commentaries, fits into the latter category. To poets of the Muromachi period, the conventions of linked verse formed what must have seemed a natural basis for analysis. But the sheer volume and detail of the rules of composition must have made both creation and interpretation into highly self-conscious acts. One suspects that for Sōgi and his followers the idea of reading a text was as much a question of strategy as was the idea of writing one, although one must add that the notion of adopting other strategies probably never occurred to poets in a backward-looking age.

Of course this means that other approaches to the genre are possible. It is almost always true, for instance, that some verses in any orthodox sequence can be read as *haikai*. Furthermore, if one allows allusions not recognized by a classical reading, that is, to Nō plays, the later imperial *uta* anthologies, and especially the great works of *renga* poets themselves, any *hyakuin* can be read with new reverberations of meaning. We have already seen Sōgi's debt, acknowledged by commentaries or not, to Shinkei, Senjun, Nōa, and Ryōa in selected verses of the Komatsubara sequence. To allow such "modern" allusions into the process of interpretation may be anathema to traditionalists, but it would serve to emphasize something about linked verse that is often overlooked—that in its diction, tone, thematics, and intertextual references it shows itself as much a part of its own time as of times past.[3]

Another approach to the *hyakuin* that suggests itself is the autobiographical. One scholar has shown that linked verse was sometimes used by courtiers to express their personal frustrations.[4] And even a master like Sōgi appears occasionally to speak in his own voice, as in this famous verse from *Yuyama sangin hyakuin* in which he laments his fate as a *rengashi* who must remain always on the outer fringes of the *waka* world.

51	Waka no ura ya	Waka Bay:
	isogakuretsutsu	hidden among its shorelines,
	mayou mi ni	my spirit wanders.[5]

Thus, the poet breaks out from behind his masks, identifying himself as a particular person in a particular time—an indulgence of the sort that most poets probably allowed themselves in the convivial atmosphere of the *za,* among friends and acquaintants who knew their private joys and troubles well. Such revelations, then, are rare finds, the discovery of which requires a knowledge of the poet's personal life that is seldom available; and just as well, since too many of them would narrow the appeal of the poetry in the same way as does a reading of *The Waste Land* that makes much of that symbolic work into a literary reconstruction of actual arguments between Mr. Eliot and his deranged wife. But when on occasion a glimpse of the poet (or of a group of poets sharing a mood, setting, or situation) does appear as one of the visions of a *renga* sequence, the reader wants at least to be able to acknowledge it—something the traditional conventions of the genre make it difficult to do.

For the modern reader, however, even more seductive than these interpretive possibilities are modes of reading that promise a holistic approach which can make the entire *renga hyakuin* speak in one thematic or dramatic voice. Since rules exist to be broken, for example, one can easily attempt to characterize any text by its aberrations. Even a work as conventional as Sōgi's 1492 sequence contains some departures from the conventions as outlined in the handbooks. The pattern of the moon verses in that sequence, for one thing, is irregular: whereas the handbooks state that this most indispensable of images should appear only once in each of the eight sides of a *hyakuin*, Sōgi's text presents the moon twice in the third and seventh sides and not at all in the fourth and eighth. The intervals are thus erratic, even if the total number of appearances matches the number prescribed in the rules. As far as the moon goes, then, Sōgi's sequence may at least be called unusual. And virtually every other work in the *renga* canon betrays some such irregularities, which can be taken as distinctive features of the texts in which they occur.

There is, however, a problem with these distinctive aberrations: namely, that their effect is seldom great enough to justify using them as the basis for a truly comprehensive interpretation. As the chart at the end of the translation shows, the 1492 sequence is by and large an ordinary example of the genre which reflects the dominance of the rules in every facet of its articulation. One can point to sequences of seasonal imagery, perhaps, or to clusters of lexical categories; but no pattern is sufficiently erratic to force a singular personality on the whole. The most one can say about the moon verses in the sequence is that they form a slightly unexpected pattern—but not one that challenges the eclectic nature of the work as a whole. Sōgi's sequence, even if viewed with expectations radically different from those embodied in a classical reading, is clearly not a study of the moon. Within the context of a classical reading, such small abberations are easily assimilated into a larger orthodoxy.

Thus, the idea of characterizing a *hyakuin* by reference to its slight irregularities can end in critical distortion. Yet the idea of capsulizing a text within one neat thematic statement is perhaps the most persistent of critical urges. Indeed, it is an urge that finds expression even within the *renga* tradition itself. There is the old custom, for instance, of referring to famous texts—which were originally titled only with notation as to the date—by highly connotative names: *Three Poets at Minase, Three Poets at Yuyama,* and so on. And even more pervasive is the tendency among modern scholars to speak of certain *hyakuin* as uniquely forlorn in tone, when in fact they should say that the very nature of the genre's vocabulary makes such a tone inevitable in every sequence. One might even say that the somber tone of most *renga* sequences is another product of the rulebooks, which assure by their restrictions the dominance of the darker thematic topics of the poetic spectrum—Love, Lamentation, Travel, and, above all, Autumn.[6] Shinkei puts the matter the way it should be put: "This Way takes evanescence and lamentation as the aim of both word and heart."[7]

It is instructive to note, moreover, that within the tradition of *renga* criticism even the most famous sequences tend to be known best for their deft handling of convention. *Minase sangin hyakuin,* for instance, has been seen by masters primarily as a work of *conventional* perfection—not as a unique text with a distinctive personality so much as an example of what the conventions can do for those who know how to make best use of them. Concerned more with establishing standards of orthodoxy than with finding idiosyncrasies, the typical medieval poet-commentator never attempted to sum up a *renga* sequence in general terms. And perhaps there is a lesson in this for modern readers of the genre. For when one prepares to read a work in a way other than the one designed by the tradition that produced it, one must ask at what price the act will be done. Culler, for instance, shows how easily a simple newspaper article can be read as poetry; but he does not argue that a critic might want to reverse that process, except perhaps as a pedagogical exercise, and read a poem as a piece of journalism.[8] Similarly, it may be that linked-verse criticism has denied itself holistic interpretations not because they are impossible but rather because they fail to display the true richness of the *renga* text. What Barthes gives as a general credo for critics seems to describe the attitude of a classical reading exactly: "The critic is not responsible for reconstructing the work's message but only its system."[9] In linked verse all facets of a complex literary act are represented in each text of the genre, which means that no one text has a specific message. Any interpretive approach that fails to recognize this fact will end up trivializing the object it attempts to enhance.

Still, there are some modern modes of interpretation that suggest themselves to anyone acquainted with linked verse—read classically or otherwise. One such, perhaps the most interesting of all, is described by Culler:

> The expectations enshrined in the conventions of genre are, of course, often violated. Their function, like that of all constitutive rules, is to make meaning possible by providing terms in which to classify the things one encounters. What is made intelligible by the conventions of genre is often less interesting than that which resists or escapes generic understanding, and so it should be no surprise that there arises, over and against the *vraisemblance* of genre, another level of

vraisemblance whose fundamental device is to expose the artifice of generic conventions and expectations.[10]

At first it may seem that this is simply another statement of the idea of using aberration as a foundation for analysis, but Culler's final words raise the possibility of an even more interesting critical prospect; that the most self-consciously conventional of texts may be interpreted reflexively, as a kind of commentary on its own artifice. And as the idea of *hon'i*, among others, makes clear, in linked verse we have the most self-conscious of genres.

An idea of how such a reflexive interpretation could create new levels of meaning within the *hyakuin* can be hinted at by re-examining the third verse of Sōgi's sequence of 1492 from a new perspective.

Machiizuru	The awaited moon
toyama no tsuki ni	appears over the foothills
kumo kiete	as clouds clear away.

Sōboku's commentary on this scene is merely a paraphrase: "This is the moon awaited after an evening shower. As the third verse of the sequence, it is a matchless effort." But a less cautious approach might well attach more interest to the question of who is waiting for the moon to appear. Is it some imagined traveler? A nameless speaker who represents the court's fetish of moon-viewing? Probably it is just this kind of persona that is implied by the inherited wisdom of the genre. But is it not possible, putting the rulebooks aside for a moment, to see the speaker as the intended reader (or auditor) of Sōgi's sequence, who has been tutored to expect the moon early in the first verses of a *hyakuin*? Or perhaps simply as Sōgi himself informing his audience that the awaited moon is now at hand?[11] A reflexive interpretation would obviously favor these latter readings, seeing the entire verse as an ironic comment placed in the text for the appreciation of those able to recognize its wit.

There is obviously no place in a classical reading per se for the idea of narrative irony. The typical ancient commentator is barely willing to acknowledge his own role in the interpretation of the text, let alone the place of an interloper making knowing remarks about his own compositions. Thus, it is only as a possible but as yet unrealized mode of interpretation that a reflexive reading may be mentioned. Furthermore, one must also recognize that even so seemingly radical a departure from conventional strategy owes its possibility to the rules as surely as does the classical approach itself. The very idea of a reflexive reading assumes a superior knowledge of generic conventions. In the following example from a sequence by Sōgi and Sōi, for instance one can point to the possiblity of ironic play in seasonal references; but at the same time one must admit that such play depends for its effect on the very categories it seems to subvert.

1	Uguisu wa	A bush warbler's call
	kiri ni musebite	is stifled by the mists
	yama mo nashi	that cover the hills.
		Sōi
2	Ume kaoru no no	The fragrance of plum blossoms
	shimo samuki koro	fills fields still cold with frost.
		Sōgi
3	Moesomuru	The growing grasses
	kusa no kakio wa	along the bamboo fence
	irozukite	take on a new color.[12]
		Sōi

A conventional reading will quickly interpret these three verses as expressions of the Spring category. But the trained eye will also see an ironic pattern at work in all three scenes, each of which presents first a Spring image (bush warbler, plum blossoms, and new grass) and then an Autumn image (mist, frost, and changing colors), making the sequence seem like a playful contradiction in terms. Once again, however, it must be pointed out that the contradiction is recognizable only in terms of well-known conventions. It is not a "dangerous" interruption of the text, in other words, because it does not contravene the rules so much as it uses them to create a sense of tension within verses that appear strictly "normal" on the surface.

It is for this reason that one must be skeptical about the idea of any new approach entirely supplanting the classical approach. There is a certain improbability involved in the notion of divorcing anything from its past—and this is particularly true when the past is well known. Culler and Barthes are correct when they insist that a genre is constituted by expectations that are always open to change; and they have shown, with great imagination, the possibility of defying such expectations in both writing and reading. But changing expectations according to critical fiat remains only a theoretical strategem. One would be hard-pressed to find a case in which such a change has taken place. The whole concept of genre, after all, rests in the authority of a community. And this means that most new readings are little more than supplements to old ones—important, but seldom truly revolutionary.

Further speculation could perhaps yield other ways to read linked verse, some of which might even succeed to a larger extent in escaping the conceptual framework of the rulebooks[13] But as a last defense of the conventional approach one may say that a rule-based reading of the *hyakuin* does its job very well, and in fact does it in ways that should be particularly interesting to modern critics. One must ask, for instance, whether any new mode of reading could claim to surpass the ability of a classical reading of linked verse to escape what Vladimir Nabokov calls "the absurdity of beginnings and ends."[14] And what other approach to the *renga* text could succeed equally well in revealing the self-conscious dimensions of literary interpretation? Conservative though their orientation may be, the rules of linked verse do serve to identify the *renga* as a literary game. And as critics like Barthes are quick to argue, it is precisely this sense of the text as a field of semantic play that sustains the literary enterprise.

Classical commentaries provide ample evidence of the kind of play that animates a rule-based reading. In their most characteristic form these are rather cryptic annotations focusing on predictable concerns, linking technique and allusion being chief among them. Only seldom, in fact, do the old commentaries make critical, as opposed to technical, statements. Instead, their purpose seems to be to draw attention to the way the conventions of the genre have been realized in individual texts. But the effect of this philological labor is finally to highlight the process of ceaseless reinterpretation that so characterizes the *renga* ethos. Great commentators of the tradition, no matter what their intentions, ask for what many modern critics ask—the participation of the reader in the creative act.[15] Rather than closing the text, they open it up continually to new possibilities—although always within strict limits. Change, the most apparent motivating principle in all *renga* criticism, demands of the reader a flexible mind that suspects above all else the idea of permanent meaning.

Needless to say, this does not mean that a classical reading can claim to be "free" in anything but a relative sense. On the contrary, a classical reading makes the reader a consumer in terms of conventions that are remarkably explicit. The distinctive thing about a rule-based reading, however, is that the very conventions that produce closure also resist it. A few verses from Sōgi's 1492 sequence once again provide a useful illustration.

| 21 | Harenoboru
kiri no mura ashi
kaze miete | The fall mist rises
from the reeds along the shore
where the wind appears. |
| 22 | Mata kakimidare
shigurete zo yuku | Again it brings disarray—
a passing winter shower. |

The most a conventional reading can say *with authority* about these verses is that together they present a late autumn or early winter landscape occupied by various phenomena: Waters, Rising Things, Plants, and Falling Things. Since the conventions of the genre dictate only these most basic elements of interpretation, however, there is room for the imaginative comment of Sōboku quoted earlier: "The mists of a passing shower clear away from the reeds, leaving all covered with dew. But as the wind blows the dew into the air, the disarray resembles another shower."

In this way a simple scene is given another dimension, literal becoming figurative in a movement that results in a complex link between verses that
otherwise might be passed over without comment. And this is a constant
feature of interpretation in a classical reading of the *hyakuin*, the very
feature that may be said to keep a rule-based strategy from descending into
pure formalism. For, since the poetics of the genre honor change and complexity, rather than thematic unity, as the aesthetic goals of their work, the
only final limit to signification at the level of the individual link is imagination—albeit an "educated" imagination that recognizes traditional metaphors and associations. It is for this reason that there is always a demand
for new interpretation in linked verse: because of the demand for constant
adjusting and readjusting of viewpoints that, in circular fashion, makes the
whole idea of "linking" possible in the first place.

As support for such a contention one need only turn to the
next verse of the 1492 sequence, which gives the shower of verse 22 another
figurative extension, this time as tears:

23   Furisuteshi   Who can tug at them now—
       sode wa ta ga yo ni   these sleeves that have cast aside
       hikaruran   the cares of the world?

Thus, in linked verse the reader, while still a consumer, is
at least a creative consumer. To return to Fish's comment, the reader of a
sequence such as the 1492 *dokugin* who approaches the text with the rules
as a key to interpretation will always be aware of what he is doing. Literally
open at the seams, every *renga* sequence asks the reader's participation,
demanding only that he be guided by the rules and by one universal principle: the indeterminacy of meaning, or to put it less forcefully, the dependence of meaning on an ever-changing context.

We can therefore say that a rule-based reading of the *renga*,
despite its overtly traditional foundations, represents a striking example of
what Barthes terms the Text—a characterization usually reserved, one must
add, only for modern, experimental works:

> The Text . . . practices the infinite deferral of the signified [*le
> recul infini de signifie*]: the Text is *dilatory;* its field is that of
> the signifier. The signifier must not be conceived as "the
> first stage of meaning," its material vestibule, but rather, on
> the contrary, as its *aftermath* [*apres-coup*]. In the same way,
> the signifier's *infinitude* does not refer back to some idea of
> the ineffable (of an unnameable signified) but to the idea of
> play. The engendering of the perpetual signifier within the
> field of the text should not be identified with an organic
> process of maturation or a hermeneutic process of deepen-

ing, but rather with a serial movement of dislocations, over-lappings, and variations.[16]

This is not the *hyakuin* as a Sōgi or a Sōboku would describe it. It seems almost certain, in fact, that when classical commentators set about their task they fully intended to establish a final reading rather than to "liberate" their texts from the burden of signification. Yet we have seen that it is in the nature of linked verse to resist closure. With each new verse, a conventional reading of the *hyakuin* revokes whatever temporary authority it has given and creates new "dislocations, overlappings, and variations."

"We can add to our knowledge, but we cannot subtract from it," says Authur Koestler of the world of scientific knowledge.[17] One might say the same thing about the practice of interpretation. We cannot empty our minds each time we confront a new genre. Among other things, this means that any "reconstructed" reading must be suspect by virtue of what it fails to say. For the modern reader of the *hyakuin*, whose mind is filled with Bashō, Saikaku, and Kawabata, not to mention Freud, Marx, and Barthes, the experience of interpretation is inevitably different than it was for a Muromachi monk-poet. Yet the rulebooks of the *renga* tradition make it possible for all readers of this one genre to at least frame their approaches in similar ways. Categorization, distancing, allusion, a sense of orthodoxy, and all the other conventions of a classical reading can guide a reader today as surely as they did Sōboku in his commentary on the sequence of 1492. And if eventually all paths through the text must diverge, well and good; for in linked verse divergence is an integral part of the game. The virtue of a rule-based reading is that it offers no final and comprehensive message, but what Jorge Luis Borges calls "the esthetic fact"–that "imminence of a revelation that does not take place . . ."[18] This in itself ensures that the *renga*, read within the terms of its own tradition, will always provide a highly rewarding literary experience.

APPENDIXES

APPENDIX A

A NOTE ON THE TRANSLATION OF SHŌHAKU'S RULEBOOK OF 1501

No annotated text of the 1501 work is available in modern printed form, although some Edo commentaries do exist in manuscript. For my translation I have used the text presented in *Renga hōshiki kōyō*, which has been edited and indexed by Hoshika Sōichi and Yamada Yoshio. To establish the sources of the various entries in the work—which are ultimately attributable to Yoshimoto, which to Kanera, and which to Shōhaku—I have relied on the index to that text and in addition cross-checked each of the entries with copies of Yoshimoto's and Kanera's rules (see Okami Masao, *Yoshimoto rengaronshū*, pp. 7–59).

In cases where the meaning of a word or phrase is unclear—and there are many such cases indeed—I have relied on fifteenth-century *renga* handbooks and dictionaries as far as possible, turning to *Mugonshō* and to *Ubuginu* for assistance when needed. Lastly, I have looked to a number of twentieth-century studies of the rules, notably to Ijichi Tetsuo's edition of *Hekirenshō* (*NKBZ* 51, pp. 15–61), Kidō Saizō's edition of *Renri hishō* (*NKBT* 66, pp. 55–65), and to Konishi Jin'ichi's *Sōgi*, Yamada Yoshio's *Renga gaisetsu*, and Fukui Kyūzō's *Renga no shiteki kenkyū*. I have also found *Nihon kokugo daijiten*, the Japanese answer to *OED*, a great help on some occasions, particularly when the editors of that dictionary have used Shōhaku's text as a source in establishing fifteenth-century usage. Even after all this, however, many sections of the rulebook remain obscure. The language of the work, a late brand of Sino-Japanese (*hentai kanbun*), is itself a problem at times; and Shōhaku's cryptic style sometimes seems to assume a background knowledge that a twentieth-century reader cannot be expected to possess. Final clarification of many points must await further attention by Japanese scholars.

APPENDIX B

There are eight manuscript texts of the 1492 sequence listed in Etō Yasusada's *Sōgi no kenkyū* (p. 280); several of these give the date of the work's composition and note the place of authorship. Variations among the texts are all minor in nature. For my translation I have used the *Rengaki* (A *renga* record) version as printed in Kaneko Kinjirō, "Entoku yonen Sōgi dokugin nanimichi hyakuin chū, honkoku," *Kodai chūsei kokubungaku* 1:29–39 (February 1977). *Rengaki* is a late-sixteenth-century manuscript containing three annotated works—the solo sequence of 1499, *Yuyama Sangin hyakuin,* and the Komatsubara *dokugin.* It is the only extant text of the latter with a verse-by-verse commentary.

In matters of interpretation, I have relied on the rules of the genre first of all, turning to Sōboku's words as a source of corroboration and support. In the matter of allusions, however, I have depended heavily on Sōboku's help. During the preparation of this book, Professor Kaneko Kinjirō's fully annotated version of the text (see Kaneko, *Sōgi meisaku hyakuin chūshaku,* pp. 289–356) appeared in print, allowing me a final opportunity to check my interpretations against those of a senior scholar who approaches the text in a similar way.

NOTES
GLOSSARIES
BIBLIOGRAPHY
INDEXES

The following abbreviations have been used in the notes and in the translation of Sōgi's sequence. References to poems from the imperial *waka* anthologies are to numbers as given in [*Shinpen*] *Kokka taiken*.

GRJ [*Shinkō*] *Gunsho ruijū.*

KRRS Kidō, ed., *Rengaronshū 2.*

MGS *Mugonshō.*

NKBT *Nihon koten bungaku taikei.*

NKBZ *Nihon koten bungaku zenshū.*

NKT *Nihon kagaku taikei.*

NST *Nihon shisō taikei.*

RGS *Renjugappekishū.*

RGY *Renga yoriai.*

RRS 1, 2 Ijichi, ed., *Rengaronshū,* 2 vols.

S *Renga shinshiki* (Shōhaku's Rulebook of 1501).

UG *Ubuginu.*

YKBS Yamagishi et al., eds., *Katsura no Miya-bon sōsho Renga* 1.

ZGRJ *Zoku Gunsho ruijū.*

KKS *Kokinshū.*

GSS *Gosenshū.*

SGSS *Shoku gosenshū.*

SIS *Shūishū.*

SKS *Shikashū.*

SKKS *Shin kokinshū.*

SZS *Senzaishū.*

WRS *Wakan rōeishū.*

NOTES

CHAPTER 1: INTRODUCTION

1. The various texts of the 1492 sequence do not make it clear whether Sōgi actually composed the work at Komatsubara or perhaps sent the finished work there after writing it in Kyoto (see Kaneko Kinjirō, "Entoku yonen Sogi dokugin nanimichi hyakuin chū, honkoku," *Kodai chūsei kokubungaku* 1:29–39 [February 1974]; Kaneko, *Sōgi meisaku hyakuin chūsaku,* pp. 291–294; and Tsurusaki Hirō, "Renga to Yukawa Masaharu," *Wakayama-kenshi kenkyū* 5:1–9 [February 1977] for discussions of the relevant documents). Because there is no irrefutable indication that he did not make the trip, I have chosen to follow the colophon of the text with commentary by Sōboku in assuming that the sequence was actually written at Masaharu's estate. It should be stressed, however, that the issue of where the poet was when he composed his work is a purely academic one, the resolution of which would not affect a conventional reading in any substantial way.

2. See Tsurusaki for details about Masaharu's life.

3. Text available in Etō Yasusada, *Sōgi no kenkyū,* pt. 2, pp. 260–263.

4. Tsurusaki, p. 7.

5. The famous solo sequence of 1499 (ed. Kaneko, in *NKBZ* 32, pp. 157–215) and a sequence composed at Sanageyama in 1476 (text in Etō, *Sōgi no kenkyū,* pt. 2, pp. 179–182). For a translation of the 1499 work, see Earl Miner, *Japanese Linked Poetry,* pp. 227–271.

6. Jonathan Culler, *Structuralist Poetics,* p. 126.

7. Miner, p. 61.

8. Culler, *Structuralist Poetics*, p. 171. Obviously thematic unity *is* present in the most basic unit of *renga* composition, the *tsukeku*, or two-verse "link." My point here is that the *hyakuin* is unusual because it is structured around the ideal of thematic disunity of the whole work—an uncommon stance for a genre that still claims to be "literary" rather than, say, musical in essence.

9. For details on the historical developments that led to Kanera's work, see pp. 23–27.

10. Culler, *Structuralist Poetics*, p. 116.

11. Roland Barthes, *S/Z*, p. 20.

12. Ibid., p. 4.

13. Ibid., p. 5.

CHAPTER 2: THE EVOLUTION OF LINKED VERSE AS A POETIC GENRE

1. *Renri hishō*, ed. Kidō Saizō, in *NKBT* 66, p. 35.

2. *Toshiyori zuinō* (Toshiyori's essential teachings, 1111–1113), ed. Hashimoto Fumio, in *NKBZ* 50, p. 54.

3. *SIS* 1183.

4. The term "hidden topic" (*kakushidai*) refers to a "genre of acrostic poem in which the successive syllables of a 'hidden topic' were worked into the poem either as the first syllables of successive lines or extending over two or more words in a given line." Robert H. Brower and Earl Miner, *Japanese Court Poetry*, p. 508.

5. Unfortunately, no early *fushimono* sequences have survived. The verses quoted here are taken from the *Itai senku* (One-thousand-verse sequence in the old style, 1456), a fifteenth-century work undertaken in a conscious attempt to reproduce what by that time had become nothing but a historical curiosity. See Ijichi Tetsuo, *Renga no sekai*, pp. 30–31.

6. For a historical consideration of the *fushimono*, see Kaneko, *Tsukubashū no kenkyū*, pp. 41–66.

7. Kidō Saizō, *Rengashi ronkō* 1, pp. 185–186.

8. Yoshimoto's *Hekirenshō* (Some warped ideas on linked verse, 1345) says that the *fushimono* is seldom a feature in all the verses of a sequence; *Renri hishō*, written just four years later, revises that statement to state that it is virtually never part of all the verses of a sequence. For details, see Kaneko, *Tsukubashū no kenkyū*, p. 202.

9. *Yakumo mishō*, in *NKT* supplement 3, pp. 203–206.

10. Brower and Miner, pp. 403–411.

11. Both Konishi Jin'ichi and Shimazu Tadao put Love, Travel, Lamentation, Buddhism, and Shinto under the general heading of Miscellaneous (see Konishi, *Sōgi*, and Shimazu, ed., *Rengashū*), a practice followed also by Earl Miner (see Miner, *Japanese Linked Poetry*). This kind of subdivision seems to be a late development, however, and is not often found in fifteenth-century anthologies.

12. *Shinsen tsukubashū kinen hyakuin* (One hundred verses in supplication for the success of the New Tsukuba collection). Shimazu, ibid., pp. 298–301.

13. *RGS* 901. Numbers here refer to item numbers within Kidō's edition of the work and not to page numbers.

14. Kanera's book is the most extensive of *renga* handbooks in terms of its attention to categories and *yoriai*. Preoccupation with matters of a similar nature,

however, is one feature of most *renga* treatises, beginning with those of Yoshimoto in the mid-fourteenth century and extending into the Edo period. Kanera's work should therefore be seen as a codification of the conventional wisdom held in varying degrees by most *waka* and *renga* poets of the late medieval period. Handbooks and treatises by Asayama Bontō (1349–1427), Sōzei (d. 1455), and Shinkei (1406–1475), all writing well before Kanera's compilation, show an identical concern for categories and associations; indeed, these may have served as some of the sources of Kanera's own work.

15. Other categories listed in Kanera's book—Heavenly Objects, Landmarks, Seashells, Food, and so on—are not treated by the rules in similar fashion. The presence of these irrelevant categories raises the question of whether Kanera's book was really intended primarily for the use of *renga* poets or for more general reference. Statements by Kanera in the preface to the work, however, make it clear that he undertook the compilation in response to requests made by linked-verse poets. It appears, therefore, that Kanera's groupings are arranged to suit the practical demands of a handbook rather than to correspond exactly to *renga* categories.

16. *Sōi Sōgi Yuyama ryōgin* (Sōi and Sōgi at Yuyama, 1482), in Shimazu, ed., *Rengashū*, pp. 189–190.

17. For a survey of classical Japanese lexicography, see Don Clifford Bailey, "Early Japanese Lexicography," *Monumenta Nipponica* 15.1:1–52 (Spring 1960).

18. Instances of *hon'i* that appeal to a sense of "proper" treatment or decorum are so numerous in both *waka* and *renga* criticism that they scarcely need mention. Usage of the work to refer to authorial intent, on the other hand, is less frequent. For one example, see the Muromachi-period commentary on verse 11 of *Yuyama sangin hyakuin*, ed. Kaneko, in *NKBZ* 32, p. 154.

19. See *KRRS*, p. 423. Kidō uses *Shogaku yōshashō* (Directions for beginners), a text with a different title but virtually identical contents.

20. Ibid., p. 454.

21. *Sōgi shoshinshō* (Notes for the inexperienced, 1473), in *KRRS*, p. 416.

22. Donald Keene, *Essays in Idleness: The Tsurezuregusa of Kenkō*, p. 118.

23. *RGS* 899.

24. *Yodo no watari*, in *KRRS*, p. 289.

25. *Shihōshō* (The way to the treasures, 1585), in *RRS* 2, p. 233.

26. For an introduction to how *yoriai* developed from *waka* sources as well as to how *waka* can be used to form associations, see *Katahashi* (Fragments, 1476?), a short work by one of Sōgi's teachers, Senjun (1411–1476). See *RRS* 1, pp. 271–280.

27. *KKS* 409.

28. Text available in Kaneko Kinjirō and Yamauchi Yōichirō, *Kamakura makki renga gakusho.*

29. Kidō Saizō and Shigematsu Hiromi, *Renga yoriashū to kenkyū*, 1, p. 163.

30. *RGS* 549.

31. The source of the association between dream and "to retell" is a scene in *Genji monogatari* (see Edward G. Seidensticker, tr., *The Tale of Genji* 2, p. 573). The source of the association between dream and "floating bridge" is likewise *Genji monogatari*, the last chapter of which is entitled "The Floating Bridge of Dreams"; dream and "straight path" owe their relationship to a poem by Fuji

wara no Toshiyuki (*KKS* 558); finally, the association between dream and "butterfly" is based on a famous story from the *Chuang-tzu* in which the Taoist philosopher falls asleep, dreams he is a butterfly, and then awakes unsure about whether he is now a man who was just dreaming he was a butterfly or a butterfly dreaming he is a man.

32. *Yuyama sangin hyakuin*, in *NKBZ* 82, p. 153.

33. In his analysis of the genre, Konishi Jin'ichi undertakes an elaborate analogy with musical structures. Konishi, *Sōgi*, pp. 96–108.

34. Octavio Paz et al., *Renga: A Chain of Poems*, pp. 18–19.

35. See note 9, this chapter.

36. *NKT* supplement 3, p. 204.

CHAPTER 3: THE RULES OF COMPOSITION

1. The rulebooks of Teika and Tameie are among those listed in the catalogue of the Reizei House Library. Works by Fujiwara no Yukiie (1223–1275) and Fujiwara no Nobuzane (1177–1265) are also on the list. See Kidō, *Rengashi ronkō* 1, pp. 185–186, for details.

2. *Ōan shinshiki* is actually a later title for what was known at the time as *Renga shinshiki* (New rules of linked verse). In order to avoid confusion with Shōhaku's *Renga shinshiki tsuika narabi ni Shinshiki kon'an tō*, I have used the former title throughout this study. A text of the work is available in Okami Masao, *Yoshimoto rengaronshū*, pp. 7–23.

3. For a good summary of the process by which Yoshimoto's rulebook came into being and the motives behind that process, see Shimazu, *Renga no kenkyū*, pp. 175–201.

4. *Ōan shinshiki* represents the third of Yoshimoto's attempts to standardize the rules, the first being an appendix to *Hekirenshō* (ed. Ijichi Tetsuo, in *NKBZ* 51, pp. 46–61) and the second an appendix to *Renri hishō* (see *NKBT* 66, pp. 56–67)—two treatises written in 1345 and 1349, respectively. Both works show that there were a number of different and competing rule systems at the time.

5. *Renri hishō*, in *NKBT* 66, p. 36.

6. Kanera is notorious for saying that he had surpassed even the famous Sugawara no Michizane (845–903) in a number of ways. Nagashima Fukutarō sees Kanera's work in court lore and his compilation of the *Kon-an* as particular evidence of a desire to best Yoshimoto. See Nagashima, *Ichijō Kanera*, pp. 97–98, 155.

7. Okami's text of *Ōan shinshiki (Yoshimoto rengaronshū)* contains the *Kon-an* as an appendix (pp. 18–23) as well as the rules section of Kanera's *Renga shogakushō* (Notes for beginners in linked verse, 1447–1456).

8. Sōzei was official Renga Master of the Ashikaga government at the time. A note at the end of the *Kon-an* says that Kanera consulted with Sōzei while writing his rules, and it seems certain that he would also have consulted other major figures as well.

9. Kidō, *Rengashi ronkō* 2, pp. 495–516.

10. See translation of rules, Section III.

11. For bibliographic information on *Mugonshō*, see the Bibliography.

12. Again, for bibliographic information on *Ubuginu*, see the Bibliography.

13. Esperanza Ramirez-Christensen, "The Essential Parameters of Linked Poetry,"

in *Harvard Journal of Asiatic Studies* 41:557 (December 1981).

14. I owe this translation to Karen Brazell and Lewis Cook. See Konishi, "The Art of Renga," tr. Karen Brazell and Lewis Cook, *The Journal of Japanese Studies* 2.1:33–61 (Winter 1975).

15. *Tōfu renga hiji*, ed. Ijichi, in *NKBZ* 51, p. 176.

Notes to the Rulebook of 1501

1. By beginning his rulebook with a section on rhyme, a poetic category usually considered irrelevant to the Japanese tradition, Yoshimoto acknowledges a debt to the example of Chinese linked verse (*lien-chü*). Instead of phonetic rhyming, however, his discussion centers on the question of clashing among the final words in adjacent verses, encouraging a good blend of verses, ending with both nouns (*mono no na*) and inflective words (*kotoba*). Exactly what is meant by the latter word is not clear in Yoshimoto's statement, but Ijichi Tetsuo argues that it must refer to inflective words (chiefly verbs and adjectives) and to suffixes such as those mentioned by Yoshimoto himself: *tsutsu*, *keri*, etc. (See supplementary notes to *Renri hishō*, in *NKBT* 66, p. 245.)

2. Here again the rulebook is unclear, but the most likely meaning of Shōhaku's statement is that clashing is not a problem between nouns formed from the *ren'yōkei* (the conjunctive). This interpretation is given in *MGS* (p. 92) and followed also by Konishi Jin'ichi (Konishi, *Sōgi*, p. 251).

3. *Kogaru*, "to burn," is homophonous with *kogaru*, "to be rowed." The third verse in the series described thus interprets the second verse in a new light, linking "boat" to "row." Were "autumn leaves" to be used, on the other hand, it would constitute a link with the first verse (since autumn leaves are said to "burn" with color)—an example of repetition. The basic principle involved is simple: the third verse in any series must avoid an obvious relationship with the first.

4. The link between "the world" (*yo*) and "bamboo" (*take*) is once again based on a homophonous relationship between another word pronounced *yo*, meaning "joint" (of bamboo in this case), and *yo*, "the world." These two words in fact form a conventional association used in linking, according to *RGS* 561.

5. *Renga shogakushō* (Notes for beginners in linked verse, 1569?), a mid-sixteenth-century commentary on the rules, explains the term "escape-poem" (*nigeuta*) this way:

> If one links "Akashi Bay" to a verse that contains the word "morning mist" and then continues in a third verse with "a boat fades behind the isles," all three of the verses will be alluding to the same foundation poem. [*KKS* 409: In the dim light / of the spreading morning mist / on Akashi Bay / a boat fades behind the isles / and my heart follows in its wake.] Even if there were no intent on the part of the first poet to allude to this poem, the phrase "morning mist" nevertheless amounts to an allusion when seen in the context of the second verse. Without the foundation poem as a backdrop, in fact, there would be no basis for linking "Akashi Bay" to "morning mist" in the first place. As for what an "escape-poem" is, this will explain it: to link "the isles appear" to "as my boat rows by" would cause no problem at all, because the second link would then be based on allusion to a different foundation poem. [*SKS* 899: As my boat rows by / on its long oversea journey, / from the far distance, / through the straights at Nagato, / the Yamato isles appear.]

(Cited in Ijichi's supplementary notes to *Renri hishō*, in *NKBT* 66, pp. 243–244.) Part of the reasoning here may depend on the fact that both *KKS* 409 and *SKKS* 899 would have been recognizable to any Japanese poet as works attributed to the great Man'yō-period poet Hitomaro; but the gist of the argument is that the second poem, while fitting nicely with the link already described in the first part of the example, introduces a different source of allusion—an "escape" from the problem of recurrence.

6. *MGS*, p. 149, seems to attribute this statement to Kanera, but I have followed Hoshika and Yamada's index, Konishi (*Sōgi*, p. 254), Fukui Kyūzō (*Renga no shiteki kenkyū*, p. 131), and the text of Kanera's work used by Okami (*Yoshimoto rengaronshū*), in tracing the statement to Shōhaku.

7. *Horikawa-In hyakushu* is an anthology of sixteen different hundred-poem *uta* anthologies by Minamoto no Toshiyori (d. 1129), Fujiwara no Mototoshi (1056–1142), and others, compiled in 1104 by order of the Retired Emperor Horikawa. *GRJ* 8, pp. 65–107.

8. Poems appealed to for precedent were called *hikiuta* or *shōka*. Such precedents were, as is apparent from this whole section of the rules, of great importance in linked verse. Allusion was restricted to *waka* sources, and the same was generally true for references to poems made in attempts to establish usage. In a *renga* session, a poet was free to refer to such precedents in defense of a verse's syntax, style, or vocabulary. Some commentaries on *hyakuin* from Sōgi's time even refer to great examples of *renga* of the past in order to establish precedent.

9. The name Go-Fukō-on was one of Nijō Yoshimoto's pseudonyms. The source of this particular statement, however, is uncertain. It does not appear in original manuscripts of *Ōan shinshiki* or its appendices, nor does it come up in any of Yoshimoto's other rulebooks, handbooks, or treatises. The idea that, contrary to Yoshimoto's advice, allusion to *Genji monogatari* should generally not extend over three verses is also voiced in Sōgi's *Bun'yō* (Cutting through leaves, 1488). See *KRRS*, p. 221.

10. The source of this rebuttal is also not certain. *MGS*, p. 149, again attributes it to Kanera, but Hoshika and Yamada (*Renga hōshiki kōyō*), Konishi (*Sōgi*, p. 248), and Fukui (*Renga no shiteki kenkyū*, p. 132) all give the statement as Shōhaku's.

11. The problem of what is "essence" (*tai*) and what "attribute" (*yū*) is a complex one. In even the most lucid explanation the criteria finally appear to be somewhat arbitrary, and there are more discrepancies and disagreements among rulebooks on this topic than on most others. For a fairly complete account of the problem, see Nagayama Isamu, "Renga ni okeru taiyū," *Gengo to bungei* 1:22–33 (1962). A list of essential and attributive vocabulary in the major lexical categories is given in Shōhaku's rules (see Section XVIII). The "extracategorical" cases given by Yoshimoto show the abstract principle at work, although there is little indication that such abstract restrictions were paid much heed by later poets.

12. *Yobukodori. Bontō-an sode no shita* (Notes from Bontō's sleeve pocket, 1384) insists that this is a metaphorical epithet meaning "lovely woman" (see Shimazu, *Renga no kenkyū*, p. 394), but *MGS*, p. 127, takes it to mean simply "spring bird." Yoshimoto seems to take it in the latter sense.

13. Opinion is widely divided on the meaning of this term. Most modern scholars want to identify the bird it signifies with the cuckoo. *RGS* 359 gives two possible interpretations: "a baby owl" and "a beautiful bird." Bontō (Shimazu, ibid., p. 388) refers to it as a "kingfisher, a bird that makes its nest in marshes

and rivers." *MGS*, p. 23, implies that the word is simply used to refer to a bird of great beauty.

14. *Hototogisu* (*Cuculus poliocephalus*). A bird of the cuckoo family. I owe the translation "wood thrush" to Robert H. Brower (see Brower, *Fujiwara Teika's Hundred-Poem Sequences of the Shōji Era, 1200*, p. 56).

15. There is some confusion here as to whether "demon" should be considered an *Animal* or a *Living Thing* (*shōrui*). The point of Shōhaku's comments is that the word is really in a category of its own. Old Chinese dictionaries do tend to associate "demon" with various kinds of snakes (notably the adder and the cobra), which were anciently classified as *Insects* (see Morohsahi Tetsuji, *Dai kanwa jiten* 12, p. 676).

16. *Kogarashi*. Literally, "tree witherer"—a cold blast of winter wind.

17. *Naruko*. A device consisting of bamboo rattles suspended across a field with rope that could be pulled by the field guard in order to scare birds and animals away from crops.

18. *Hita* (also *hiki-ita*). Another device used to frighten birds.

19. *Toboso*. Originally a word used to refer to a pivot used in hinging a door, but by the Muromachi period it seems to have referred to the door itself.

20. An old term for *kirigirisu*, "field cricket."

21. A proverb, probably of Chinese origin, suggesting the unruliness of human passions.

22. A saying from *Chuang-tzu:* "Man's life under heaven—it passes like a white colt by a gap in the wall." See Burton Watson, *The Complete Works of Chuang Tzu*, p. 330, for another translation.

23. See note 37, this chapter.

24. *Sono akatsuki*. The Buddhist moment of enlightenment.

25. *Samidare*. Rains of the fifth lunar month, Japan's rainy season.

26. *Mume no ame* (modern *tsuyu*). Virtually synonymous with *samidare*. The new green growth on the flowering plum emerges at about the same time as the rains; hence the appellation. *MGS*, p. 41: "If *samidare* has already been introduced, then *mume no ame* should not be used in the same sequence."

27. These are different pronunciations of the same Chinese character.

28. In linked verse there are three established meanings for the word *furusato*: (1) an abandoned capital or imperial residence; (2) an old town (or townhouse) where the person is presently living; (3) the "home" one has left behind in travel (see *RGS* 176).

29. *Yado*, here translated as "lodge," and *yadori*, here translated as "lodging," are different pronunciations of the same Chinese character, but there is a subtle difference in nuance as well. *Yado* usually refers to a more permanent kind of residence, while *yadori* indicates a temporary lodging such as a travelers' inn.

30. A place where dew accumulates is in poetry said to be a "lodging for the dew" (*tsuyu no yadori*).

31. *Niwa no oshie*. Teachings passed down from father to son or from master to disciple. The term originated from an incident in the Confucian *Analects* in which the Master stops his son in the garden and cautions him to spend more time in study of poetry and ritual. See Waley, *The Analects of Confucius*, pp. 207–208.

32. *Nokoru kari*. *MGS*, p. 23, defines the term to refer only to geese late in returning from Siberia in autumn: "*Nokoru kari* is in the *Autumn* category. These

are geese who return late, after lingering along the way. This is something about which people are often mistaken." Shōhaku's comment, on the other hand, seems to say that the word was also used to refer to geese that left late for the continent in spring.

33. An archaic term for *saru* (*Macaca fuscata*), the Japanese monkey.

34. The reference here is to *otoko*, "male," and not to "man" in the more general sense.

35. Saohime. The Goddess of Spring.

36. Hashihime. Protector of bridges, especially of the famed Uji Bridge.

37. Both readings refer to the same bird.

38. *Tama no o.* A conventional epithet (*makura-kotoba*) that usually carries the implication "of short duration." *Sōgi sode no shita*, in *KRRS*, p. 249.

39. *Kozue no aki.* An ornamental term for the ninth lunar month.

40. *Chiri no yo.* A Buddhist pejorative for the vulgar world.

41. *Nori no shi.* A Buddhist monk.

42. An archaic term for "ocean."

43. *Kami no ku* and *shimo no ku*. The upper (seventeen-syllable) and lower (fourteen-syllable) parts of an *uta*. In linked verse the terms were often used to refer to the alternating long and short verses of a sequence.

44. *Nori no mushiro.* A straw mat upon which Buddhist masters sat while expounding the Law; by extension, the Law itself.

45. *Na no kami.* One of the specific, "named" gods of the Shinto pantheon: Amaterasu no Ōmikami, "The Sun Goddess," etc.

46. *Nisemono no hana.* Metaphorical uses of the word "blossom," such as "blossoms of snow." The word *nisemono* is used in this sense throughout the rulebook.

47. *Yo no hana.* Generally a reference to cherry blossoms blooming late in the third lunar month or early in the fourth. Shimazu Tadao, however, takes the term to indicate blossoms other than the cherry. See Shimazu, ed., *Rengashū*, p. 387.

48. *Hana momiji.* This compound may refer to the most characteristic beauties of spring and autumn, but it can also indicate "bright red leaves."

49. Those who contended that "blossoms" should be counted as a three-instance word were no doubt insisting on the authority of *Ōan shinshiki*, which puts *hana* in the category of words that may appear only three times in a *hyakuin*. In Yoshimoto's earliest treatise, however, *hana* appears with the comment that it is common to use the word once in each of the four sheets of a sequence (see *Hekirenshō*, in *NKBZ* 51, p. 49). This comment probably describes general practice in the mid-fifteenth century as well. It should be noted, nonetheless, that there were exceptions to this rule even in Sōgi's time. Until the sixteenth century there seems to have been no absolute rule making the appearance of the word *hana* obligatory in each sheet. For details, see Kidō, *Rengashi ronkō* 2, p. 515, and Shimazu, ed., *Rengashū*, pp. 385–388.

50. Fujiwara. The first character in this famous family name was of course "wisteria."

51. The word "willow" (*yanagi*), unless otherwise qualified, would indicate the Spring category (*RGS* 889).

52. *Sakura momiji.* The autumn leaves of the cherry tree.

53. *Kusa no momiji.* The colored blades of dying autumn grasses.

54. *Momiji no hashi*. In autumn a "bridge of autumn leaves" was said to span the River of Heaven (the Milky Way). According to the Tanabata legend, it was over this bridge that the Weaver Maiden and the Herd Boy traveled for their once-a-year tryst on the night of the seventh day of the seventh lunar month.

55. *Hama ogi*, probably synonymous with *ashi*, or "marsh reed" (*Phragmites communis*), as a link by Gusai (*Tsukubashū* 1333) shows:

Kusa no na mo	Even the grasses
tokoro ni yorite	are known by different names
kawaru nari	in different places.
Naniwa no ashi wa	The *ashi* of Naniwa
Ise no hamaogi	are *hamaogi* in Ise.

56. *Obana*. The flowering ear of the miscanthus.

57. *Suguro no susuki*. In spring, fields were burned to produce rich soil, leaving the "charred stubble" of the miscanthus behind.

58. *Hoya*. A roof thatched with reeds of one sort or another, often with miscanthus.

59. *Shio yaku*. Fires were used in the distillation of salt from sea brine.

60. *Takitsuse*. "Roaring rapids" might be a better translation. "Falling rapids" is meant to show the homophonous relationship between *takitsuse* and *taki*, "waterfall" or "cascade."

61. *Kano kishi*. A Buddhist term for the next life or enlightenment.

62. *Tamazusa*. An epithet for "letter."

63. *Sugaru*. An ancient word for "deer."

64. *Kaseki* is another old word for "deer." "To present a stag" (*ka o sashite*), however, is a phrase used to indicate a deceptive ploy or stratagem. The term comes from a famous incident in the history of the Chinese Ch'in dynasty (221–206 B.C.) in which an evil minister tested the loyalty of his subordinates by presenting a stag to the emperor and asking all to accept it as a horse. See *Shih chi* 1, p. 273.

65. "Turning the Wheel of the Law" is a metaphor for the teaching of Buddhist doctrine. Soon after achieving enlightenment, the historical Buddha is said to have "set in motion the Wheel of the Law" through his preaching.

66. *Mizuguruma wa shizen no koto ni ya*. An obscure phrase, perhaps meaning "Water wheel should only be counted if it should happen to appear." The word is indeed rarely seen in linked verse.

67. *Tsuri no tomoshibi*. A lamp held by a cord attached to its top.

68. *Nori no tomoshibi*. A phrase used metaphorically, meaning that the Buddhist Law lights the way to salvation like a lamp in the night; also, a metaphor for one who is "illuminated"–i.e., well-versed in the Way. Finally, it can be used more literally to refer to a lamp used in Buddhist ceremony.

69. *Haru no yuki*. A term that may be taken either as spring snow or as a metaphor for falling blossoms.

70. Kidō, *Rengashi ronkō* 2, 510, quotes another text of Shōhaku's work, the last part of which says "just as in the *honshiki*"–a term used to refer to rules in use before Yoshimoto's time. *Hekirenshō* (*NKBZ* 51, p. 50) and *Renri hishō* (*NKBT* 66, p. 58) list "snow" among things that may appear four times in a sequence but add a statement to the effect that the word should really only be used three times, with "spring snow" counting as a fourth instance. Shōhaku, perhaps appealing to rules in use before Yoshimoto, disregards the last restriction,

saying that "snow" may appear four times without qualification—with "spring snow" counting in that number only if it is used.

71. See Section IX for previous reference. The Japanese word here is *ariake* and refers to the moon remaining in the sky after daybreak during the latter half of the lunar month.

72. *Haru, aki o tomuru.* In poetry, barrier-gates (*seki*) are sometimes described as "halting" the seasons in their progress.

73. Again, this sentence is unclear. Yoshimoto's rules originally stated that "barrier-gate" should be used "once as such, once in the name of a *Famous Place*, once in connection with *Love*, and once in connection with either *Autumn* or *Spring*" (see Okami, *Yoshimoto rengaronshū*, p. 10). Shōhaku's comments confuse this scheme and finally seem to restrict the word to three rather than four appearances (see *MGS*, p. 92).

74. *Tsuki no kōri.* A metaphor for moonlight.

75. The word "bell," although not technically in the *Buddhism* category, is generally associated with the precincts of Buddhist temples. Shōhaku's point is that, in cases where categorization by lexical content is difficult, context should govern interpretation.

76. *Soradanome.* A metaphorical phrase meaning "to put one's trust in something unreliable."

77. According to *MGS*, p. 15, the phrase "birds referred to in the context of hunting" indicates the pheasant, while "birds that sleep on the water" (*ukinedori*) means a kind of waterfowl. "Night bird," a word already listed several times in other entries, is a euphemism for "cock."

78. *Nisemono no tama.* Again, a reference to metaphorical uses of a term: "jewels of rain," "jewels of dew," etc.

79. *Ya.* The word can also refer to the proprietor of a shop.

80. *Ukiyo*, "the floating world," and *yo no naka*, "this world of ours," are very similar in meaning, as Shōhaku's subsequent comment suggests. Both words tend to be used in the context of *Love* or *Lamentation*.

81. "Named" instances of the "world" (*na no yo*) would include "the world of dust," "the world of dreams," etc.

82. *Ao-ume, momiji nado wa shizen no koto taru beshi.* Earlier (see note 65) Shōhaku indicated that instances of "water wheel" occur only rarely; here he seems to be saying much the same thing.

83. *Mihashi.* May be used as an honorific of general reference ("the venerable bridgeway"), but usually refers to the stairway leading into the *Shishinden*, the main ceremonial building of the Imperial Palace.

84. "Yume no ukihashi." The title of the last chapter of *Genji monogatari*, which leaves Ukifune, and the conclusion of her story, in uncertainty. By extension, the phrase is often used to connote a sense of melancholy and uncertainty over life in the dreamlike world.

85. *Hama bisashi.* The eaves of a house on the seashore. Also used to describe the rustic dwellings of fisherfolk. *MGS*, p. 11, says that the term is also used to refer to a place on the beach that the surf has hollowed out, making the appearance of overhanging eaves.

86. *Kumo no uebito.* High members of the court aristocracy, specifically *tenjōbito* (courtiers) granted audience privileges in the Imperial Residence.

87. *Kumoi no niwa.* The garden of the Imperial Palace.

88. *Ararebashiri.* A song sung at court during New Year festivities. The tune was accompanied to the tapping of feet; hence, perhaps, the title.

89. *Sono.* A crop garden, or at least a large, forested garden, as opposed to the small, ornamental gardens (*niwa*) attached to residences.

90. *Shika oi.* Evidently the idea of chasing deer from the crops places a verse in the *Plants* context, according to Shōhaku's thinking.

91. *Kokoro no matsu* and *kokoro no sugi.* Both terms refer to the idea of steadfastness. The pine and the cedar are both evergreens that never change color or attitude. "Cedarlike heart, pinelike heart—both mean a heart that is steadfast." *Sōgi sode no shita,* in *KRRS,* p. 253.

92. *Shitamoe.* Literally, "undergrowth." The word refers to new growth emerging in the fields each spring. What the word clashes with is not made clear in Shōhaku's comment, but *MGS,* p. 85, says that it should be separated from words in the *Plants* category by at least two verses, an interpretation that would seem to be supported by the word's appearance in this part of the rules.

93. Plain of Floating Islands. A swampy area south of Mt. Ashitaka in Suruga province (eastern Shizuoka prefecture).

94. *Ikeru o hanatsu.* A term referring to the Hōjōe, a yearly ceremony of the eighth lunar month in which fish and birds were "set free" from tanks and cages in a gesture intended to compensate for lives taken in war. The most famous of these rites, at least in the fifteenth century, was the one performed at the Iwashimizu Hachiman Shrine, a Shinto shrine dedicated to the God of War. Originally the ritual seems to have been Buddhist in affiliation; later, under the influence of medieval eclecticism, it became a Shinto observance. *MGS,* p. 4, puts the word in three categories: *Shinto, Waters,* and *Autumn.*

95. *Uma no hanamuke.* A parting banquet or gift for travelers.

96. Tsu no kuni no Naniwa is a place located in what is now Ōsaka; Yamashiro in Toba is a place in Kyoto. Both place-names are frequently used as double entendres: Naniwa because it contains the interrogative pronoun *nani,* or "what," and Toba because it can be extended to form the word *towanu,* the negative inflection of *tou,* "to ask."

97. Shinobu District is located in ancient Michinoku, now Fukushima Prefecture. In poetry, the name is often used as a pun, *shinobu* meaning "to yearn for in secret." This basic meaning pertains to all the references to the word in Shōhaku's lists.

98. Again, a place-name in the Shinobu District, Fukushima Prefecture.

99. The name of a hill located in what is now Osaka.

100. *Furusato,* "home town," contains the character for old (*furu*); hence the clash.

101. As part of the New Year festivities held on the first day of the rat (*ne no hi*) in the first month of the lunar year, courtiers traditionally went out into the fields and pulled pine seedlings for good luck. For details, see William H. and Helen Craig McCullough, *A Tale of Flowering Fortunes: Annals of Japanese Aristocratic Life in the Heian Period,* 1, pp. 378–379.

102. Otowayama is the name given to one of the thirty-six peaks of the Higashi-yama area of Kyoto; Otonashigawa refers to the headwaters of the Kumano River in ancient Kii (modern Wakayama prefecture). The clash here arises because of the presence in both place-names of the word *oto,* "sound."

103. *Kure.* Variously translated herein as "end," "to come to a close."

104. Shadow would clash with *ko no shita,* "under the trees," but not with "under the moon" or "under the heavens." See *MGS,* p. 24.

105. *Kinuginu* is a word referring to the parting of lovers after a night's tryst. The words clash because both mean "parting."

106. *Omoi* and *hi*. The clash here arises partly because "musing" is often treated in metaphorical terms that suggest "burning" and partly because of the homophony existing between the last syllables of *omo(h)i* and *hi*.

107. It is not clear from Yoshimoto's statement what *shi* clashes with, but *UG*, p. 184, indicates that it clashes with another instance of itself.

108. *Yumiharizuki* and *toshi no ya*. The former is a descriptive term for the crescent moon, the latter a metaphor for the swift passage of time.

109. *Kure*. The word is a part of the compounds *yūgure*, "nightfall," and *yūmagure*, "dusk." *Kure* itself may also be used to refer to the close of day; hence the clash with "evening shower."

110. *Akekure*. Again, the clash is between "evening" and the word *kure*, here rendered as "late."

111. *Tsukihi*. A metaphorical expression meaning "time."

112. A Sino-Japanese dictionary compiled in the mid-Heian period by Minamoto no Shitagō (911–983).

113. Both "clan way" (*ie no kaze*) and "storm" (*arashi*) contain the character for "wind" as a component; hence the clash.

114. The first character in the place-name Kiso is the character for "tree" or "wood."

115. A treatise by the poet-scholar Kenshō (b. 1130).

116. *Hotori*, pronounced *be* in compounds. In this latter form the word appears in both *nobe*, "fields," and *yamabe*, "mountains"; hence the clash.

117. The second character in Awaji is the character for "path."

118. The final syllable of *nageki* is homophonous with *ki*, "wood."

119. The last syllable of *katami* is homophonous with *mi*, the stem of the verb *miru*, "to see." *Nagame*, "gaze," does not clash with *katami* because it contains no homophonous syllable.

120. An adverbial intensifier meaning "never at all."

121. *Omiyaru* and *omou*. The two words are nearly identical in meaning in many cases, although the former is often used in the sense of "to think about (someone or something)."

122. The implication of this statement is that identical forms of any inflected word should be separated by at least two verses.

123. Shikishima is an archaic name for the Japanese islands, and *Shikishima no michi*, "the Way of Shikishima," is a synonym for *uta no michi*, "the Way of Poetry."

124. *Moji amari*. *Uta* verses traditionally had thirty-one syllables, and *renga* verses seventeen or fourteen. In some cases, however, poets chose to exceed traditional restrictions in order to produce special effects.

125. Here the word "*waka* treatises" seems to refer to such works in the general sense and not to one text in particular.

126. *Azumaya*. A chapter title in *Genji monogatari*. The word may also refer to an Eastern-style garden bower or kiosk. The clash with Azumaji, "the Eastern Road," arises from the fact that both words contain *Azuma*, "the east," as a component.

127. *Nuru*. The verb form "to recline" or "to lie down" as opposed to the noun "sleep."

128. *Sōmon no yosutebito.* A term referring to hermit-monks, as opposed to simple recluses.

129. *Sanji gana.* Words of three syllables in which at least two syllables are constituted by identical vowels or consonants: *chikaki, fukaki, nagara, bakari,* etc. For other examples, see *MGS,* p. 83.

130. "Words that must be separated by at least five verses" is intended as translation of *jisari* in the phrase *tada wa jisari naru beshi.* What is meant by the term is not made clear in Shōhaku's remarks, but it seems certain that it is a contracted form of *dōjisari,* meaning "the same word must be separated from another instance of itself." *MGS,* p. 70, uses *dōjisari* in a context in which Shōhaku uses only *jisari.* Yamada, *Renga gaisetsu,* p. 114, interprets the term in the same way.

131. The word *ato* has a wide variety of meanings: bird tracks, brush marks, ruins, remains, memento, scar, etc. Why these two usages are singled out is not clear. The phrase "bird tracks," however, may sometimes be used to refer to an awkward hand in calligraphy, and that fact may be more important in this case than the presence of *ato* in both expressions.

132. *Kokonoe.* An epithet for the Imperial Palace compound.

133. *Miyako* and *Ōmiya.* Both contain the word *miya;* hence the clash.

134. See note 54. The Tanabata stars correspond to Western Vega and Altair.

135. "Ink-dyed robes" (*sumizome goromo*) were worn by recluses and hermits as well as by true priests. *MGS,* p. 116, puts the word in the *Lamentation* category and not in *Buddhism;* and the same is true of *UG,* p. 195.

136. The work cited here is *Mototoshishō,* presumably referring to a treatise by Fujiwara no Mototoshi. Shōhaku's reference to it is meant to support Kanera's placing of "moss robes" and "ink-dyed robes" among words that must be separated by more than one verse—an entry that does not appear in the 1502 text. Thus Shōhaku's comment may be interpreted as an attempt to compensate for an earlier oversight.

137. In Kanera's statement, the middle character of both *asazukuhi* and *yūzukuhi* is the character for "moon." Those to whom Shōhaku refers use a different character—*tsuku,* "to be connected or attached"—in an attempt to avoid the kind of clashing Kanera describes.

138. *Ama no iwafune,* according to Japanese legend, refers to a stone boat in which the gods row down to earth from the Plain of Heaven; *amanogawa fune* is a boat that plies the waters of the River of Heaven.

139. *Kawaoto no ame.* A metaphorical phrase describing the sound of gurgling river water as "the patter of raindrops."

140. Thus "clouds of blossoms" clashes with both "clouds" and "blossoms."

141. Since *nami no hana,* "blossoms on the waves," is generally used as a figurative expression meaning "whitecaps," there is no clash with words in the *Plants* category.

142. *Nisemono.* See note 46, this chapter.

143. In other words, in the case of compounds that can be taken literally as well as figuratively (i.e., "snow on the waves"), the compound will clash with both its constituents; those that can only be taken figuratively (i.e., "snowfall of blossoms"), on the other hand, will not clash with both constituents.

144. *Tai-yū no hoka.* Literally, to be "outside the *tai-yū* distinction." The principle involved in the progression of phenomena in these categories can be

summarized as follows: once both "essential" and "attributive" words have been introduced in sequence, the first category introduced may not be returned to in a third verse. Thus, essential–essential–attributive or attributive–attributive–essential involve no problems, but interrupted progressions such as essential–attributive–essential are not allowed. The "neutral" category makes for a partial escape from this restriction, for attributive–essential–neutral affords another possibility, as Yoshimoto's example suggests. No series can extend over more than three verses, however; and the series neutral–essential (or attributive)–neutral is as contrary to the principle as the other examples listed above.

145. Suma and Akashi are both coastal regions on the Inland Sea near modern Kobe.

146. These place-names refer to Suma no Ueno and Akashi no Oka, inland regions of the same areas mentioned in the previous note. See *MGS*, p. 122.

147. Naniwa and Shiga are both *Famous Places*, the one located on the coast at modern Ōsaka and the other on the shores of Lake Biwa. Yoshimoto's *Hekirenshō* implies that the two places are not necessarily in the *Waters* category "because they are places where *yamazato* (mountain towns) are also located" (*NKBZ* 51, p. 53). *MGS*, p. 120, says that the names of *Famous Places* on the coastline are generally not in the *Waters* category, but that Akashi and Suma are given exceptional status because of their longstanding association with the sea in the *waka* tradition.

148. *Komo.* Sometimes translated as "water-oat."

149. *Kakehi.* A bamboo water conduit.

150. *Miyakodori.* A type of waterfowl. For a description, see Helen Craig McCullough, tr., *Tales of Ise*, p. 205.

151. *Tomaya.* A rustic hut with a roof of thatched sedge or cogon grass.

152. Namidagawa, "river of tears," is usually used figuratively, but occasionally refers to a specific place.

153. *Iwahashi.* A bridge of stepping stones.

154. *Takitsuse.* See note 60, this chapter.

155. Uji no Kawashima. An island in the Uji River.

156. As mentioned above in note 93, the word "island" (*shima*) is generally considered to be in both the *Mountains* and *Waters* categories. River islands, however, seem to escape the former categorization.

157. Hasedera. Located at Hase in the mountains of Nara Prefecture.

158. Kiyomidera. A temple located in Kiyomi City, Shizuoka Prefecture (ancient Suruga Province), that stands on what is believed to be the ancient site of the Kiyomi Barrier-Gate. Now pronounced Seikenji.

159. Naniwadera. The Shitennōji in modern Ōsaka.

160. The Kiso Road ran through ancient Shinano (now Nagano Prefecture) from Torii Pass to Magome Pass. The Suzuka Road ran through the Suzuka Mountains in ancient Ise, Iga, and Ōmi (now Mie and Shiga Prefectures). Both were major highways during the Muromachi period.

161. Yoshino refers to the mountainous area of central Nara Prefecture famous for its cherry blossoms; Ono is the Ōhara area north of Kyoto.

162. Tsuru no Hayashi. The grove of sala trees where the historical Buddha, Sakyamuni, passed away. The appellation stems from a miraculous event at the

moment of his death in which the trees of the grove turned white as the color of the crane.

163. Washi no Mine. The Japanese name for Sanskrit Gradhvakūta, a famous mountain in northern India where Sakyamuni expounded *The Lotus Sutra*.

164. Muro no Yashima. Another name for the area of the Ōmiwa Shrine in Tochigi City, Tochigi Prefecture (ancient Shimotsuke). The meaning of the name is unclear, but scholars connect it with *kamado*, "hearth" or "furnace." The steam rising off a nearby pond was often compared to smoke in poetry; hence the etymology.

165. Katsuragi. A mountain on the border between ancient Kawachi and Yamato (modern Ōsaka and Nara).

166. Matsushima is a group of islands lying off the coast of central Miyagi Prefecture (ancient Rikuzen). *RGS* 95 notes that the word "island" is in both the *Mountains* and *Waters* categories, so Shōhaku is not the first to place the word in both contexts.

167. Taminoshima, in modern Osaka, and Mishima, a town on the Izu peninsula, both contain the word "island" in their names but are nonetheless inland areas.

168. Koi no yama. Like Namidagawa in note 152, this place-name is usually used figuratively. There was, however, a place called Koi no yama in Uzen Province (Yamagata Prefecture), a reference to which would fall into the *Famous Places* category.

169. *Matsu no hana*. The term may refer to the pollen clusters that appear on the pine each spring, but *Bontō-an sode no shita* (Shimazu, *Renga no kenkyū*, p. 383) says the pine "blossoms" once every one hundred years.

170. *Aratama no toshi*. A conventional epithet for the new year.

171. Kasuga Matsuri. A festival held at the Kasuga Shrine in Nara during the third and eleventh lunar months. The Kasuga Shrine was the family shrine of the Fujiwara clan and the Kasuga Festival was thus one of the most lavish events of the court calendar.

172. The main Shinto festival of the court year was the Aoi Matsuri, held at the Kamo Shrine in the fourth lunar month each year. Festivals held at the Iwashimizu Hachiman Shrine in the third lunar month and additional Kamo Festivals held in the eleventh month were referred to as *rinji no matsuri*—"extraordinary" or "special" events, although in the Heian period these too were held on a regular basis. For details, see McCullough and McCullough, *A Tale of Flowering Fortunes*, pp. 408–409.

173. *Agatameshi*. Appointments to provincial posts were made at the court during the spring months.

174. See note 88 above.

175. *Suma no miharae*. While in exile at Suma, Genji and a few attendants go to the shoreline to undertake a ritual cleansing of their troubles and woes, as was customary practice on the day of the snake in the third lunar month. In contrast to the festive atmosphere of the court, Genji's rite is a sad and somber one, and it is cut short by a storm that eventually leads to his removal to Akashi. See Seidensticker, tr., *The Tale of Genji* 1, p. 245.

176. Because it took place on the day of the snake—anciently the third day of the third lunar month.

177. *Kokoro no hana*. A conventional phrase referring to the fickleness of the human heart, which like a flower fades quickly. The most famous statement of the idea is in Ono no Komachi's poem (*KKS* 797):

Iro miede	What is it that fades
utsurou mono wa	without any change in color?
yo no naka no	It is the flower
hito no kokoro no	of the heart of those who love
hana ni zo arikeru	in this world of ours.

178. *Shirao no taka.* A hunting hawk whose tail feathers have been artificially lengthened with swan or crane feathers.

179. *Tsugio no taka.* Another name for the hawk of note 178 above.

180. *Kami matsuru.* A general term referring to Shinto festivals. *UG,* p. 132, says that the term is put in the *Summer* category because the Kamo Festival, held in the fourth lunar month, is the most fundamental of Shinto festivals.

181. *Sakaki toru.* Refers to a rite in the Kamo Festival in which a *sakaki* branch (a variety of anise) is passed around. The *sakaki* is the sacred tree of Shinto.

182. *Kadai.* Topics used in *waka* contests and in the composition of hundred-poem anthologies (*hyakushu uta*).

183. Probably a reference to *Keibutsushū,* a work on *waka* topics.

184. Hirano Matsuri. Festival of the Hirano Shrine of northern Kyoto. Held in the fourth and eleventh lunar months, but again put in the *Summer* category because the earlier performance was considered to be more fundamental.

185. *Suma no nagaame.* Most likely a reference to the rainy season spent by Genji at Suma. See Seidensticker, tr., *The Tale of Genji* 1, pp. 231–32.

186. *Hato fuku.* A signal-whistle used in hunting, accomplished by placing the palms of the hands together and blowing between them to imitate the cooing of a dove. *Yakumo mishō,* p. 375.

187. *Hisagi.* Also pronounced *kisasage. Catalpa ovata,* a broad-leafed deciduous tree.

188. *Uragare.* A term referring to the withered ends of grasses and shrubs.

189. *Shinobugusa (Polypodium lineare).* In poetry, the plant is most often encountered in the context of a pun, *shinobu* meaning "to yearn for in secret."

190. *Hoya tsukuru.* Possibly a reference to the building of a rustic hut. *MGS,* pp. 13, 105, however, says the phrase refers specifically to the construction of a temporary hut in Shinano Province (Nagano Prefecture) on the twentieth day of the seventh lunar month as part of the Misayama Festival.

191. *Hatsutogari.* The first hawking expedition of autumn.

192. *Toyade.* The opening of the hawk's cages for the first hunt.

193. *Uzura goromo.* A patchwork robe. *Sōgi sode no shita:* "A short robe." *KRRS,* p. 251.

194. *Kaya.* Various forms of grasses and reeds used in thatching roofs.

195. *Tsukasameshi.* Appointments to important posts in the court administration were made in autumn.

196. The word "starry night" (*hoshi tsukiyo*) means literally "a moonlit night lit by the stars," or in other words a moonless night illuminated by starlight.

197. *Negai no ito.* During the Tanabata Festival, poles to which five-colored threads had been attached were presented by women as offerings to the Weaver Star, Vega.

198. *Mozu no kusaguki.* In spring, the shrike leaves the lowlands and flies into the hills, but his disappearance from farm villages was traditionally attributed to his hiding in the tall grasses; thus *mozu no,* "of the shrike," became a fixed prefix for *kusaguki,* "grass stalks."

199. According to Sōgi's *Bun'yō*, the word *susamajiki*, here translated as "chilling," can also mean "frightening" (see *KRRS*, p. 217). *MGS*, p. 108, says that the word indicates *Autumn* even when it is used to mean "frightening"; and this seems also to be the import of Shōhaku's comment. For a complete account of the word's usages in linked verse, see Kaneko, *Shinsen tsukubashū no kenkyū*, pp 641–690.

200. *Niwabi*. Fires used to light *kagura* dances at court; also the name of a *kagura* song.

201. *Konoha goromo*. May indicate either an actual robe made of fall leaves or a metaphorical "robe" of leaves surrounding the base of a tree. *MGS*, p. 62, says that actual robes of leaves were woven and worn by people at the time of Shen Nung, the mythical Chinese ruler who was attributed with the establishment of agriculture and husbandry.

202. Kita Matsuri. As contrasted with the Southern Festival (Minami Matsuri) at the Iwashimizu Shrine. See note 172 above.

203. *Toyo akari no sechie*. The final banquet of the Thanksgiving Festival (Daijōsai), held in the eleventh lunar month.

204. *Omigoromo*. "Purification" robes were worn by participants in the Shinjōe and the Daijōe, both imperial rites of thanksgiving held in the autumn and winter.

205. *Hikage no ito*. Cords attached to the caps of participants in the thanksgiving rites as a sign of their "taboo" status.

206. *Toshi no uchi ni haru tatsu*. In the lunar calendar, spring occasionally began in the twelfth month of the old year, especially during years when an intercalary month had been added to the regular twelve-month scheme.

207. *Asaji*. A variety of grass, usually growing in thickets.

208. *Ukisu*. A nest of reeds and dead leaves built among floating marsh grasses.

209. *Midori tatsu* and *wakamidori*. Both terms refer to new spring growth on trees and shrubs.

210. *Shioya*. A hut on the beach where salt is distilled from seawater.

211. *Ie o izuru*. A euphemism for taking the tonsure as a Buddhist priest.

212. *Sato kagura*. *MGS*, p. 72: "Any *kagura* taking place outside the palace is "town kagura."

213. *Momoshiki*. A decorative expression for the Imperial Palace.

214. *Kumo no ue*. Again, a decorative expression for the Imperial Palace.

215. See note 132, this chapter.

216. *Sugi no mado*. A window shutter made of cedar wood.

217. *Sugegasa*. A large sedge hat used for protection from the sun and rain during travel.

218. *Shiba toru*. Brush was gathered for firewood.

219. *Saibara*. A type of folk song popular at court throughout the classical period.

220. *Hanazome no koromo*, "blossom-dyed robes," for instance, would be in the *Spring* category. See *MGS*, p. 6.

221. *Ashigamo*. The same as simple *kamo*, "mallard."

222. *Ashitazu no*. A pillow word for "to cry."

223. *Take no miya*. The Ise Shrine, according to *Sōgi sode no shita*. *KRRS*, p. 257.

224. Sue no Matsuyama. A famous mountain in Miyagi Prefecture (ancient Rikuchū).

225. *Yomogiu no yado.* Nearly always a reference to the "Wormwood" chapter of *Genji monogatari.* See Seidensticker, tr., *The Tale of Genji* 1, p. 290.

226. *Mugura no yado.* An abandoned house.

227. *Yūgao no yado.* Again, usually a reference to the "Evening Faces" chapter of *Genji monogatari.* See Seidensticker, tr., *The Tale of Genji* 1, p. 57.

228. *Kayaribi.* Incense burned as a mosquito deterrent. I owe the translation to Donald Keene (see Keene, tr., *Essays in Idleness,* p. 19).

229. *Matane.* To go back to sleep after waking in the night.

230. *Isaribi.* Fires used to attract fish at night.

231. *Ukinedori.* Ducks and wild geese, which sleep while afloat on the water.

232. *Kokoro no tsuki.* The heart of one who has attained a state of Buddhist enlightenment.

233. *Kokoro no yami.* Attachments to the world that keep the heart from attaining salvation, particularly the attachment of parents to their children.

234. See note 24, this chapter.

235. *Yume no yo.* The present world, the world of illusion according to Buddhist doctrine.

236. *Tsune no tomoshibi.* Lamps kept burning continuously in front of Buddhist and Shinto altars.

237. *Akehatete.* The period immediately following dawn.

238. *Akesugite.* Another reference to the period just after dawn.

239. *Asaborake.* The faint, murky light of predawn.

240. *Kane no kasumu. MGS,* p. 24, indicates that this phrase referred to the tolling of the evening bell, but Shinkei in his *Shiyō shō* (Notes on my own use of the rules, 1471) says that it means simply "a bell ringing in the distance" (see Kidō, *Rengashi ronkō* 2, p. 497).

241. *Jibun ni arazu. RGS* 72 in fact lists "gloaming" (*yoi*) as a time of day. Shōhaku's rather enigmatic comment may mean that the word should not be counted among *Nocturnal Things.*

242. *Higurashi* (translated elsewhere as "cicala"). Sometimes used to refer to a variety of cricket and sometimes to the idea of "spending a day." It contains the word *higure,* "dusk"; hence the clash.

243. The first character in the compound *shigure,* "showers," is the character for "time."

244. *Kinuginu.* The characters in this compound, "the morning after," mean "robes," but Yoshimoto treats the concept rather than the characters in this case.

245. The Ikuta Shrine in what is now Kobe. Once famous for the grove of trees that surrounded it.

246. *Kakushi-dai.* A *waka* topic woven into the words of a verse so as to be "hidden" from obvious view.

247. The last syllable of *maki,* "black pine," is homophonous with the word *ki,* "tree."

248. *Unohana.* Also called Deutzia. The translation "white hydrangea" is from Brower, *Fujiwara Teika's Hundred-Poem Sequence,* p. 53.

249. *Ama obune* is a pillow word meaning "fisherman's skiff." It is usually attached to words beginning with *hatsu* (as in Mount Hatsuse) because the latter term can be interpreted as "to moor."

250. Tatsutahime. The Goddess of Autumn. Tatsuta is an area in Nara Prefecture famous for its autumn leaves.

251. *Hekirenshō* (see *NKBZ* 51, p. 57), for instance, says that a verse ending with the particle *ni* should not be followed by a verse ending with *te,* but stresses that such clashing exists only between the grammatical particles and not between sounds. Thus a verse ending with the word *koromode* ("sleeve") would pose no problems.

252. *Azuma asobi.* Originally performed in the eastern provinces around modern Tokyo. From the mid-Heian period on, these "entertainments" were held mainly at court. The dances were performed by four or six dancers and accompanied by flutes and stringed instruments playing tunes derived in the most part from eastern folk songs.

253. "Motomeko." The title of one of the most famous songs used in *azuma asobi.*

254. *No no miya.* Temporary shrine of the High Priestess of Ise and the Kamo Virgin; located west of the capital.

255. See Section XVI of Shōhaku's rules, p. 66.

256. *Sakuratai.* There are two theories concerning the origin of this name. One has it that the fish are in season around the time the cherry is in bloom; the other, that the fish's stripes are cherry pink in color.

257. *Sakuragai.* Named so because of its pink color, according to *MGS,* p. 100.

258. "Sakura hito." Title of a folksong, again according to *MGS,* p. 72.

259. *Sakura no ta. Bontō-an sode no shita* (Shimazu, *Renga no kenkyū,* p. 404) identifies this as the name of a specific place in Yoshino, but *MGS,* p. 100, refers to it simply as a large stand of cherry trees.

260. *No asobi.* An outing in the country for picnicking, herb-picking, hunting, etc. Not restricted to any one season.

261. *Nerai kari.* Falcon-hunting is classed in the *Winter* category, but hunting by torch was a *Summer* activity.

262. See note 54, this chapter.

263. *Hatsu shio. MGS,* p. 106: "This refers to the first tide on the fifteenth day of the eighth lunar month, but occasionally it is also used to refer to the first tide when it occurs a little before or after that date."

264. *Irodori. MGS,* p. 105: "varieties of small birds."

265. *Omoigusa.* A general term referring to various late autumn flowers: gentian, spiderwort, maidenflower, among others.

266. *Koigusa.* Again a general term for various grasses usually used metaphorically.

267. *Shinobu-zuri.* A process of dyeing that involved "rubbing" (*suru*) robes with *shinobu,* a mosslike fern. For details, see McCullough, tr., *Tales of Ise,* p. 200.

268. *Misogi.* A Shinto ritual in which, on the last day of the sixth lunar month, imperial princes and court officials ceremonially cleansed the court of impurities.

269. *Harau.* To purge or cleanse. Also a word with Shinto denotations, but referring to no specific event in the court calendar.

270. *Ma.* Written with a variety of different characters, all homophonous with the middle syllable of *yamagure.*

271. *Ki moji.* The examples Shōhaku gives (*fukaki* and *asaki, tōki* and *chikaki*) are adjectives ending in the attributive form; both sets are also antonyms. *UG,* p. 155, says that verbs ending in *ki,* the attributive form of the past suffix *shi,*

should be separated by at least two verses, although adjectives ending in *ki* do not clash at all.

272. *Nani no ji* and *iku no ji*.

273. *Tami no kamado*. A metonym for the common people, subjects of the emperor.

274. This refers not to a river (*kawa*), but to the Yokawa area of Mount Hiei, the great center of Tendai Buddhism located northeast of the capital.

275. *Yomogi ga soma*. A thicket of mugwort grown so tall that it might be taken for a stand of timber (*Sōgi sode no shita*). See *KRRS*, p. 268.

276. *Yamagatsu*. A general term for peasants, hunters, and woodsmen who live in the mountains.

277. The word "mountain bird" (*yamadori*) appears in Yoshimoto's work with the gloss, "This is in the *Miscellaneous* category."

278. In Ssu-ma Ch'ien's *Book of History*, Confucius meets Lao Tzu, and this comment is supposed to summarize his impressions of the Taoist master. Confucius says that he can understand the activities of birds, fish, and beasts well enough to hunt them down. "But when it comes to the dragon," he adds, "I know nothing of how it flies on the wind through the clouds of heaven. Today I have seen Lao Tzu, and indeed he is a dragon!" See *Shih chi* 7, p. 2140.

279. *Kakekotoba*. A technique by which one sequence of sounds can be made to produce different sets of words by different parsings.

280. *Mari no niwa*. A courtyard or garden area used for the court game of kickball (*kemari*).

281. *Kuni no umi*. A reference both to lakes such as Ōmi no Umi (Lake Biwa) and to ocean bays such as Ise no Umi. See *MGS*, p. 50.

282. The most famous of all medieval highways was the Eastern Road (Azumaji).

283. Shōhaku here seems to be alluding to *Sōgi sode no shita* (*KRRS*, p. 269). Elsewhere in the same text, however, Sōgi contradicts himself by saying that one may drop *Love* after one or two verses (pp. 239–240). In practice, *Love* was dropped after only one verse quite often.

284. *Higata*. The exposed mudflats of a beach at ebb tide.

285. *Miru*. A variety of seaweed.

286. *Me*. Another variety of sea plant.

287. *Ukikusa*. Marsh grass that floats on the surface although rooted underwater.

288. As noted earlier (note 11 above), there are a number of discrepancies among rulebooks concerning distinctions between "essences" and "attributes." Some words are classified identically in almost all sources: e.g., waves, water, and salt are all considered "attributive" in Yoshimoto, Kanera, and Shōhaku. On the other hand, "hermit's cavern" is "essential" in Yoshimoto and "attributive" in Shōhaku.

289. *Muro no to*. The cave of an ascetic.

290. The compound does not refer to any individual person but rather to the general concept of parents and children.

291. *Sōzu*. Written with the characters for "priest," but referring to scarecrows guarding crops. See *MGS*, p. 33.

292. *Kodama*. A tree spirit.

293. *Hana no aruji*. A person who owns a cherry grove, and thus a word in the

Human Relations category. Likewise, *tsuki no tomo* is in the category because it refers to friends who enjoy the moonlight together.

CHAPTER 4: READING BY THE RULES

1. The illustration appears in the text of *Shichijū-ichi ban shokunin uta-awase* (Seventy-round poem contest of the various professions), a mock poem contest of the late Muromachi period that presents poems by various professionals of the time, ranging from artists and poets to woodworkers and barrel-makers. For a text of the work that includes Mitsunobu's illustration, see *GRJ* 22, p. 180.

2. For a description of this short work, entitled *Renga kaiseki nijū-go kin* (Twenty-five rules for conduct in the *za*, 1489), see Okuda Isao, *Rengashi: sono kōdō to bungaku*, pp. 44–47.

3. Such commentaries exist for many of the most famous works of the *renga* canon, including *Minase sangin hyakuin, Yuyama sangin hyakuin,* and the solo sequence of 1499. The best study of *kochū* is Kaneko, *Renga kochūshaku no kenkyū*. Kaneko, ed., *Renga kochūshaku shū* contains commentaries on some of the more important personal anthologies, including several on Sōgi's *Wakuraba* (Old leaves, 1485) and *Shitakusa* (Undergrowth, 1496). Most commentaries are alike in focusing primarily on explication of linking technique; some of the more detailed ones also draw attention to allusions and to pertinent categories.

4. See p. 59.

5. *Kochiku* (Orphaned bamboo). Kaneko, ed., *Renga kochūshaku shū*, p. 547.

6. *RGS* 899. In Shōhaku's rules "Parting Love" is treated as a subcategory of *Love*. See p. 47.

7. *RGS* 899 treats "to visit in a dream," "to meet in dreams," and "to come in dreams" as in the *Love* category. *MGS* notes that "in general, the word dream indicates *Love* as a category" (p. 79).

8. *Shunmusō chū* (A commentary on Shōhaku's Spring dream, date uncertain). For a text with medieval commentary, see Kaneko, ed., *Renga kochūshaku shū*, p. 286.

9. According to the commentary attached to Shōhaku's verse, the snipe beats its wings a hundred times each morning to shake off the night's frost. Ibid., p. 286.

10. *Eishō jūnen nigatsu Botanka Sōseki ryōgin* (One-hundred verses by the Master of Peony House and Sōseki, written during the second lunar month, tenth year of the Eishō era, 1513). *KBS*, p. 240.

11. *MGS*, p. 100.

12. *KRRS*, p. 268.

13. *Sōchō kawa* (Sōchō's talks on poetry, 1490). Kidō and Shigematsu, *Renga yoriaishū to kenkyū* 2, p. 9.

14. See p. 50.

15. A return to *Spring* as a single category might also appear to be a possibility here, but Shōhaku's rulebook (p. 67) prohibits such a progression: "If a simple *Autumn* verse is followed by a verse that involves both *Autumn* and *Love*, then one should not return to a simple *Autumn* scene in a third verse (the same holding for all other cases of this sort)." The principle invoked is a variation of the idea of *rinne*, or improper recurrence, and is also articulated in the rules' discussion of Essential and Attributive words. See note 144, Chapter 3, for details.

16. *KBS,* p. 240.

17. *Mino senku,* p. 128. The verses quoted are the beginning two in the seventh *hyakuin* of the sequence.

18. See, for instance, *Renri hishō* (*NKBT* 66, pp. 54–55). Handbooks of Sōgi's time also dictate that the link between the first verse (*hokku*) and the second (*waki*) should be particularly close.

19. See Sōgi's *Shoshinshō* (*KRRS,* pp. 413–414); Sōseki's *Renga shoshinshō* (Notes for those inexperienced in linked verse, 1528?) in Ijichi, ed., *Rengaron shinshū* 1, pp. 233–234; and Jōha's *Shihoshō* (*RRS* 2, pp. 242–244).

20. *Nagabumi,* in *RRS* 2, p. 189.

21. *Yashima Kobayashi-an naniki hyakuin* (One hundred verses at Yashima Kobayashi Temple; in *KBS,* pp. 208–209). The commentary is thought to have been written by Sōboku himself on the basis of notes left by Sōchō.

22. *Tenbun jūyonen nigatsu nanibito hyakuin* (One hundred verses from the second lunar month of the fourteenth year of the Tenbun era, 1545), in *KBS,* p. 305.

23. *Sōi Sōgi Yuyama ryōgin,* p. 177.

24. Ibid., Shimazu includes Sōgi's commentary in his headnotes.

25. Shimazu, for instance, admits that without Sōgi's commentary he would never himself have arrived at such an interpretation.

26. Shimazu, ed., *Rengashū,* p. 178.

27. Ibid.

28. *Asaji. KRRS,* p. 317.

29. See p. 42.

30. Noa's verse comes from *Chikurinshō* (Poems by poets of the bamboo grove, no. 2208), an anthology compiled in 1474 by Sōgi in commemoration of the "seven sages" of linked verse in the generation before his: Chiun (d. 1448), Sōzei, Gyōjo (1405–1469), Nōa, Shinkei, Senjun, and Sōi. Sōgi's own verse is *Shinsen tsukubashū* 3038.

31. The poem is by the T'ang poet Tai Shu-lun (732–789). See *San t'i shi* 1, p. 61.

32. For a more detailed discussion of the idea of the "golden age" among *renga* poets, see Carter, "Mixing Memories: Linked Verse and the Fragmentation of the Court Heritage," forthcoming in the *Harvard Journal of Asiatic Studies* 48.1 (June 1988).

33. *Shinsen tsukubashū* 3805.

34. *SKKS* 588.

35. *Shinsen tsukubashū* 425–426.

36. *SKKS* 38.

37. For details on the *haikai* movement in the Muromachi period, see Shimazu, *Rengashi no kenkyū,* pp. 199–217, and *Renga no kenkyū,* pp. 327–373.

38. *Minase sangin hyakuin,* ed. Ijichi Tetsuo, in *NKBT* 39, p. 351.

39. Miner, *Japanese Linked Poetry,* p. 196.

40. See, for instance, Konishi, *Sōgi,* p. 199. Konishi characterizes many of Sōchō's attempts as "lacking in movement."

41. Quoted in Araki Yoshio, *Sōgi,* p. 100. For original statement, see *Sanetaka-kō ki* (Lord Sanetaka's diary), Vol. 1, part 2, p. 716.

42. The word is listed on p. 43.

43. *RGS* 816 does indeed list "rooftiles" as a word conventionally associated with "demon," but gives no explanation behind the association.

44. *Tsukuba mondō* (Tsukuba queries, 1372), ed. Kidō Saizō, in *NKBT* 66, p. 86.

45. Yoshimoto's scheme is taken from *Tsukuba mondō* (see previous note), Senjun's from *Katahashi* (*RRS* 1, p. 279), and Sōboku's from *Tōfū renga hiji* (*NKBZ* 51, p. 164). In *Nagabumi* (*RRS* 2, p. 189), Sōchō quotes Sōgi as saying that truly unusual verses should not be introduced until after verse 22, but it is clear from a reading of Sōgi's own works that the restrictions on striking categories (Love, Buddhism, Lamentation) applied only to the first ten verses of a sequence in his time. His breakdown might be something like this: Verses 1–10, *jo;* verses 11–22, transition; verses 23–92, *ha;* and verses 93–100, *kyū.*

46. *Baikunshō* (Plum-scented notes, 1510), in Ijichi, ed., *Rengaron shinshū*, p. 200.

47. *Katahashi,* in *RRS* 1, p. 279.

48. This tendency to view the final verses of a sequence as a return to the pace of the prelude is even more pronounced in late sixteenth-century handbooks. See *MGS*, p. 155, and Jōha's *Renga kyōkun* (A *renga* primer, date uncertain), in *RRS* 2, p. 269.

49. In Shōhaku's version of the rules, the word "blossoms" is simply listed among the things that may appear up to three times in a *hyakuin,* but custom seems to have demanded that the word appear once in each of the sheets of a sequence (see note 49, Chapter 3). The rule about moon verses is also at work in most Muromachi *renga* sequences, although again clear statement that the moon *must* appear in all but the last side of the eight sides of a sequence does not come until the late fifteenth century. Yoshimoto's *hyakuin* generally follow the convention, however, as do those involving masters of Sōgi's time. For a clear statement of the idea, see Kensai's *Baikunshō* (Ijichi, ed., *Rengaron shinshū* 1, p. 200).

50. Translations for these terms are Earl Miner's. See *Japanese Linked Poetry*, p. 72.

51. For a discussion of early definitions of Design and Ground as well as a summary of Muromachi views, see Carter, "Renga kyokusei jidai no ji, mon," *Bungaku gogaku* 87:51–58 (May 1981).

52. *Kyūshū mondō,* in *RRS* 1, pp. 84–85.

53. *Yuyama sangin hyakuin,* in *NKBZ* 32, p. 162.

54. Ibid.

55. The thirteenth-century *waka* treatise *Kirihioke* (The paulownia brazier) states that no *waka* sequence (*hyakushu uta*) should contain more than ten Design verses (*NKT* 4, p. 288), a number that has been cited as appropriate for the *hyakuin* as well. In point of fact, however, Yoshimoto in *Tsukuba mondō* says that to be able to produce just two or three truly outstanding verses in a sequence is the mark of a true master (*NKTB* 66, p. 87). Since Yoshimoto does not specify how many poets would be involved in the ideal sequence, this statement may be said simply to confuse the issue; but it does indicate that the true Design verses in a *hyakuin* were seldom many in number. Later poets, depending on their own skills and personalities, thus may have produced more Design verses; but the ideal was clearly to produce only a relatively small number of truly outstanding verses.

56. *Hitorigoto* (Talking to myself, 1468), ed. Shimazu Tadao, in *NST* 23, p. 471. The terms used by Shinkei are *jirenga,* "background links," and *jōku,* "strong verses." Among other synonyms used to refer to Design verses are *sakotsu* and *shūitsu*—"well built verses," and "excellent verses."

57. *Kyōchūshō*, in *ZGRJ* 17, pp. 1237–1240.

58. The words *honoka* and *honobono* (both meaning "faintly") have traditionally been associated with plants that come into ear (*ho*), such as the miscanthus. The association is based on the homophonic relationship between the words, and in addition on the fact that miscanthus plumes are said to sway "faintly" in the wind.

59. For centuries, scholars believed that all of the verses in Sōboku's work were Sōgi's, but Ogawa Tatsuzō has shown that in fact the work contains verses by Shōei, Kensai, Sōchō, Shōhaku, and Sōseki as well. See Ogawa, "Sōboku rengaronsho Kyōchūshō ni tsuite," in *Renga to sono shuhen*, ed. Hiroshima chūsei bungei kenkyū-kai, pp. 91–117.

60. Ibid.

61. *Azuma mondō* (East country queries, 1470), ed. Kidō Saizō, in *NKBT* 66, p. 232.

62. See Culler, *On Deconstruction: Theory and Criticism after Structuralism*, pp. 35–39.

63. Sōgi, for instance, includes a statement about how to conduct oneself in the presence of courtiers—an experience with which he was well acquainted—in his *Azuma mondō. NKBT* 66, p. 225.

64. Quoted in Ijichi, *Sōgi*, p. 52. The original statement comes from *Sanetaka-kō ki*, Vol. 1, pt. 2, pp. 714–715.

65. *Sanetaka-kō ki*, Vol. 1, pt. 2, p. 715.

66. Ibid.

67. Konishi, *Sōgi*, p. 78.

68. Oscar Wilde, *The Picture of Dorian Gray*, p. xxxiii.

69. *Meiō hachinen Sōgi dokugin nanihito hyakuin* (Solo sequence of 1499), in *NKBZ* 32, p. 218.

70. *Kanshō ninen kugatsu nijūsannichi nanihito dokugin hyakuin* (A solo sequence composed on the twenty-third day of the ninth lunar month of the second year of the Kanshō era, 1461), in Etō, *Sōgi no kenkyū*, pt. 2, p. 13.

CHAPTER 5: THE ROAD TO KOMATSUBARA

1. Tsurusaki, "Renga to Yukawa Masaharu," p. 7.

2. *Oi no susami*, in *KRRS*, p. 162.

3. Araki, *Sōgi*, pp. 243–266, provides the most striking example of the tendency to attribute personality traits on the basis of rather flimsy evidence. He even claims to know why Sōgi liked the *yamabuki* in the first place: "The reason Sōgi loved the globeflower was doubtless because its blossoms are pure and clean without being cold, displaying warm colors but never in a common way—because they retain a shy forlornness in the midst of vividness and conceal a sense of impermanence behind a bright facade" (p. 252).

4. Donald Keene, *Some Japanese Portraits*, p. 29. For a fairly complete account of Sōgi's professional life, see Carter, *Three Poets at Yuyama*, pp. 12–53.

5. There are, of course, notable exceptions to the rule of anonymity in linked verse. Sōchō, for instance, has left us a rather substantial portrait of himself as a personality, although even in his case one may claim that what he tells us about himself is calculated to fit the ideal of the unorthodox monk—a

pattern learned from his Zen teacher, Ikkyū. Furthermore, Sōchō's portrait comes primarily from his diaries and not from his work in the "serious" tradition of linked verse.

6. Maria Corti, *An Introduction to Literary Semiotics*, p. 118.

7. For a study of the contributors to *Shinsen tsukubashū*, see Kaneko, *Shinsen tsukubashū kenkyū*, pp. 480–587. Kaneko shows in these pages and elsewhere in his book that the anthology of 1495 was truly a reflection of its times in that it included work chiefly by *renga* masters and their patrons in the capital and the provinces. Kidō, *Rengashi ronkō* 1, pp. 475–480, comes to a similar conclusion, pointing out that nearly 50 percent of the authors represented in the work come from the military classes. Thus, while the largest number of poems have been contributed by professional poets and members of the imperial family and the court aristocracy, military types are also exceptionally conspicuous contributors to the collection.

8. *Tsukuba mondō*. NKBT 66, pp. 81–82.

9. Discussions of Japanese poetic theory generally tend to de-emphasize what James J. Y. Liu calls the pragmatic view of literature (see Liu, *Chinese Theories of Literature*, pp. 106–116) common among Chinese poets and their readers. But works as early as the *Kokinshū* Preface (905) define poetry as a medium that "without exertion, moves heaven and earth, stirs the feelings of gods and spirits invisible to the eye, softens the relations between men and women, calms the hearts of fierce warriors" (Brower and Miner, *Japanese Court Poetry*, p. 3). Further supported by the tenets of Neo-Confucianism—a philosophy especially popular among Zen monks—this view of poetry as a force for moral order was of considerable importance in the Muromachi period, although never quite sufficiently powerful to supplant the aesthetic theories prevalent among the court aristocracy. Yoshimoto's statement appears in a section of *Tsukuba mondō* written in response to the question of whether linked verse could be considered an aid to good government. His conclusion is that, while for many the composition of poetry is little more than an aesthetic pursuit, linked verse of courtly elegance—meaning linked verse that abides by standards of decorum and propriety—is an aid to the maintenance of order, indirectly at least.

10. Etō, *Sōgi no kenkyū*, pt. 1, pp. 155–65. Recently, Fujiwara Masayoshi has presented an argument similar to Etō's, insisting in fact that Sōgi's original decision to adopt linked verse as a profession was greatly influenced by the idea that courtly literature could be a force for peace in the world. See Fujiwara Masayoshi, *Sōgi josetsu*, pp. 127–130, 136–141.

11. Kidō, *Rengashi ronkō* 1, pp. 401–403.

12. Ijichi, *Sōgi*, pp. 263–264, gives what details we know about Sōgi's activities during these months. Kaneko, *Shinsen tsukubashū no kenkyū*, pp. 332–346, shows that as early as 1489 Sōgi and Kensai were making plans for a second imperial anthology (a *jun-chokusenshū*, or collection of the second order) of linked verse.

13. For details about the texts of the 1492 sequence, see Appendix B.

14. Kaneko, *Shinsen tsukubashū no kenkyū*, p. 537, gives 1518 as the probable year of Masaharu's death.

15. Quoted in Tsurusaki, "Renga to Yukawa Masaharu," p. 7.

16. Ibid., p. 5.

CHAPTER 6: SŌGI'S SOLO SEQUENCE OF 1492

1. *Imamichi.* The road from the capital to Shiga over Mt. Hiei.
2. *Nishi no michi.* The road west from the capital.
3. *Kakuremichi.* A shortcut or secret path.
4. *Kumoiji.* The path of geese, the moon, or the sun across the sky.
5. *Yami no michi.* A metaphor for the dark "way" through life.
6. *Futamichi.* Diverging roads.
7. *Azumaji.* Old name for the Tōkaidō, a famous post-road running from the capital to the Kantō.
8. Shinto. The native religion of Japan.
9. *Me no michi.* The field of vision.
10. *Chidō.* For the text of the collection of *fushimono* from which these examples are taken, see Hoshika and Yamada, pp. 11–20.
11. *Renga shoshinshō.* Ijichi, *Rengaron shinshū* 1, p. 264.
12. *Shogakushō. KRRS,* p. 424.
13. Keene, tr., *Essays in Idleness,* p. 175.
14. *Tōfū renga hiji,* in *NKBZ* 51, p. 181. See also *Tsukuba mondō* (*NKBT* 66, p. 103) and Sōgi's *Azuma mondō* (*NKBT* 66, pp. 235–236).
15. *UG,* p. 155.
16. See p. 60.
17. There are two families of *Shitakusa* texts, one traceable to a "first edition" compiled by Sōgi between 1491 and 1493 and the other from a revision compiled in 1496. This *tsukeku* is in both texts, nos. 907–908 in the former and 895–896 in the latter. See Ijichi and Kaneko, eds., *Sōgi kushū,* pp. 289, 339.
18. Ikeda Kikan, *Heian jidai no bungaku to seikatsu,* p. 339.
19. *RGS* 88.
20. See p. 44.
21. *Chikurinshō* 1043–1044.
22. Kidō and Shigematsu, *Renga yoriaishū to kenkyū,* 1, p. 285 and 2, p. 17.
23. *MGS,* p. 51.
24. *NKBZ* 7, p. 49.
25. *Oi no susami. KRRS,* pp. 148, 150.
26. Ijichi and Kaneko, eds., *Sōgi kushū,* p. 70.
27. Keene, tr., *Essays in Idleness,* p. 199.
28. Etō, *Sōgi no kenkyū,* pt. 1, pp. 369–406.
29. *Sōgi sode no shita. KRRS,* p. 269.
30. *Renri hishō. NKBZ* 66, p. 60.
31. *Renga shogakushō. RRS* 2, p. 303.
32. See note 31, Chapter 4, for reference.
33. See Carter, "Renga ni okeru honkadori," in Kaneko, ed., *Renga kenkyū no tenkai,* pp. 121–131.
34. *Wakakusayama. GRJ* 13, p. 98.
35. Quoted in Shinkei's *Sasamegoto* (Whisperings, 1463), ed. Kidō Saizō, in *NKBT* 66, p. 171. For what information there is on Ryōa, see Kaneko, *Tsukubashū no kenkyū,* pp. 559–560.

36. *Oi no susami. KRRS*, p. 152.

37. *Shirakawa kikō.* Kaneko, *Sōgi tabi no ki shichū*, p. 9.

38. *MGS*, pp. 8-9.

39. Keene, tr., *Essays in Idleness*, p. 115.

40. *Asaji. KRRS*, pp. 337-374.

41. *Azuma mondō. NKBT* 66, p. 213.

42. *Shōtetsu monogatari* (Tales of Shōtetsu), ed. Hisamatsu Sen'ichi, in *NKBT* 65, p. 176.

43. *Oki* is a pivot word meaning "to arise" in verse 63 but also meaning "offing" or "offshore" when that verse is linked to verse 62.

44. *Yamato monogatari*, ed. Takahashi Shōji, in *NKBZ* 8, pp. 405-406.

45. *Kachō yosei* (In a setting of flowers and birds, 1472). See Ii Haruku, ed., [*Matsunaga-bon*] *Kachō yosei*, p. 71.

46. *MGS*, p. 79.

47. See p. 50.

48. Text available in Kimura Miyogo, "Chikuba kyōgin shū."

49. Seidensticker, tr., *The Tale of Genji* 2, p. 867.

50. See *S* III (p. 42).

51. *SKKS* 362.

52. *Shihōshō. RRS* 2, pp. 234-235.

53. *Eikyū hyakushu. GRJ* 8, p. 119.

54. *Makura no sōshi* (Pillow book), ed. Matsuo Satoshi and Nagai Kazuko, p. 63. For a translation of the pertinent section, see Ivan Morris, *The Pillow Book of Sei Shōnagon* 1, p. 1.

55. Arthur Waley, *The Analects of Confucius*, p. 83.

CHAPTER 7: A FINAL WORD

1. Umberto Eco, *The Role of the Reader: Explorations in the Semiotics of Texts*, p. 9.

2. Stanley Fish, "Interpreting the *Variorum*," in his *Is There a Text in This Class?*, p. 167.

3. For a study of *renga* diction in the age of Sōgi, see Carter, "Waka in the Age of Renga," *Monumenta Nipponica* 36.4:425-444 (Winter 1980).

4. Itō Kunio, "Go-Sukō-In to Fushimi no Miya rengakai," pp. 241-251.

5. *Yuyama sangin hyakuin. NKBZ* 32, p. 168.

6. An early rule made the appearance of the moon, nearly always an Autumn symbol, obligatory in at least seven of the eight sides of a sequence. And, since each time the moon appears, Autumn usually comes with it, this means that as a category Autumn—which must continue over at least three verses in each occurrence—will generally be the major category of at least twenty-one verses in every *hyakuin*. The rules make it possible for Autumn to be the major category of up to forty-five verses.

7. *Sasamegoto. NKBT* 66, p. 139.

8. Culler, *Structuralist Poetics*, pp. 160-61.

9. Barthes, *Critical Essays*, p. 260.

10. Culler, *Structuralist Poetics*, p. 148.

11. Although in Jōha's time the moon usually appeared in either verse 5 or 7 of the first side of a sequence, in the later fifteenth century it generally was

introduced earlier. The moon verse comes before verse 5, for instance, in forty-one of fifty-three sequences listed in Etō, *Sōgi no kenkyū*, pt. 2.

12. *Sōi Sōgi Yuyama ryōgin*, pp. 175–176.

13. A *renga* experiment by four Western poets—Octavio Paz, Jacques Roubaud, Eduardo Sanguinetti, and Charles Tomlinson—writing in four different languages shows that radically new approaches to linked verse are possible. These four poets, while sharing a common cultural attitude, clearly do not employ an explicit set of conventions to guide the process of composition. The result resembles certain characterizations of the Japanese genre as a "multiple stream of consciousness" in which the links between stanzas are so "free" as to escape signification by conventional means. See Paz et al., *Renga: A Chain of Poems*.

14. Vladimir Nabokov, *Lectures on Literature*, p. 380.

15. Shimazu Tadao has argued that *kochū* provide evidence that *renga* links could scarcely be understood even by medieval readers without commentary establishing authorial intent; but Kaneko Kinjirō refutes this contention by showing that the writing of commentaries was a phenomenon that characterized all genres of the late Muromachi period (see Kaneko, *Renga kochūshaku no kenkyū*, pp. 9–17, for a rehearsal of the disagreement). The presence of instructional comments in most *kochū* supports Kaneko's view, showing that the purpose of commentaries was to teach composition and not to establish meaning. Whether seen as instruction or interpretation, ancient commentaries remain a testament to the self-consciousness of a classical reading.

16. Barthes, "From Work to Text," in Josue V. Harari, ed., *Textual Strategies*, p. 76.

17. Arthur Koestler, *The Sleepwalkers*, p. 19.

18. Jorge Luis Borges, *A Personal Anthology*, p. 92.

GLOSSARY A

Akashi	明石	Fukakusa	深草	
Akazome Emon	赤染衛門	*fushimonoshū*	賦物集	
Ariwara no Narihira	在原業平	*fushimono renga*	賦物連歌	
Asayama Bontō	朝山梵燈	*Genji monogatari*	源氏物語	
		Gensei	玄清	
Ashikaga Yoshimasa	足利義政	Gensen	玄宣	
—— Yoshimitsu	義満	Go-Fukō-on	後普光園	
—— Yoshimochi	義持	*Gosenshū*	後撰集	
—— Yoshinori	義教	Go-Toba	後鳥羽	
Bashō	芭蕉	Gusai	救済	
Biwako	琵琶行	Gyōjo	行助	
bugyō	奉行	*Gyokuyōshū*	玉葉集	
Chiun	智蘊	*ha*	破	
Chuang-tzu	荘子	*haikai*	俳諧	
daruma uta	達磨歌	Hana no Gosho	花の御所	
dōi no renga	同意の連歌	Hatakeyama	畠山	
dōjisari	同字去	*Heike monogatari*	平家物語	
dokugin	独吟	Henjō	遍昭	
Eshun	恵俊	*hentai kanbun*	変体漢文	
Fūgashū	風雅集	Hiei	比叡	
		hikiuta	引歌	
Fujiwara no Ietaka	藤原家隆	Hino Tomiko	日野富子	
—— Nobuzane	信実	*hokku*	発句	
—— Shunzei	俊成	*hon'i*	本意	
—— Tameie	為家	*honka*	本歌	
—— Tameuji	為氏	*honshiki*	本式	
—— Tameyo	為世	Hosokawa	細川	
—— Teika	定家	*hyakuin*	百韻	
—— Toshiyuki	敏行	*hyakushu uta*	百首歌	
—— Yukiie	行家			

Ichijō Kanera 一条兼良

Iga 伊賀

Ikeda 池田

Ikkyū 一休

Ise 伊勢

Ise monogatari 伊勢物語

Itai senku 異体千句

ji 地

jirenga 地連歌

jo 序

jo-ha-kyū 序破急

jōku 定句

Joren 静蓮

Juntoku *tennō* 順徳天皇

jun chokusenshū 准勅撰集

kadai 歌題

kakekotoba 掛詞

Kakinomoto Hitomaro 柿本人麻呂

Kakitsu no Ran 嘉吉の乱

kakushidai 隠題

kami no ku 上の句

Kamo 賀茂

Kawachi 河内

Keiboku 慶卜

Keibutsushō 景物抄

keiko 稽古

kemari 蹴鞠

Kensai 兼載

Kenshō 顕昭

ki moji き文字

Ki no Tsurayuki 紀貫之

Kitabatake 北畠

Kochikusai 孤竹斎

kochū 古注

kojitsu 故実

Kokinshū 古今集

kokoro naki mono 心なきもの

kokorozuke 心付

Komatsubara 小松原

Koretaka 惟喬

kotoba 詞

kusari renga 鎖連歌

Kyōchūshō 胸中抄

kyū 急

lien-chü 聯句

Magome 馬籠

Man'yōshū 万葉集

mappō 末法

Minamoto no Shitagō 源順

—— Toshiyori 俊頼

Miyoshi Chōkei 三好長慶

moji amari 文字余

mon 文

mono no na 物の名

Mototoshi 基俊

mumon 無文

Murakami *tennō* 村上天皇

Murasaki Shikibu 紫式部

Musashino 武蔵野

nadokoro 名所

Nagayasu 長泰

Nara 奈良

nigeuta	逃歌
Nijō Yoshimoto	二条良基
nō	能
Nōa	能阿
Nōin	能因
Obasute	姨捨
Oda Nobunaga	織田信長
Ōhara	大原
Ōmi	近江
Ōmiwa	大三輪
omoshiroshi	面白し
omote	面
Ōnin no Ran	応仁の乱
Ono no Komachi	小野小町
Ōuchi	大内
Ōyodo	大淀
Po Chü-i	白居易
renga	連歌
Renga kaiseki nijū-go kin	連歌会席二十五禁
renga kaishi	連歌懐紙
Renga shogakushō	連歌初学抄
Rengaki	連歌記
Rikuchū	陸中
rinne	輪廻
Ryōa	良阿
saibara	催馬楽
Saigyō	西行
sakotsu	作骨
sakushu	作手
Sanekuni	実國

sanji gana	三字仮名
Sanjōnishi Sanetaka	三条西実隆
Sarashina	更科
sato dairi	里内裏
Satomura Jōha	里村紹巴
Sei Shōnagon	清少納言
Senjun	専順
seri	世理
Shigeno no Naishi	しげののないし
Shichijū-ichi ban shokunin uta-awase	七十一番職人歌合
Shiga	志賀
shimo no ku	下の句
Shinano	信濃
Shinkei	心敬
Shin kokinshū	新古今集
Shinsen tsukubashū	新撰莵玖波集
shitashisugitaru	したしすぎたる
Shiyōshō	私用抄
Shōei	紹永
Shogaku yōshashō	初学用捨抄
Shōhaku	肖柏
shōka	証歌
Shōkokuji	相國寺
Shoku gosenshū	続後撰集
Shōtetsu	正徹
shōrui	生類
shuhitsu	執筆
shūitsu	秀逸
Shun'e	俊恵(法師)
Sōboku	宗牧

Sōchō	宗長		*Ubuginu*	産衣
Sōgi	宗祇		*uchikoshi o kirau*	打越を嫌う
Sōi	宗伊		Uesugi	上杉
Sōseki	宗碩		Uji	宇治
Ssuma Chien	司馬遷		*ukare*	うかれ
Sugawara no Michizane	菅原道真		*umon*	有文
Suma	須磨		*ura*	裏
Suō	周防		*ushin*	有心
			uta	歌
Takayama Sōzei	高山宗砌		*waka*	和歌
tai	体		*Wamyō ruijushō*	和名類聚抄
Tai Shu-lun	戴叔倫		*Yakumo mishō*	八雲御抄
Tatsuta	竜田		Yamato	大和
Tenji *tennō*	天智天皇		*Yamato monogatari*	大和物語
Tokugawa Ieyasu	徳川家康		*yōen*	妖艶
Tomooki	友興		Yokawa	横川
torinashizuke	取成付		*yoriai*	寄合
tōrinne	遠輪廻		Yoshida no Kenkō	吉田兼好
Toyotomi Hideyoshi	豊臣秀吉		Yoshino	吉野
tsukeai	付合		*yū*	用
tsukeku	付句		Yukawa Masaharu	湯川政春
Tsukubashū	菟玖波集		Zeami	世阿弥
tsumaru	つまる			
Tsurezuregusa	徒然草			

GLOSSARY B

Glossary to Shohaku's Rulebook of 1501

The following is an English-Japanese glossary to the rulebook of 1501 which lists all the words in Shohaku's work with the exception of technical vocabulary (i.e., *kakushi-dai*, "hidden topics," etc.) already listed in glossary A. All categories and Japanese terms are in italics. Romanized readings follow Hoshika and Yamada, *Renga hōshiki kōyō* (1936) wherever possible.

Abandon (v), *sutsuru*　捨

Abandon the world (v), *yo o sutsu*　捨世

Abandoned soul, *sutsuru mi*　捨身

Above the clouds, *kumo no ue*　雲の上

Afar, *ochi*　おち / をち

After dawning, *akesugite*　明過て

Akashi (pn)　明石

Alone, *hitori*　独

Ancient, *inishie*　古

Animals, ugokimono　動物

Announcement of Capital Appointments, Tsukasameshi　つかさめし

Announcement of Provincial Appointments, Agatameshi　縣召

Arrow, *ya*　矢

"Arrowlike" year, *toshi no ya*　年の矢

Autumn, aki　秋

Autumn chill, *aki samushi*　秋寒

Autumn of the Treetops, Kozue no aki　梢の秋

Autumn paddies, *aki no ta*　秋田

Autumn robes, *akisari goromo*　秋去衣

Autumn wind, *akikaze*　秋風

Awaji (pn)　淡路

Azalea, *tsutsuji*　躑躅

Bamboo, *take*　竹

Bamboo blinds, *sudare*　簾

Bamboo grass, *sasa*　篠

Bamboo hut, *sasa no io*　篠庵

Bamboo leaves, *take no ha* 竹の葉

Barrier-gate, *seki/seki no to* 關 / 關戸

Bay, *ura* 浦

Be (v), *ari* 有

Be born (v), *umaru* 生

Be lost in thought (v), *mono omou* 物思

Beach, *iso* 磯

Bead/jewel, *tama* 玉

Bear, *kuma* 熊

Beasts, kedamono 獸

Become (v), *naru* なる / 成

Bed, *toko* 床

Bedchamber, *neya* 閨

Before dawn, *ariake* 有明

Bell, *kane* 鐘

Bell cricket, *suzumushi* 鈴虫

Beneath, *moto* もと

Bird, *tori* 鳥

Bird rattle, *naruko* なるこ

Bird tracks, *tori no ato* 鳥跡

Bird's lodging, *tori no yadori* 鳥のやどり

Bird's nest, *tori no su* 鳥巢

Birds and beasts, *tori-kedamono* 鳥獸

Birds, tori 鳥

Bitter (adj), *tsurashi* つらし

Black pine, *maki* 槇

Blossoming grasses, *kusa no hana* 草の花

Blossom, *hana* 花

Blossoms and red leaves, *hana momiji* 花紅葉

Blossoms left on withered grasses, *kusakare ni hana nokoru* 草枯花残

Blossoms on the waves, *nami no hana* 波の花

Boat, *fune* 舟 / 船

Bogwood, *umoregi* 埋木

Bonfire, *takibi* 焼火

Border guard, *sekimori* 關守

Born, to be, *umaru* 生

Boulder, *iwa* 岩

Bow/long-bow, *yumi* 弓

"Bowlike" moon, *yumiharizuki* 弓張月

Break of day, *shinonome* しのゝめ

Bridge, *hashi* 橋

Bridge of red leaves, *momiji no hashi* 紅葉橋

Bridge of stones, *iwahashi* 岩橋

Brush door, *shiba no to* 柴戸

Brush-burning, *shiba taku* 柴焼

Brush-gathering, *shiba toru* 柴取

Brushwood, *tsumagi* 爪木

Buddhism, shakkyō 釋教

Buddhist temple, *tera* 寺

Burn (v), *kogaru* こがる

Burnt-over field of reeds, *ogi no yakebara* 荻の焼原

Bush warbler, *uguisu* 鶯

Caged hawks, *toyo taka* 鳥屋鷹

Calling bird, *yobukodori* 呼子鳥

Camelia, *tsubaki* 椿

Cap, *kammuri* 冠

Capital bird, *miyakodori* 都鳥

Capital, the, *miyako* 都

Cascade, *taki* 瀧

Cascade of blossoms, *hana no taki* 花の瀧

Cascade of tears, *namida no taki* 涙の瀧

Catalpa, *hisagi* 楸

Cathay, Morokoshi (pn) もろこし

Cave, *hora* 洞

Cavern, *iwaya* 岩屋

Cedar window, *sugi no mado* 杉の窓

Charcoal-burning, *sumi yaku* 炭焼

Charcoal kiln, *sumigama* 炭竈

Charred stubble, *suguro* すぐろ

Chasing deer from the paddies, *shika oi* 鹿追

"Cherry-Blossom Man," *Sakura hito* (song title) 櫻人

Cherry blossom, *sakura* 櫻

Cherry seabream, *sakuradai* 櫻鯛

Cherry shell, *sakuragai* 櫻貝

Child, *ko* 子

Chill of night, *yosamu* 夜寒

Chilling (adj), *susamaji* 冷

Cicada, *semi* 蝉

Cicala, *higurashi* 日晩

Clan way, *ie no kaze* 家風

Clapper, *hita* ひた

Close of . . . *kure* 暮

Cloth dyed in moss-fern design, *shinobu-zuri* 忍摺

Cloth-bleaching, *nuno sarasu* 布曝

Clothing, irui 衣類

Cloud, *kumo* 雲

Cloud up (v), *kumoru* くもる

Clouds of blossoms, *hana no kumo* 花の雲

Cock, *niwatori* 雞 庭鳥

Cogon grass, *asaji* 淺茅

Cold (adj), *samushi* 寒

Color of the fields, *no no iro* 野色

Color of the mountains, *yama no iro* 山色

Colored birds, *irodori* 色鳥

Come to a close, *kure* 暮

Constant flame, *tsune no tomoshibi* 常燈

Cool (adj), *suzushi* 涼

"Counterfeit" blossoms, *nisemono no hana* 似物の花

"Counterfeit" jewels, *nisemono no tama* 似物の玉

"Counterfeit" snow, *nisemono no yuki* 似物の雪

Cracks in the ice, *kōri no hima* 氷のひま

Crane, *tazu/tsuru* 田鶴/鶴

Crane Grove, Tsuru no Hayashi (pn) 鶴林

"Crane in the reeds," *ashitazu* 蘆田鶴

Crane's nest, *tsuru no su* 鶴巣

Crossing Shiga Mountain, *Shiga no yamagoe* 志賀の山越

Cry (v), *naku* 泣(鳴)

Cup water in one's hands (v), *aka musubu* 閼伽結

Current, *nagare* 流

Cypress grove, *hinohara* 檜原

Dark (adj), *kurashi* くらし

Darkness of the heart, *kokoro no yami* 心のやみ

Dawn, *akatsuki* 曉

Dawn moon, *ariake no tsuki* 有明の月

Dawning, *ake* 明

Day, *hi* 日

Day of the Rat, Ne no hi 子日

Daybreak, *akebono* 曙

Daytime, *hiru* ひる

Death, *shi* 死

Decayed wood, *kuchiki* 朽木

Deep (adj), *fukashi* 深

Deer, *shika* 鹿

Demon, *oni* 鬼

Dew, *tsuyu* 露

Dew accumulating, *tsuyu fukete* 露ふけて

Dew on the sleeves, *sode no tsuyu* 袖の露

Dew on withered fields, *kareno no tsuyu* 枯野の露

Dewy drizzle, *tsuyu-shigure* 露時雨

Dewy frost, *tsuyu-jimo* 露霜

Die (v), *shinu* 死

Dike, *tsutsumi* 堤

Dim (adj), *oboro* 朧

Distant (adj), *toshi* 遠

Door, *to* 戸

Door of black pine, *maki no to* 槇木戸

Door of cherry blossoms, *sakurado* 櫻戸

Dove whistle, *hato fuku* 鳩吹

Dragon, *tatsu* 龍

Dream, *yume* 夢

Driftwood, *nagareki* 流木

Drizzle, *kosame* 小雨

Dryad, *kodama* 小玉

Dusk, *yūmagure* 夕ま暮

Dust, *chiri* 塵

Dwarf bamboo, *ozasa* 小篠

Dwellings, kyosho 居所

East, the, Azuma (pn) あづま

"The Eastern Cottage," *Azumaya* (chapter title, *Genji monogatari*) 東屋

Eastern dances, *azuma asobi* 東遊

Eastern Road, Azumaji (pn) 東路

Eaves, *noki* 軒

Echo, *hibiki* 響

Edgestone, *migiri* 砌

Emergence of the new moon, *mikazuki no izuru* 三日月の出

Empty illusion, *sorame* 空目

End, *sue* 末

End of autumn or spring, *haru/aki no kure* 春/秋の暮

Enter (v), *iru* 入

Environs, *sotomo* 外面

Ephemeral, *hakanashi* はかなし

Evening, *yūbe, yū* 夕

Evening frost, *yūshimo* 夕霜

Evening moon, *yūzuki* 夕月

Evening shower, *yūdachi* 夕立

Evening sun, *yūzukuhi* 夕月日

Evening wind, *yūkaze* 夕風

Extraordinary Festival of the Iwashimizu Hachiman Shrine, *Iwashimizu no rinji matsuri* 石清水臨時之祭

Extraordinary Festival of the Kamo Shrine, *Kamo no rinji matsuri* 賀茂臨時祭

Eye, *me* 目

Faint dawnlight, *asaborake* 朝ぼらけ

Falling leaves, *ochiba* 落葉

Falling pine needles, *matsu no ochiba* 松落葉

"Falling" rapids, *takitsuse* 瀧津瀬/たきつ瀬

Falling Things, furimono 降物

Famous Places, nadokoro 名所

Far shore, *kano kishi* 彼岸

Faraway, *haruka* 遙

Father, *chichi* 父

Fawn, *ka no ko* 鹿の子

Fence, *kaki/kakio* 垣/墻

Ferry boat, *watashibune* 渡舟

Festival of the Gods, Kami matsuri 神祭

Festival of Abounding Light, Toyoakari no Sechie 豊明節會

Field, *no/nobe* 野/野邊

Field cricket, *kirigirisu* 蛬

"Field Cricket," *Kirigirisu* (*kagura* title) 蛬

Fields changing color, *no no irozuku* 野の色付

Fire, *hi* 火

Firefly, *hotaru* 螢

Firewood, *takigi* 薪

First bird-hunt, *hatsu togari* 初鳥狩

227

First storm, *hatsu arashi* 初嵐

First tide, *hatsu shio* 初鹽

Fish, *uo* 魚

Fisherman, *ama* 海士

"Fisherman's skiff...," *ama obune* 海士小舟

Fishing, *tsuri* 釣／釣垂

Fishing fire, *isari* いさり

Fishnet, *ami* 網

Floating bridge, *ukihashi* 浮橋

"Floating Bridge of Dreams," *Yume no ukihashi* 夢の浮橋 (Chapter title, *genji monogatari*)

Floating grass, *ukikusa* 薄草

Floating nest, *ukisu* 浮巢

Floating wood, *ukiki* 浮木

Floating world, *ukiyo* 浮世

Flock of birds, *muratori* 村鳥

Floor, *yuka* 床

Flower of the heart, *kokoro no hana* 心'の花

Flowers of the pine, *matsu no hana* 松の花

Flowers of words, *kotoba no hana* 詞の花

Fodder, *magusa* 秣

Foot of the mountain, *fumoto* 麓

"Forgetting" grass, *wasuregusa* 忘草

Former world, *saki no yo* 前世

Friend, *tomo* 友

Friends of the moon, *tsuki no tomo* 月の友

Frog, *kawazu* 蛙

Frost, *shimo* 霜

Frosty brow, *mayu no shimo* 眉の霜

Fuji's snows, *Fuji no yuki* 富士雪

Fujiwara (clan name) 藤原

Fulfilled Love, au koi 逢戀

Full dawning, *akehatete* 明はてて

Fulling block, *kinuta* 磌／砧

Funaoka Mountain, Funaoka yama (pn) 舟岡山

Future prospects, *aramashi* あらまし

Garden, *niwa* 庭

Garden fires, *niwabi* 庭火

Garden in the clouds, *kumoi no niwa* 雲居庭

Garden orchard, *sono* 圃

Garden precepts, *niwa no oshie* 庭訓

Gate, *kado* 門

Gaze, *nagame* ながめ

Gloaming, *yoi* 宵

Globeflower, *yamabuki* 欵冬

Gloom of night, *yūyami* 夕闇

Go-between, *nakadachi* 媒

Gods, *kami* 神

Gossamer, *kagerō* 蜻蛉

Grass, *kusa* 草

Grass-cutting, *kusa o karu* 草をかる

Grass hut, *kusa no iori* 草の庵

Grasses where the shrikes hide, *mozu no kusaguki* 鵙草莖

Grasses, kusa 草

Great Shrine, Ōmiya 大宮

Grebe, *niho* 鳰

Green, *ao* 青

Green-growth, *midori* 緑

Green plum, *aoume* 青梅

Green willows, *aoyagi* 青柳

Greenery, *kusaki* 草木

Grief, *uki* 憂

Grieved soul, *ukimi* 憂身

Grievous (adj), *monoushi* 懶

Grove, *mori* 森

Growing chilly, *yaya samushi* やゝさむし

Grow dark (v), *kururu* 暮

Grow warmer (v), *ataka naru* あたゝかなる

Guide, *shirube* しるべ

Gull, *kamome* 鷗

Hail, *arare* 霰

"Halting" autumn or spring, *haru/aki o tomuru* 春秋をとむる

Handcart, *teguruma* 輦

Hanging lamp, *tsuri no tomoshibi* 釣の燈

Harbor, *minato* 湊

Hard-hearted (adj), *tsurenashi* つれなし

Hart, *sugaru* すがる

Harvesting sea grass, *me o karu* 和布刈

Hase Temple, Hasedera (pn) 長谷寺

Hawk, *taka* 鷹

Haze, *kasumi* 霞

Haze over (v), *kasumu* かすむ

Hazy bell sound, *kane no kasumu* 鐘のかすむ

Heart of cedar, *kokoro no sugi* 心の杉

Heart of pine, *kokoro no matsu* 心の松

Hearths of the people, *tami no kamado* 民のかまど

Heavens, *ama* 天

Hedge, *magaki* 籬

Hedge of mist, *kiri no magaki* 霧の籬

Hermit of the Priestly Way, Sōmon no yosutebito 桑門の世捨人

Hermit's cavern, *muro no to* 室戸

Hermitage, *kakurega* 隠家

Heron, *sagi* 鷺

Hidden, *kakure* かくれ

Highway, *koshiji* 越路

Hill, *oka* 岡

Hirano Festival, Hirano matsuri 平野祭

Home/hometown, *furusato* 故郷

Honored Presence, *mimashi* みまし

Horse, *uma* 馬

House, *sumika* 栖

House in the mugwort patch, *yomogiu no yado* 蓬生宿

House of the evening faces, *Yūgao no yado* 夕顔宿

How, *ika ni*　いかに

How many, *iku*　幾、

Human Relations, jinrin　人倫

Hundred-layered, *momoshiki*　百敷

Hunting, *kari*　狩

Hunting by torch, *nerai kari*　ねらひかり

Hunting with young hawks, *kotaka-gari*　小鷹かり

Hut, *io/iori*　いほ/庵

Hut in the blossoming grasses, *hana no kusa no io*　花の草の庵

Ice, *kōri*　氷

Ice-beads on the eaves, *noki no tamamizu*　軒の玉水

Icehouse, *himuro*　氷室

Icehouse snow, *himuro no yuki*　氷室雪

Ice needle, *taruhi*　たるひ

Icicle, *tsurara*　つらゝ

Icy tears, *namida no kōri*　涙の氷

Idle words, *soragoto*　空事

Ikuta Grove, Ikuta no Mori (pn)　生田林

Image, *omokage*　おも影

Imperial Residence, Kōkyo　皇居

Imperial Lustration, Misogi　御祓

Imperial Seat, Omashi　御座

Incense, *kaori*　薫

Ink-dyed robes, *sumizome no koromo*　墨染衣

Ink-dyed sleeves, *sumizome no sode*　墨染袖

Inkstone-water, *suzuri mizu*　硯水

Inlet, *e*　江

Insect, *mushi*　蟲

Insects, mushi　蟲

Iris, *kakitsubata*　杜若

Island, *shima*　嶋/島

Ivy, tsuta　蔦

GLOSSARY B

Japanese poetry, *uta* 歌

Jewel/bead, *tama* 玉

Jewel string of life, *tama no o* 玉緒

Jeweled missive, *tamazusa* 玉章

Time of day, *jibun* 時分

Join (v), *au* 逢

Kaodori, kaodori 貌鳥

Kaseki, kaseki かせき

Kasuga (pn) 春日

Kasuga Festival, Kasuga matsuri 春日祭

Keepsake, *katami* 形見

Kickball garden, *mari no niwa* 鞠の庭

Kiso (pn) 木曽

Kiso Road, Kisoji (pn) 木曽路

Kiyomi Temple, Kyomidera (pn) 清水寺

Know (v), *shiru* 知

Komo reed, *komo* 薦

Koromode Grove, Koromode no Mori (pn) 衣手杜

Koromogawa (pn) 衣川

Lamentation, jukkai 述懐

Lamp, *tomoshibi* 燈

Lamp of the Law, *nori no tomoshibi* 法の燈

Late and soon, *akekure* 明暮

Late blossoms, *yo no hana* 餘の花

Late cherry blossoms, *osozakura* おそ櫻

Law, the, *nori* 法

Laying the fan aside, *ōgi o oku* 扇ををく

Leaf, *ha* 葉

Leave home and family (v), *ie o izuru* 家を出

Leaves of grass, *kusa no ha* 草の葉

Leaves of words, *koto no ha* 言の葉／ことの葉

Letter, *fumi* 文

Lie, *itsuwari* 偽

Life, *inochi* 命

Light and shadow, *kōin* 光陰

Light snow, *awayuki* 淡雪

Lightning, *inazuma/inabikari* 稲妻/雷

Little bird, *kotori* 小鳥

Living, *ikuru* 生死

Living Things, shōrui 生類

Lodge, *yado* 宿

Lodging, *yadori* やどり

Lodging for the dew, *tsuyu no yadori* 露のやどり

Lonely (adj), *sabishi* さびし

Long (adj), *nagashi* 永

Long day, *nagakihi* 永日

Long rains at Suma, *Suma no nagaame* 須磨のなが雨

Longbow/bow, *yumi* 弓

Long-tailed hawk, *tsugio no taka* 繼尾鷹

Look back (v), *kaerimiru* 顧見

Lotus, *hachisu* 蓮

Love, koi 戀

Love grass. *koigusa* 戀草

Lovingly, *koishiku* 戀しく（こひしく）

Lustration of the Snake, Jōshi no harae 上巳の祓

Maidenflower, *ominaeshi* 女郎花

Man, *otoko* 男

Man in the moon, *katsura no otoko* 桂男

Maple tree, *kaede* 楓

Mark, *shirushi* しるし

Marsh reeds, *ashi* 蘆

Master, *aruji* 主（あるじ）

Master of the blossoms, *bana no aruji* 花のあるじ

Mat of grass, *kusa no mushiro* 草莚

Mat of moss, *koke no mushiro* 苔莚

Mat of rice-stalks, *ina mushiro* 稲莚

Mat of the Law, *nori no mushiro* 法莚

Meadow, *ono* 小野

Midair, *nakazora* 中空

Mifune Mountain, Mifuneyama (pn) 御舟山

Miscanthus, *susuki/obana* 薄/尾花

Miscellaneous, zō 雑

Mishima (pn) 三島

Mist, *kiri* 霧

Molting hawks, *ke kōru taka* もかふる鷹

Molting willows, *yanagi chiru* 柳ちる

Monkey, *saru* 猿

Month, *tsuki* 月

Moon, *tsuki* 月

Moon and sun, *tsukihi* 月日

Moon-frost, *tsuki no shimo* 月の霜

Moon-ice, *tsuki no kōri* 月の氷

"Moonlike" heart, *kokoro no tsuki* 心の月

Moon-snow, *tsuki no yuki* 月の雪

Moonlight from the *sake* cup, *sakazuki no hikari* さか月の光

Moonlit evening, *yūzukuyo* 夕月夜

Mooring at Mt. Hatsuse, *ama-obune hatsuseyama* 海士小舟泊瀬山

Morn and eve, *asayū* 朝夕

Morning, *asa/ashita* 朝/あした

Morning after, *kinuginu* 衣々（きぬぎぬ）

Morning frost, *asashimo* 朝霜

Morning glory, *asagao* 槿朝

Morning moon, *ashita no tsuki* 朝月

Morning sun, *asazukuhi* 朝月日

Morning wind, *asakaze* 朝風

Mosquito incense, *kayaribi* 蚊遣火

Moss fern, *shinobugusa* 忍草

Moss robes, *koke no koromo*　苔衣

Mother, *haha*　母

Mountain, *yama/yamabe*　山／山邊

Mountain bird, *yamadori*　山鳥

Mountain cherry, *yamazakura*　山櫻

Mountain crest, *onoe*　尾上

Mountain of snow, *yuki no yama*　雪山

Mountain of Love, *koi no yama*　戀山

Mountain pass, *soba*　そば

Mountain path, *yamaji*　山路

Mountain Princess, Yamahime　山姫

Mountains, sanrui　山類

Mountain rustic, *yamagatsu*　山がつ

Mount Asama (pn)　淺間

Mount Fuji (pn)　富士

Mount Katsuragi (pn)　葛城

Mud hen, *kuina*　水鶏

Mugwort, *yomogi/yomogiu*　蓮生

Muro no Yashima (pn)　室八嶋

Musing, *omoi*　思火

Name, *na*　名

"Named" god, *na no kami*　名神

"Named" insect, *na no mushi*　名蟲

Naniwa in Tsu, Tsu no Kuni no Naniwa (pn)　津の國のなには

Naniwa Temple, Naniwadera (pn)　難波寺

Near (adj), *chikashi*　近

Net of haze, *kasumi no ami*　霞の網

New green-growth, *midori tatsu*　緑立

New leaves, *wakaba*　若葉

New moon, *mikazuki*　三日月

New pine-growth, *matsu no midori*　松の緑

New sprouts, *shitamoe*　下もえ

Next world, *nochi no yo* 後の世・後世
Next-door, *tonari* 隣
Night, *yo/yoru/sayo* 夜／さ夜
Night growing late, *yo no fukuru* 夜の更る
Night bird, *yoru no tori* 夜鳥
Nightfall, *yūgure* 夕暮
Nine-Fold Enclosure, Kokonoe (pn) 九重
Nocturnal Things, yabun 夜分
Noon, *hiru* ひる
Noon and night, *yoru-hiru* よる、ひる
Northern Festival, Kita matsuri 北祭
Number one, *ichi moji* 一文字

Oak, *kashiwa* 柏
Ocean/sea, *umi* 海
Offing, *oki* 沖
Oka (in Akashi), (Akashi no) Oka (pn) 明石の岡
Old/old age, *oi* 老
Old capital, *furusato* 故郷
Old man, *okina* 翁
Open up, *ake* 明
"Opening" of the day, *yo no akuru* 夜の明
Opening the door, *to o akuru* 戸をあくる
Opening the birdcages, *toyade* 鳥屋出
Orange blossom, *tachibana* 橘
Otonashigawa (pn) 音無川
Otowayama (pn) 音羽山
Our sovereign's reign, *kimi ga yo* 君が代
Outing in the fields, *no asobi* 野遊

Paddy, *ta* 田
Paddy hut, *ta no io* 田庵
Paddy of cherry trees, *sakurada* 櫻田
Paddy-plowing, *oda kaesu* 小田返

Pains, *nageki* 歎

Palace Bridge, Mihashi 御階

Palace in the Bamboo, Take no Miya (pn) 竹宮

Parent, *oya* 親

Parent and child, *oya-ko* 親子

Parting, *wakare* 別

Parting Love, wakaruru koi 別戀

Passing shower, *murasame* 村雨／急雨

Passion flower, *omoigusa* 思草

Past, *mukashi* 昔

Path, *michi* 道

Pathmarker, *shiori* しをり

Paulownia, *kiri* 桐

Peak, *mine* 嶺

Peony, *botan* 牡丹

Person, *hito* 人

Pheasant, *kigisu/kiji* 雉子

Piercing the soul, *mi ni shimu* 身にしむ

Pillar of black pine, *makibashira* 槇木柱

Pillow, *makura* 枕

Pillow of bamboo grass, *sasa no makura* 篠枕

Pillow of grass, *kusamakura* 草枕

Pine, *matsu* 松

Pine-Bay Mountain, Matsurayama (pn) 松浦山

Pine cricket, *matsumushi* 松蟲

Pine gate, *matsu no to* 松門

Pine Island, Matsushima (pn) 松島

Pine Mountain in Sue, Sue no Matsuyama (pn) 末松山

Pine wind, *matsukaze* 松風

Pining Love, matsu koi 松戀

Pivot door, *toboso* 樞

Plantain, *bashō* 芭蕉

Plants, uemono 植物

Pleading threads, *negai no ito* 願絲

Plover, *chidori* 千鳥

Plucking young greens, *na tsumu* 菜摘

Plum blossom, *mume* 梅

Plum rains, *mume no ame* 梅雨

Pole-fishing, *tsuritaru* 釣垂

Pond, *ike* 池

Pony, *koma* 駒

Present a stag (v), *ka o sashite* かをさして

Princess of the Bridge, Hashihime 橋姫

Pronoun "I," *ware* 我

Proverb, *kotowaza* 諺

Pull (v), *hiku* ひく

Pure water, *shimizu* 清水

Purification robes, *omigoromo* 小忌衣

Purify (v), *harau* はらふ

Push (v), *osu* おす

Put asunder (v), *waku* 分

Putting on a thatched roof, *hoya tsukuru* 穂屋をつくる

Quail, *uzura* 鶉

Quail robes, *uzura goromo* 鶉衣

Quail's bed, *uzura no toko* 鶉の床

Rain, *ame* 雨

Rain cloak, *mino* 蓑

Rain hat, *kasa* 笠

Raindrops, *amasosogi* あまそゝぎ

Rain of tears, *namida no ame* 涙の雨

Rains of the fifth month, *samidare* 五月雨

Rainy night, *amayo* 雨夜

Reality, *utsutsu* うつつ

Recesses of Ono, Ono no oku (pn) 小野奥

Recesses of Yoshino, Yoshino no oku (pn) 芳野奥

Recline (v), *nuru* ぬる

Recoil (v), *kaeru* 歸

Red leaves, *momiji* 紅葉

Red leaves of grass, *kusa no momiji* 草の紅葉

Red plum, *kōbai* 紅梅

Reed fire, *ashibi* 蘆火

Reed hut, *ashiya* 蘆屋

Reed mallard, *ashigamo* あし鴨

Reeds, *ogi* 荻

Reign, *yo* 代

Reign of the Gods, *kamiyo* 神代

Release of Living Things, Ikeru o Hanatsu 救生

Relying on the empty sky, *soradanome* 空だのめ

Remain behind (v), *nokoru* 殘

Remains, *ato* 跡

Reminiscence, kaikyū 懷舊

Resent (v), *uramu* うらむ

Resentment, *urami* うらみ

Residence, *sumai* 住居

Return (v), *kaeru* 歸

Returning to sleep, *matane* 又寝

Rice plant, *inaba/oshine* 又寝 / をしね

Rice seedlings, *sanae* 早苗

Rising Things, sobikimono 從物

River, *kawa* 川 / 河

River of tears, *namida gawa* 涙川

River of Heaven, Ama no Kawa (pn) 天河

River rainfall, *kawaoto no ame* 河音の雨

Robe, *koromo, kinu* 衣

Robe of haze, *kasumi no keramo* 霧の衣

Robe of leaves, *konoha-goromo* 木葉衣

Robe of mist, *kasumi no koromo* 霞衣

Robes, ishō 衣裳

239

Robes of Sao Princess, *Saohime no koromo* 佐保姫の衣

Robes of the Weaver Maiden, *Tanabata-goromo* 織女衣

Rock, *ishi* 石

Roof tiles, *iraka* 甍

Rope, *nawa* 繩

Rope bridge, *kakehashi* 梯

Rough-hewn year, *aratama no toshi* 荒玉年

Ruins, *ato* 跡

"Running Hail," *Ararebashiri* (song title) あらればしり

Rusty trout, *sabi ayu* さびあゆ

Sacrifice, *nie* 贄

Sad (adj), *kanashi* かなし

Salt, *shio* 鹽

Salt-burning, *shio yaku* 鹽焼

Salt hut, *shioya* 鹽屋

Sand, *masago* 真砂

Sandbar, *su* 州

Sao Princess, Saohime 棹姫

Sash, *obi* 帯

Scarce (adj), *sukunashi* すくなし

Scarecrow, *sōzu* そうづ

Sea/ocean, *umi* 海

Sea grass, *me* 和布

Sea pine, *miru* 海松

Search out (v), *tadoru* たどる

Seas, *umi* 海

Seaway, *unaji* 海路

Seaweed, *moshiogusa* 藻鹽草

Sedge, *suge* 菅

Sedge hat, *sugegasa* 菅笠

See (v), *miru* 見

Seedling bed, *nawashiro* 苗代

Seed-scattering, *tane maku* 種まく

Self, *mi* 身

Setting of the dawn moon, *ariake no iru* 有明の入

Shade/shadows, *kage* 陰/影

Shallow (adj), *asashi* 淺し

Shiga (pn) 志賀

Shining Things, hikarimono 光物

Shinobu no Oka (pn) 忍のをか

Shinobu no Ura (pn) 忍の浦

Shinobu no Yama (pn) 忍の山

Shinto, jingi 神祇

Shinto music, *kagura* 神樂

Shinto shrine, *miyai* 宮居

Ship, *fune* 舟

Ship of the River of Heaven, Amanokawa Fune 天河舟

Ship of Amanoiwa, Amanoiwa Fune 天磐舟

Shoes, *kutsu* 沓

Shop, *ya* 屋

Shore, *nagisa* 渚

Shore reeds, *hama ogi* 濱荻

Shorebank, *kishi* 岸

Shoreline eaves, *hama-bisashi* 濱庇

Short (adj), *mijikashi* 短

Shoulder sash, *hire* ひれ

Shower of autumn leaves, *konoha no ame* 木葉の雨

Shower of pine-wind, *matsukaze no ame* 松風の雨

Shower of tears, *namida no shigure* 涙の時雨

Showers, *shigure* 時雨

Shrine, *miya miyai* 宮/宮居

Shrine in the Fields, Nonomiya (pn) 野の宮

Skiff, *obune* 小舟

Skirt of the mountain, *susono* すそ野

Sky, *sora* 宮

Sleep, *ne* 寝

Sleep (v), *nemuru* 眠(寝)

Sleeping alone, *hitorine* 独寝

Sleeping waterfowl, *ukinedori* 浮寝鳥

Sleeve-drenching waters, *sode yuku mizu* 袖行水

Sleeves, *sode* 袖

Slope, *saka* 坂

Slow day, *osoki hi* 遅日

Smoke, *keburi* 煙

Smoke rising from one's thoughts, *omoi no keburi* 思煙

Smoke rising from the breast, *mune no keburi* 胸の煙

Snow, *yuki* 雪

Snow on the waves, *nami no yuki* 波の雪

Snowfall of blossoms, *hana no yuki* 花の雪

Snowy temples, *kashira no yuki* 頭雪

"Something for the horse," *uma no hanamuke* 馬のはなむけ

"The Sought-After Child," *Motomeko* (song title) 求子

Soul, *tamashii* 魂

Sound, *oto* 音

Source of the pure waters, *shimizu ga moto* 清水がもと

Southern Festival, Minami matsuri 南祭

Spring, haru 春

Spring, *izumi* 泉

Spring bird, *haru no tori* 春鳥

Spring chill, *haru samushi* 春寒

Spring coming in the midst of the old year, *toshi no uchi ni haru tatsu* 年内立春

Spring haze, *kasumi* 霞

Spring moon, *haru no tsuki* 春月

Spring rain, *harusame* 春雨

Spring snow, *haru no yuki* 春雪

Spring wind, *harukaze* 春風

Stable, *umaya* 驛

Stag, *saoshika* さをしか

Stand, *hara* 原

Stand of bamboo grass, *sasahara* 篠原

Stand of mugwort, *yomogi ga soma* 蓬杣

Stand of pines, *matsubara* 松原

Star, *hoshi* 星

Starry night, *hoshi tsukiyo* 星月夜

Storm, *arashi* 嵐

Straw mat, *mushiro* 莚

String (v), *haru* 張

Suma (pn) 須磨

Suma Lustration, Suma no miharae/misogi 須磨の御祓

Sumac, *haji* 櫨

Summer, natsu 夏

Summer moon, *natsu no tsuki* 夏月

Sumo Wrestling Matches, Sumō 相撲

Sun, *hi* 日

Sunset, *iriai* 入相

Sun-shaded cords, *hikage no ito* 日蔭絲

Suzuka Road, Susukaji (pn) 鈴鹿路

Swamp, *numa* 沼

Sweetflag, *ayame* 菖蒲

Sweetflag under the eaves, *noki no ayame* 軒菖蒲

Take on a chill (v), *sayuru/saekaeru* 冴

Takeda (pn) 竹田

Takekawa (pn) 竹川

Taking leave, *nagori* 名残

Taking the blossoms as a master, *hana o aruji* 花をあるじ

Taking the moon as a master, *tsuki o aruji* 月をあるじ

Taking the *sakaki* branch, *sakaki o toru* 榊取

Taminoshima (pn) 田蓑島

Tanabata Festival, Tanabata 七夕

Tanakami Grove, Tanakami no Mori (pn) 田上杜

GLOSSARY B

T'ang Kingdom, Karakuni (pn) 唐國

Tarrying wild goose, *nokoru kari* 殘雁

Tatsuta Princess, Tatsutahime 立田姫

Teacher of the Law, *nori no shi* 法師

Tears, *namida* 涙

Tears of dew, *namida no tsuyu* 涙の露

That dawning, *sono akatsuki* 其曉

Thatch, *kaya* 萱

Thatched roof, *hoya* 穗屋

Thatched hut, *tomaya* 蓬屋

Thicket, *yabu* 藪

Thing, *mono* 物

Think (v), *omou* 思

Think about (v), *omoiyaru* 思やる

This morning, *kesa* けさ

This world of dust, *chiri no yo* 塵世

This world of ours, *yo no naka* 世の中（世中）

Those who dwell in the clouds, *kumo no uebito* 雲上人

Thunder, *kaminari* 雷

Tide, *shio* 潮（汐）

Tideland, *higata* 干潟

Tiger, *tora* 虎

Timber, *soma* 杣

Time, *toki* 時

Time of . . ., *koro* 比

Tip, *moto-sue* 本末

Toba in Yamashiro, Yamashiro no Toba (pn) 山しろのとは（ぬ）

Today, *kyō* 今日

Tomorrow, *asu* 明日

Town, *sato* 里

Town *kagura, sato kagura* 里神樂

Tracks of the brush, *fude no ato* 筆跡

Tranquil (adj), *nodoka* 長閑

Transience, *mujō* 無常

Travel, *tabi* 旅

Travel robe, *tabi koromo* 旅衣

Traveler's sleep, *tabine* 旅寝

Tree, *ki* 木

Tree-cutting, *ki o kiru* 木をきる

Trees, *ki* 木

Treetops, *kozue* 梢

Trickling from the eaves, *noki no shizuku* 軒のしづく

Trickling from the mountains, *yama no shizuku* 山の滴

Trout, *ayu* 鮎

Truth, *makoto* 真

Twilight, *tasogare* たそがれ

Two people, *futari* ふたり

Typhoon, *nowaki* 野分

Ueno (in Suma), (Suma no) Ueno (pn) 須磨の上野

Uji no Kawashima (pn) 宇治川島

Ukishimagahara (pn) 浮島原

Ukita Grove, Ukita no Mori (pn) 浮田杜

Under, *shita* 下

Under-cord, *shita-himo* 下紐

Valley, *tani* 谷

Valley door, *tani no to* 谷戸

Vicinity, *hotori* ほとり

Village, *mura* 里

Vine, *mugura* 葎

Visit (v), *tazunu* 尋

Voice, *koe* 聲

Voice of the reeds, *ogi no koe* 荻の聲

Vulture Peak, Washi no Mine (pn) 鷲の聲

Waking (from sleep), *nezame* 寝覺

Wall, *kabe* 壁

Warm day, *atatataki hi* 温日

Warming of the waters, *mizu no nurumu* 水のぬるむ

Washing water, *te arau mizu* 手洗水

Water, *mizu* 水

Water bucket, *shitahi* 下樋

Water oat, *makomo* 真薦

Water pipe, *kakehi* 縣樋

Water wheel, *mizuguruma* 水車

Water's edge, *migiwa* 汀

Waterfowl, *mizutori* 水鳥

Waters, suihen 水邊

Wave, *nami* 波

Waves of blossoms, *hana no nami* 花の波

Way of the word, *koto no ha no michi* こ×の葉の道

Way of poetry, *uta no michi* 歌の道

Way of Shikishima, *Shikishima no michi* 敷島の道

Weed-choked house, *mugura no yado* 葎の宿

Wet sleeves, *sode nururu* 袖ぬる

What, *nani* なに

Wheel, *kuruma* 車

Wheel of the Law, *nori no kuruma* 法の車

When, *itsu* いつ

Where, *izuku* いづく

Wherefore, *nado* など

Which, *izure* いづれ

White hair, *shiraga* 白髪

White hydrangea, *unohana* 卯花

White-tailed hawk, *shirao no taka* 白尾鷹

Who, *tare* 誰

Why, *nazo* なぞ

Wild boar, *i* 猪

Wild geese, *kari* 雁

Willow, *yanagi* 柳

Wind, *kaze* 風

Wind, to, (verb) *kuru* くる

Wind of spring, *haru no kaze* 春の風

Window, *mado* 窓

Winter, fuyu 冬

Winter moon, *fuyu no tsuki* 冬月

Winter tree, *fuyuki* 冬木

Winter showers, *fuyu no shigure* 冬時雨

Winter-withered fields and hills, *fuyugare no noyama* 冬枯の野山

Wisteria, *fuji* 藤

Withered tips, *uragare* 裏枯

Withering wind, *kogarashi* 木枯

Woman, *onna* 女

Wood, *ki* 木

Wood thrush, *hototogisu* 郭公 / 時烏

Woodcutter, *kikori* 樵夫

Woodsman, *somabito* 杣人

Word, *kotoba* 詞

World, *yo* 世

World of dreams, *yume no yo* 夢世

Year, *toshi* 年

Years of age, *yowai* 齢

Yesterday, *kinō* 昨日

Yokawa (pn) 横川

Young (adj), *wakashi* 若

Young green-growth, *wakamidori* 若緑

Young greens, *wakana* 若菜

Young sea grass, *wakame* 若和布

Young trout, *waka ayu* 若鮎

247

BIBLIOGRAPHY

Place of publication is Tokyo unless otherwise indicated.

Araki Yoshio 荒木良雄. *Sōgi* 宗祇 (A biography of Sōgi). Sōgensha, 1941.

Ariyoshi Tamotsu 有吉保, Fujihara Haruo 藤平春男, and Hashimoto Fumio 橋本不美男, eds. *Karonshū* 歌論集 (An anthology of *waka* treatises). Nihon koten bungaku zenshū series, Vol. 50. Shōgakkan, 1975.

Asaji 淺茅. In Kidō Saizō 木藤才蔵, ed., *Rengaron shū 2* (A collection of *renga* treatises 2). Chūsei no bungaku series, Vol. 14. Miyai Shoten, 1982.

Azuma mondō 吾妻問答. In Imoto Nōichi and Kidō Saizō, eds., *Rengaron-shū, Haironshū* 連歌論集、俳論集. Nihon koten bungaku taikei series, Vol. 66. Iwanami Shoten, 1961.

Baikunshō 梅薫抄. In Ijichi Tetsuo, ed., *Rengaron shinshū 1* 連歌論新集. Koten Bunko, 1956.

Bailey, Don Clifford. "Early Japanese Lexicography," *Monumenta Nipponica* 15.1:1-52 (Spring, 1960).

Barthes, Roland. *S/Z*. Tr. Richard Miller. New York, Hill and Wang, 1974.

——. *Critical Essays*. Tr. Richard Howard. Evanston, Northwestern University Press, 1977.

——. "From Work to Text." In Josue V. Harari, ed., *Textual Strategies*. Ithaca, Cornell University Press, 1979.

Bontō-an sode no shita 梵燈庵袖下. In Shimazu Tadao, *Renga no kenkyū*. Kadokawa Shoten, 1973.

Borges, Jorge Luis. *A Personal Anthology*. New York, Grove Press, 1967.

Brower, Robert H. *Fujiwara Teika's Hundred-Poem Sequence of the Shōji Era, 1200*. *Monumenta Nipponica* Monograph series, No. 55. Sophia University, 1978.

—— and Earl Miner. *Japanese Court Poetry*. Stanford, Stanford University Press, 1960.

BIBLIOGRAPHY

Bun'yō 分葉. In Kidō Saizō, ed., *Rengaronshū* 2. Chūsei no bungaku series, Vol. 14. Miyai Shoten, 1982.

Carter, Steven D. "Waka in the Age of Renga," *Monumenta Nipponica* 36.4:425–444 (Winter 1980).

———. "Renga kyokusei jidai no ji, mon" 連歌極盛時代の地文 (*Ji* and *mon* in the golden age of linked verse), *Bungaku gogaku* 87:51–58 (May 1981).

———. *Three Poets at Yuyama.* Japan Research Monograph 4. Berkeley, Institute of East Asian Studies, 1983.

———. "Renga ni okeru honkadori" 連歌に於ける本歌取リ (Allusion in linked verse). In Kaneko Kinjirō, ed., *Renga kenkyū no tenkai* 連歌研究の展開 . Benseisha, 1985.

———. "Mixing Memories: Linked Verse and the Fragmentation of the Court Heritage," *Harvard Journal of Asiatic Studies* 48.1 (forthcoming June 1988).

Chikuba kyōginshū. See Kimura Miyogo, ed., "Chikuba kyōgin shū" below.

[*Kōhon*] *Chikurinshō* 校本竹林抄 (Poems by poets of the bamboo grove, a collated text). Ed. Hoshika Sōichi [also read Muneichi]. Iwanami Shoten, 1937.

Corti, Maria. *An Introduction to Literary Semiotics.* Tr. Margherita Bogat and Allen Mandelbaum. Bloomington, Indiana University Press, 1978.

Culler, Jonathan. *Structuralist Poetics.* Ithaca, Cornell University Press, 1975.

———. *On Deconstruction: Theory and Criticism after Structuralism.* Ithaca, Cornell University Press, 1982.

Dai kanwa jiten 大漢和辞典 (The great Chinese-Japanese dictionary). Comp. Morohashi Tetsuji 諸橋轍次 13 vols. Taishūkan Shoten, 1955–1960.

Eco, Umberto. *The Role of the Reader: Explorations in the Semiotics of Texts.* Bloomington, Indiana University Press, 1979.

Eikyū hyakushu 永久百首 . In [*Shinkō*] *Gunsho ruijū* [新稿]群書類従 (Classified series of collected texts, newly collated.), Vol. 8. Comp.

Hanawa Hokinoichi 塙 保己一 and ed. Kawamata Keiichi 川俣 馨一 . 2nd ed. Meichō Fūkyū-Kai, 1977–1978.

Eishō jūnen nigatsu Botanka Sōseki ryōgin 永正十年二月牡丹花宗碩両吟 (One hundred verses by the Master of Peony House and Sōseki, written during the 2nd lunar month, 10th year of the Eishō era, 1513). In Yamagishi Tokuhei et al., eds., *Renga 1* 連歌 . Katsura no Miya-bon sōsho series, Vol. 18. Tenri City, Yōtokusha, 1968.

Entoku yonen Sōgi dokugin nanimichi hyakuin. See Kaneko Kinjirō. "Entoku yonen Sōgi dokugin nanimichi hyakuin chū, honkoku" below.

Etō Yasusada 江藤 保貞 . *Sōgi no kenkyū* 宗祇の研究 (A study of Sōgi). 2 parts. Kazama Shobō, 1967.

———. "Sōgi renga sakuhinshū shūi" 宗祇連歌作品集 拾遺 (Selected works from Sōgi's linked verse), *Tsurumi Joshi Daigaku kiyō* 9:239–312 (1971).

Fish, Stanley. "Interpreting the *Variorum.*" In his *Is There a Text In This Class?* Cambridge, Harvard University Press, 1980.

Fujiwara Masayoshi 藤原 正義 . *Sōgi josetsu* 宗祇序説 (Sōgi, An Introduction). Kazama Shobō, 1984.

Fukui Kyūzō 福井 久蔵 . *Renga no shiteki kenkyū* 連歌の私的研究 (Studies in the history of linked verse). Yūseidō, 1978.

[Shinkō] Gunsho ruijū 〔新校〕群書類從 (Classified series of collected texts, newly collated). Comp. Hanawa Hokinoichi 塙 保己一 and ed. Kawamata Keiichi 川俣 馨一 . 2nd ed. 24 vols. Meichō Fukyū-Kai, 1977–1978.

Hekirenshō. In Ijichi Tetsuo, Kuriyama Riichi, and Omote Akira, eds., *Rengaronshū, nōgakuronshū, haironshū.* Nihon koten bungaku zenshū series, Vol. 51. Shōgakkan, 1973. 僻連抄

Hisamatsu Sen'ichi 久松 潜一 and Nishio Minoru 西尾 実 , eds. *Karonshū, nōgakuronshū (Waka* treatises, *nō* treatises). Nihon koten bungaku taikei series, Vol. 65. Iwanami Shoten, 1961. 歌論集　能樂論集

Hitorigoto ひとりごと . In Shimazu Tadao et al., eds., *Kodai chūsei geijutsuron* 古代中世芸術行論 . Nihon shisō taikei series, Vol. 23. Iwanami Shoten, 1973.

Horikawa-In hyakushu 堀川院百首 . *See Eikyū hyakushu* above.

Hoshika Sōichi [also read Muneichi] 星加宗一 and Yamada Yoshio 山田孝雄. *Renga hōshiki kōyō* 連歌法式綱要 . Iwanami Shoten, 1936.

Ii Haruki 伊井春樹, ed. [*Matsunaga-bon*] *Kachō yosei* [松永本] 花鳥餘情 (The Matsunaga text of *Kachō yosei*). Genji monogatari kochū shūsei series, Vol. 1. Ōfūsha, 1978.

Ijichi Tetsuo 伊地知鐵男 . *Sōgi* 宗祇 (A biography of Sōgi). Seigodō, 1943.

——. *Renga no sekai* 連歌の世界 (The world of linked verse). Nihon rekishi sōsho series, Vol. 15. Yoshikawa Kobunkan, 1967.

——, ed. *Rengaronshū* 連歌論集 (A collection of *renga* treatises). 2 vols. Iwanami Bunko, 1953–1956.

——, ed., *Rengaron shinshū* 1 連歌論新集 (A new collection of *renga* treatises). Koten Bunko, 1956.

——, ed. *Rengashū* 連歌集 (An anthology of linked verse). Nihon koten bungaku taikei series, Vol. 39. Iwanami Shoten, 1960.

—— and Kaneko Kinjirō, eds. *Sōgi kushū* 宗祇句集 (Sōgi's personal anthologies). Kichō kotenseki sōkan, No. 12. Kadokawa Shoten, 1977.

——, Kuriyama Riichi 粟山理一 , and Omote Akira 表章 , eds. *Rengaroshū, nōgakuronshū, haironshū* 連歌論集 能樂論集, 俳論集 (*Renga* treatises, *nō* treatises, *haikai* treatises). Nihon koten bungaku zenshū series, Vol. 51. Shōgakkan, 1973.

Ikeda Kikan 池田亀鑑 . *Heian jidai no bungaku to seikatsu* 平安時代の文学と生活 (Literature and life in the Heian period). Shibundō, 1978.

Imoto Nōichi 井本農一 and Kidō Saizō, eds. *Rengaronshū, haironshū* 連歌論集 俳論集 (*Renga* treatises. *haikai* treatises). Nihon koten bungaku taikei series, Vol. 66. Iwanami Shoten, 1961.

Itō Kunio 伊藤邦生. "Go-Sukō-In to Fushimi no Miya rengakai" 後崇光院と伏見宮連歌会 (Go-Sukō-In Sadafusa and the linked-verse meetings of the Fushimi Princes). In *Renga to chūsei bungei*, 連歌と中世文芸

ed. Kaneko Kinjirō Hakase Koki Kinen Ronshū Henshū Iinkai. Kadokawa Shoten, 1977.

Kaneko Kinjirō 金子金治郎. *Tsukubashū no kenkyū* 菟玖波集の研究 (A study of *Tsukubashū*). Kazama Shobō, 1965.

——. *Shinsen tsukubashū no kenkyū* 新撰菟玖波集の研究 (A study of *Shinsen tsukubashū*). Kazama Shobō, 1969.

——. "Entoku yonen Sōgi dokugin nanimichi hyakuin chū, honkoku" 延徳四年宗祇独吟何路百韻注番羽刻 (A reprint of Sōgi's solo sequence of the 4th year of the Entoku era, with Sōboku's commentary), *Kodai chūsei kokubungaku* 古代中世国文学 1:29–39 (February 1974).

——. *Renga kochūshaku no kenkyū* 連歌古注釋の研究 (A study of ancient linked-verse commentaries). Kadokawa Shoten, 1974.

——. *Sōgi tabi no ki shichū* 宗祇旅の記私注 (A personal commentary on Sōgi's travel accounts). Ōfūsha, 1976.

——. *Renga kenkyū no tenkai* 連歌研究の展開 (The develoment of linked-verse studies), Benseisha, 1985.

——. *Sōgi meisaku hyakuin chūshaku* 宗祇明作百韻注釋 (Annotated versions of Sōgi's major hundred-verse sequences), Vol. 4 of *Kaneko Kinjirō renga kōsō* 金子金治郎連歌考叢 (*Renga* studies of Kaneko Kinjirō). Ōfūsha, 1985.

——, ed. *Renga kochūshaku shū* 連歌古注釋集 (A collection of linked-verse anthologies with ancient commentaries). Kadokawa Shoten, 1979.

—— and Yamauchi Yōichirō 山内洋一郎, eds. *Kamakura makki renga gakusho* 鎌倉末期連歌学書 (A late Kamakura-period *renga* handbook). Chūsei bungei sōsho series, Vol. 4. Hiroshima, 1965.

——, Nakamura Shunjō 中村俊定, and Teruoka Yasutaka 曎峻康隆 eds. *Renga haikai shū* (An anthology of *renga* and *haikai*). Nihon koten bungaku zenshū series, Vol. 32. Shōgakkan, 1974. 連歌俳諧集

Kanshō ninen kugatsu nijūsannichi nanihito dokugin hyakuin 寛正二年九月二十三日何人独吟百韻 (A solo sequence composed on the 23rd day of the 9th lunar month of the 2nd year of the Kanshō era, 1461). In Etō Yasusada, *Sōgi no kenkyū*. pt. 2. Kazama Shobo, 1967.

Katahashi 片端. In Ijichi Tetsuo, ed., *Rengaronshū* 1. Iwanami Bunko, 1953.

Kawaguchi Hisao 川口久雄 and Shida Nobuyoshi 志田延義、, eds. *Wakan rōeishū, ryōjin hishō* 和漢朗詠集梁塵秘抄 (Collection of songs in Chinese and Japanese/ A sheaf of secret songs). Nihon koten bungaku taikei series, Vol. 73. Iwanami Shoten, 1965.

Keene, Donald. *Some Japanese Portraits.* Kondansha, 1978.

———, tr. *Essays in Idleness: The Tsurezuregusa of Kenkō.* New York, Columbia University Press, 1967.

Kidō Saizō 木藤才蔵、. *Rengashi ronkō* 連歌史論考 (Essays on the history of linked verse). 2 vols. Meiji Shoin, 1971–1973.

———, ed. *Rengaronshū* 2 連歌論集 (A collection of *renga* treatises 2). Chūsei no bungaku series, 2nd Ser., Vol. 14. Miyai Shoten, 1982.

——— and Shigematsu Hiromi 重松裕己, eds. *Rengaronshū* 1 (A collection of *renga* treatises 1). Chūsei no bungaku series, 1st Ser., Vol. 24. Miyai Shoten, 1972.

——— and Shigematsu Hiromi, eds. *Renga yoriaishū to kenkyū* 連歌寄合集と研究 (Several handbooks of conventional *renga* associations, with a study). 2 vols. Toyohashi, Mikan Kokubun Shiryō Kankōkai, 1978–1979.

Kimura Miyogo 木村三四吾, ed. "Chikuba kyōgin shū" 竹馬狂吟集 (Crazy verses on bamboo stilts), *Biburia* 43:1–111 (October 1969).

Kirihioke 桐火桶 (The panlownia brazier). In Nihon kagaku taikei series, Vol. 4. Ed. Sasaki Nobutsuna 佐々木信綱. Kazama Shobō, 1978.

Kochiku 孤竹 (Orphaned bamboo). In Kaneko Kinjirō, ed., *Renga kochūshaku shū.* Kadokawa Shoten, 1979.

Koestler, Arthur. *The Sleepwalkers.* London, 1977.

Kokin wakashū 古今和歌集 (Collection of ancient and modern times). Ed. Ozawa Masao 小沢正夫. Nihon koten bungaku zenshū series, Vol. 7. Shōgakkan, 1971.

[*Shinpen*] *Kokka taikan* [新編]國家大觀 (Great compendium of modern poetry). Ed. Taniyama Shigeru 谷山茂、 et al. 2 vols. Kadokawa Shoten, 1983.

Konishi Jin'ichi 小西甚一. *Sōgi* 宗祇 (Sōgi: a study), Nihon shijin sen series, Vol. 16. Chikuma Shobō, 1971.

——. "The Art of Renga," tr. Karen Brazell and Lewis Cook, *The Journal of Japanese Studies* 21.1:33–61 (Winter 1975).

Kyōchūshō 胸中抄 (Notes from deep within). In Vol. 17 of *Zoku Gunsho ruijū* 続群書類従 (Classified series of collected texts, continued). Comp. Hanawa Hokiichi 塙保己一 and Hanawa Tadatomi 塙忠宝. 3rd rev. ed. Zoku Gunsho Ruijū Kansei-Kai, 1974.

Kyūshū mondō 九州問答 (Kyūshū queries). In Ijichi Tetsuo, ed., *Rengaronshū* 1. Iwanami Bunko, 1953.

Liu, James J. Y. *Chinese Theories of Literature*. Chicago, University of Chicago Press, 1975.

Makura no sōshi 枕草子 (The pillow book of Sei Shōnagon). In Matsuo Satoshi and Nagai Kazuko, eds., *Makura no sōshi*. Nihon koten bungaku zenshū series, Vol. 11. Shōgakkan, 1974.

McCullough, Helen Craig, tr. *Tales of Ise*. Stanford, Stanford University Press, 1968.

—— and William H. McCullough, trs. *A Tale of Flowering Fortunes: Annals of Japanese Aristocratic Life in the Heian Period*. 2 vols. Stanford, Stanford University Press, 1980.

Matsuo Satoshi 松尾聰, and Nagai Kazuko 永井和子, eds. *Makura no sōshi*. Nihon koten bungaku zenshū series, Vol. 11. Shōgakkan, 1974.

Meiō hachinen Sōgi dokugin nanihito hyakuin 明応八年宗祇独吟何人百韻 (Solo sequence of 1499). In Kaneko Kinjirō, Nakamura Shunjō, and Teruoka Yasutaka, eds., *Renga haikai shū*. Nihon koten bungaku zenshū series, Vol. 32. Shōgakkan, 1974.

Minase sangin hyakuin 水無瀬三吟百韻 (Three poets at Minase). In Ijichi Tetsuo, ed., *Rengashū*. Nihon koten bungaku taikei series, Vol. 39. Iwanami Shoten, 1960.

Miner, Earl. *Japanese Linked Poetry*. Princeton, Princeton University Press, 1979.

Mino senku 美濃千句 (One thousand verses at Mino). In Etō Yasusada, *Sōgi no kenkyū*, pt. 2. Kazama Shobō, 1967.

Morris, Ivan, tr. *The Pillow Book of Sei Shōnagon*. 2 vols. New York, Columbia University Press, 1967.

Mugonshō 無言抄. In *Mugonshō, shōziashū* 無言抄匠材集 (Silent notes/ Master's handbook). Nihon koten zenshū series, 5th issue. Nihon Koten Zenshū Kankō-Kai, 1936.

Nabokov, Vladimir. *Lectures on Literature*. Ed. Fredson Bowers. New York, Harcourt Brace Jovanovich, 1980.

Nagabumi 永文 (Long letter). In Ijichi Tetsuo, ed., *Rengaronshū* 2. Iwanami Bunko, 1955.

Nagashima Fukutarō 永島福太郎. *Ichijō Kanera* 一条兼良. Jinbutsu sōsho series, Vol. 31. Yoshikawa Kobunkan, 1959.

Nagayama Isamu 永山勇. "Renga ni okeru taiyū 連歌における体用 (Essence and attributes in linked verse)," *Gengo to bungei* 1:22-33 (1962).

Nihon kagaku taikei 日本歌学大系 (Great compendium of Japanese poetic writings). Ed. Sasaki Nobutsuna 佐々木信綱 and Kyūsojin Hitaku 久曽神昇. 4th ed. 10 vols., 5 supplementary vols. Kazama Shobō, 1977-1981.

Nihon kokugo daijiten 日本国語大辞典 (Great dictionary of the Japanese language). Comp. Kindaiichi Kyōsuke 金田一京助 et al. 20 vols. Shōgakkan, 1972-1976.

Nihon koten bungaku taikei 日本古典文学大系 (Great compendium of Japanese classical literature). Comp. Takagi Ichinosuke 高木市之助 et al. 102 vols. Iwanami Shoten, 1956-1968.

Nihon koten bungaku zenshū 日本古典文学全集 (Collection of Japanese classical literature). Ed. Akiyama Ken 秋山虔 et al. 51 vols. Shōgakkan, 1970-1976.

Nihon shisō taikei 日本思想大系 (Great compendium of Japanese thought). Comp. Hayashiya Tatsusaburō 林屋辰三郎 et al. Iwanami Shoten, 1970-1982.

Ōan shinshiki 応安新式. *See Renga shinshiki*.

Ogawa Tatsuzō 小川幸三. "Sōboku rengaronsho Kyōchūshō ni tsuite" 宗牧連歌論書「胸中抄」について (About Sōboku's *renga* treatise, "Notes from deep within"). In *Renga to sono shūhen*. Ed. Hiroshima Chūsei Bungei Kenkyū-Kai. Hiroshima, 1967.

Oi no susami 花のすさみ (An old man's diversions). In Kidō Saizō, ed., *Rengaronshū* 2. Chūsei no bungaku, Vol. 14. Miyai Shoten, 1982.

Okami Masao 岡見正雄, ed. *Yoshimoto rengaronshū* 良基連歌論集 (Yoshimoto's *renga* treatises). Koten Bunko, 1952.

Okuda Isao 奥田勲. *Rengashi: sono kōdō to bungaku* 連歌師：その行動と文学 (The *renga* master—his lifestyle and works). Nihonjin no kōdō to shisō, Vol. 41. Hyōronsha, 1976.

Paz, Octavio et al. *Renga: A Chain of Poems*. New York, George Braziller, 1971.

Ramirez-Christensen, Esperanza. "The Essential Parameters of Linked Poetry," *Harvard Journal of Asiatic Studies* 41:555–595 (December 1981).

Renga kyōkun 連歌教訓 (A *renga* primer). In Ijichi Tetsuo, ed., *Rengaronshū* 2. Iwanami Bunko, 1955.

Renga sahō 連歌作法 (How to compose linked verse). In Kidō Saizō and Shigematsu Hiromi, eds., *Renga yoriashū to kenkyū*, Vol. 1. Toyohashi, Mikan Kokubun Shiryō Kankō-Kai, 1978.

Renga shinshiki 連歌新式 (New rules of linked verse). In Okami Masao, *Yoshimoto rengaronshū*. Koten Bunko, 1952.

Renga shinshiki tsuika narabi ni Shinshiki kon-an tō 連歌新式追加並新式今案等 (The new rules of linked verse, with additions, new ideas on the new rules, and other comments). In Hoshika Sōichi and Yamada Yoshio, *Renga hōshiki kōyō*. Iwanami Shoten, 1936.

Renga shogakushō 連歌初学抄 (Notes for *renga* beginners). In Ijichi Tetsuo, ed., *Rengaronshū* 2. Iwanami Bunko, 1955.

Renga shoshinshō 連歌初心抄 (Notes for *renga* novices). In Ijichi Tetsuo, ed., *Rengaron shinshū* 1. Koten Bunko, 1956.

Renga to chūsei bungei 連歌と中世文芸 (Linked verse and the medieval literary arts). Ed. Kaneko Kinjirō Hakase Koki Kinen Ronshū Henshū Iinkai 金子金治郎博士古稀記念論集編集委員会. Kadokawa Shoten, 1977.

BIBLIOGRAPHY

Renga to sono shūhen 連歌とその周辺 (*Renga* and its environment). Ed. Hiroshima Chūsei Bungei Kenkyū-Kai. Hiroshima, 1967.

Renga yoriai 連歌寄合 (Notebook of conventional associations in linked verse). In Kidō Saizō and Shigematsu Hiromi, eds., *Renga yoriashū to kenkyū*, Vol. 1. Toyohashi, Mikan Kokubun Shiryō Kankō-Kai, 1978.

Renjugappekishū 連珠合璧集 (Strings of linked jewels). In Kidō Saizō and Shigematsu Hiromi, eds., *Rengaronshū* 1. Chūsei no bungaku series, 1st Ser., Vol. 24. Miyai Shoten, 1972.

Renri hishō 連理秘抄 (Treasured notes on the principles of linked verse). In Imoto Nōichi and Kidō Saizō, eds., *Rengaronshū haironshū*. Nihon koten bungaku taikei series, Vol. 66. Iwanami Shoten, 1961.

Renshōshū 連証集 (Collection of sample associations). In Kaneko Kinjirō and Yamauchi Yoichirō, eds., *Kamakura makki renga gakusho*. Chūsei bungei sōsho series, Vol. 4. Hiroshima, 1965.

San t'i shi [Japanese: *Santaishi*] 三体詩 (Poems in three styles). Ed. Murakami Tetsumi 村上哲見. 4 vols. Chūgoku koten sen series, No. 30. Asahi Shimbunsha, 1978.

Sanetaka-kō ki 実隆公記 (Lord Sanetaka's diary). Ed. Sanjōnishi Kin'osa 三条西公正 and Takahashi Ryōuzō 高橋隆三. 14 vols. 1931–1963.

Sasamegoto ささめごと (Whisperings). In Imoto Nōichi and Kidō Saizō, eds., *Rengaronshū haironshū*. Nihon koten bungaku taikei series, Vol. 66. Iwanami Shoten, 1961.

Seidensticker, Edward G., tr. *The Tale of Genji*. 2 vols. New York, Alfred A. Knopf, 1976.

Shih chi 史記 (Book of history). Ed. Chung-hua shu-chu. 10 vols. Peking, 1959.

Shihoshō 至宝抄 (The way to the treasures). In Ijichi Tetsuo, ed., *Rengaronshū* 2. Iwanami Bunko, 1955.

Shimazu Tadao 島津忠夫. *Rengashi no kenkyū* 連歌史の研究 (Studies in *renga* history). Kadokawa Shoten, 1969.

———. *Renga no kenkyū* 連歌の研究(Studies in linked verse). Kadokawa Shoten, 1973.

———, ed. *Rengashū* 連歌集 (An anthology of linked verse). Shinchō Nihon koten shūsei series, Vol. 33. Shinchōsha, 1979.

——— et al., eds. *Kodai chūsei geijutsuron* 古代中世芸術論 (Ancient and medieval literary treatises). Nihon shisō taikei series, Vol. 23. Iwanami Shoten, 1973.

Shinsen tsukubashū kinen hyakuin 新撰菟玖波集祈念百韻 (One hundred verses in supplication for the success of the New Tsukuba collection). In Shimazu Tadao, ed., *Rengashū*. Nihon koten shūsei series, Vol. 33. Shinchōsha, 1979.

Shinsen tsukubashū [Sanetaka-bon] 新撰菟玖波集 実隆本 (The Sanjōnishi Sanetaka text of New Tsukuba collection). Ed. Kaneko Kinjirō and Yokoyama Shigeru 横山重 . Kadokawa Shoten, 1970.

Shinshiki kon-an 新式今案 (New ideas on the new rules). In Okami Masao, ed., *Yoshimoto rengaronshū*. Koten Bunko, 1952.

Shirakawa kikō 白河記行 (Journey to Shirakawa). In Kaneko Kinjirō, *Sōgi tabi no ki shichū*. Ōfūsha, 1976.

Shitakusa 下草 (Undergrowth). In Ijichi Tetsuo and Kaneko Kinjirō, eds., *Sōgi kushū*. Kichō kotenseki sōkan, No. 12. Kadokawa Shoten, 1977.

Shogakushō 初学抄 (Notes for beginners). In Kidō Saizō, ed., *Rengaronshū 2*. Chūsei no bungaku series, 2nd Ser., Vol. 14. Miyai Shoten, 1982.

Shōtetsu monogatari 正徹物語(Tales of Shōtetsu). In Hisamatsu Sen'ichi and Nishio Minoru, eds., *Karonshū, nōgakuronshū*. Nihon koten bungaku taikei series, Vol. 65. Iwanami Shoten, 1961.

Shunmusōchū 春夢草注 (A commentary on Shōhaku's Spring Dreams). In Kaneko Kinjirō, ed., *Renga kochūshaku shū*. Kadokawa Shoten, 1979.

Sōchō kawa 宗長歌話 (Sōchō's talks on poetry). In Kidō Saizō and Shigematsu Hiromi, eds., *Renga yoriaishū to kenkyū*, Vol. 2. Toyohashi, Mikan Kokubun Shiryō Kankō-Kai, 1979.

Sōgi dokugin nanihito hyakuin 宗祇独吟何人百韻. *See Meiō hachinen Sōgi dokugin nanihito hyakuin.*

Sōgi shoshinshō 宗祇初心集 (Notes for the inexperienced). In Kidō Saizō, ed., *Rengaronshū* 2. Chūsei no bungaku series, 2nd Ser., Vol. 14. Miyai Shoten, 1982.

Sōgi sode no shita 宗祇袖下 (Notes from Sōgi's sleeve pocket). In Kidō Saizō, ed., *Rengaronshū* 2. Chūsei no bungaku series, 2nd Ser., Vol. 14. Miyai Shoten, 1982.

Sōi Sōgi Yuyama ryōgin 宗伊宗祇湯山両吟 (Soi and Sōgi at Yuyama). In Shimazu Tadao, ed., *Rengashū*. Shinchō Nihon koten shūsei series, Vol. 33. Shinchōsha, 1979.

Takahashi Shōji 高橋正治 et al., eds. *Taketori monogatari, Ise monogatari, Yamato monogatari, Heichū monogatari* 竹取物語、伊勢物語、大和物語、平中物語 (The tale of the bamboo cutter, tales of Ise, tales of Yamato, tales of Heichū). Nihon koten bungaku zenshū series, Vol. 8. Shōgakkan, 1972.

Tenbun jūyonen nigatsu nanihito hyakuin 天文十四年二月何人百韻 (One hundred verses from the 2nd lunar month of the 14th year of the Tenbun era, 1545). In Yamagishi Tokuhei et al., eds., *Renga* 1. Katsura no Miya-bon sōsho series, Vol. 18. Tenri City, Yōtokusha, 1968.

Tōfū renga hiji 当風連歌秘事 (Secrets of linked verse in the current age). In Ijichi Tetsuo, Kuriyama Riichi, and Omote Akira, eds., *Rengaronshū, nōgakuronshū, haironshū*. Nihon koten bungaku zenshū series, Vol. 51. Shōgakkan, 1973.

Toshiyori zuinō 俊頼髄脳 (Toshiyori's essential teachings). In Ariyoshi Tamotsu, Fujihira Haruo, and Hashimoto Fumio, eds., *Karonshū* (A collection of *waka* treatises). Nihon koten bungaku zenshū series, Vol. 50. Shōgakkan, 1975.

Tsukuba mondō 筑波問答 (Tsukuba queries). In Imoto Nōichi and Kidō Saizō, eds., *Rengaronshū, haironshū*. Nihon koten bungaku taikei series, Vol. 66. Iwanami Shoten, 1961.

Tsukubashū 菟玖波集 (Tsukuba collection). Ed. Fukui Kyūzō. 2 vols. Nihon koten zensho series. Asahi Shimbunsha, 1948–1951.

Tsurusaki Hirō 鶴崎裕雄. "Renga to Yukawa Masaharu," (Yukawa Masaharu 連歌と湯河政春.

and linked verse), *Wakayama-kenshi kenkyū* 5:1–9 (February 1977).

Ubuginu 産衣 (Baby's first clothes). In Hoshika Sōichi and Yamada Yoshio, *Renga hōshiki kōyō*. Iwanami Shoten, 1936.

Wakan rōeishū 和漢朗詠集 (Collection of songs in Chinese and Japanese). In Kawaguchi Hisao and Shida Nobuyoshi, eds., *Wakan rōeishū, ryōjin hishō*. Nihon bungaku taikei series, Vol. 73. Iwanami Shoten, 1965.

Wakuraba 若葉 (Old leaves). In Ijichi Tetsuo and Kaneko Kinjirō, eds., *Sōgi kushū*. Kichō kotenseki sōkan series, No. 12. Kadokawa Shoten, 1977.

Waley, Arthur, tr. *The Analects of Confucius*. New York, Vintage, 1938.

Watson, Burton, tr. *The Complete Works of Chuang Tzu*. New York, Columbia University Press, 1968.

Wilde, Oscar. *The Picture of Dorian Gray*. London, Oxford University Press, 1974.

Yakumo mishō 八雲御抄 (Revered notes on the art of the eightfold clouds). In Nihon kagaku taikei series, supplementary Vol. 3. Ed. Kyūsojin Hitaku. Kazama Shobō, 1978.

Yamada Yoshio 山田孝雄. *Renga gaisetsu* 連歌概説 (An introduction to linked verse). Iwanami Shoten, 1937.

Yamagishi Tokuhei 山岸德平 et al., eds. *Katsura no Miya-bon sōsho* 桂宮本叢書 (The Katsura no Miya series of texts). 2nd edition. 23 vols. Tenri City, Yōtokusha, 1968–69.

Yamato monogatari 大和物語 (Tales of Yamato). In Takahashi Shōji et al., eds., *Taketori monogatari, Ise monogatari, Yamato monogatari, Heichū monogatari*. Nihon koten bungaku zenshū series, Vol. 8. Iwanami Shoten, 1972.

Yashima Kobayashi-an naniki hyakuin 矢島小林庵何木百韻 (One hundred verses at Yashima Kobayashi Temple). In Yamagishi Tokuhei et al., eds., *Renga* 1. Katsura no Miya-bon sōsho series, Vol. 18. Tenri City, Yōtokusha, 1968.

Yodo no watari 淀渡 (Yodo crossing). In Kidō Saizō, ed., *Rengaronshū* 2. Chūsei no bungaku series, 2nd Ser., Vol. 14. Miyai Shoten, 1982.

Yuyama sangin hyakuin 湯山三吟百韻 (Three poets at Yuyama). In Kaneko Kinjirō, Nakamura Shunjō, and Teruoka Yasutaka, eds., *Renga*

Haikai shū. Nihon koten bungaku zenshū series, Vol. 32. Shōgakukan, 1974.

Zoku Gunsho ruijū (Classified series of collected texts, continued). Comp. Hanawa Hokiichi 塙保己一 and Hanawa Tadatomi 塙忠宝. 3rd rev. ed. 71 vols. Zoku Gunsho Ruijū Kansei-Kai, 1974–1975.

続群書類従

INDEX TO SHŌHAKU'S RULEBOOK OF 1501

INDEX TO FIRST LINES OF POEMS

GENERAL INDEX

ageku, 165

Akashi, 24

Akazome Emon (early 11th century): *uta* by, 145

aki. See Autumn (thematic category)

allusion: and neoclassicism, 6; as operation of classical reading, 6, 76, 85–89, 118, 123, 128, 133, 139, 150, 155–156, 172; and *yoriai,* 24–25; and linking, 27; in Shōhaku's rulebook of 1501, 42–43; as stylistic technique, 89. For examples in Komatsubara *dokugin,* see translation (115–165).

Analects: poetic allusions to, 105, 165–165; as source of Sōgi's conservatism, 111; as source of poetic allusion, 139, 164

ancient commentaries. *See kochū*

Animals (ugokimono; lexical category): and *Renjugappekishū,* 19; relevant vocabulary lists, 43, 64. For examples in Komatsubara *dokugin,* see translation (115–165) and chart on 166–170.

Araki Yoshio: and Sōgi's personality, 212 n. 3

Archbishop Henjō (816–890): *uta* by, 153

Arima hotsprings, 36

Ariwara no Narihira (825–880), 139

Asaji (Cogon grass, 1500?): on use of *honka,* 85; on allusion as stylistic technique, 89. *See also* Sōgi

Asayama Bontō (1349–1427), 191–192 n. 14, 194 n. 12–13, 203 n. 169, 207 n. 259

Ashikaga government, 1

Ashikaga Yoshimasa (1435–1490), 1

Ashikaga Yoshimitsu (1358–1408), 107–108

Ashikaga Yoshimochi (1386–1428), 108

Ashikaga Yoshinori (1394–1441), 108

associations. *See yoriai*

au koi. See Fulfilled Love (thematic sub-category)

author. *See sakushu.*

Autumn (aki; thematic category): in *waka* anthologies, 14–15; in *renga* anthologies, 14–15; and categorization, 16–17, 119, 122, 123, 127–128, 129, 143, 159, 161, 162, 176; and rules of intermission, 60, 67; relevant vocabulary lists, 63–65, 69, 70; and rules of seriation, 70; and

ji/mon, 99. For examples in Komatsubara *dokugin,* see translation (115–165) and chart on 167–170.

Azuma mondō (East Country queries, 1470): on *ji/mon,* 100; advice to *rengashi* from, 101; on use of *nadokoro,* 148. *See also* Sōgi

Baikunshō (Plum-scented notes, 1510): on *jo-ha-kyū,* 93–94. *See also* Kensai

Barthes, Roland: and reading, 7, 174–175; and "codes" of reading, 7; and "play of signifiers," 20, 176–179 passim; and "Text," 178–179. *See also S/Z*

Bashō (1644–1694), 179; and *haikai renga,* 89–90, 145; and theme of travel, 146.

Beasts (kedamono; lexical subcategory), 58, 59, 70. For examples in Komatsubara *dokugin,* see translation (115–165) and chart on 166–170. *See also Animals*

Birds (tori; lexical subcategory): and rules of intermission, 58, 59. For examples in Komatsubara *dokugin,* see translation (115–165) and chart on 166–170. *See also Animals*

Blossoms (hana; lexical/thematic subcate-gory): and rules of repetition and inter-mission, 30, 47–48, 196 n. 49, 211 n. 49; and categorization, 78; and *ji/mon,* 95–100, 98, 132, 147; as symbol of *Spring,* 159. For examples in Komatsubara *dokugin,* see translation (115–165) and chart on 166–170.

Bontō-an sode no shita (Notes from Bontō's sleeve pocket). *See* Asayama Bontō

Borges, Jorge Luis, 179

Brower, Robert H., 13, 190 n. 4. 195 n. 14, 206 n. 248, 213 n. 9

Buddha: teachings of, 144; death of in Tsuru no Hayashi, 202

Buddhism: use of term *rinne* in, 39; moon as symbol of, 127–128; and *mappō,* 144; and fishermen, 127–128, 157; and Shinto 163–164

Buddhism (shakkyō; thematic category): in *waka* anthologies, 14–15; in *renga* an-thologies, 14–15; and categorization, 21, 68, 79, 80, 123, 127–128, 144,

intermission: and development of rules, 5; defined, 31–32; and *Ōan shinshiki*, 34; and *Shinshiki kon-an*, 37; in Shōhaku's rulebook of 1501, 52–70; and categorization, 77–78. For examples in Komatsubara *dokugin*, see translation (115–165) and chart on 166–170.

irui. See Clothing (lexical category)

Ise monogatari (Tales of Ise): and allusion, 103, 139

Ise Shrine, 15

ishō. See Robes (lexical subcategory)

Itai senku (One-thousand verse sequence in the old style, 1456): *renga* from, 11

Iwashimizu Hachiman Shrine, 164

ji (*Ground*): defined, 95–100; in Komatsubara *dokugin*, 123, 124, 142, 145, 161. For other examples in Komatsubara *dokugin*, see translation (115–165) and chart on 166–170. *See also ji/mon* and *mumon*

ji/mon (*Ground* and *Design*): defined, 95–100, 211 n. 55; in Komatsubara *dokugin*, 123–124, 142, 161. For other examples in Komatsubara *dokugin*, see translation (115–165) and chart on 166–170.

jingi. See Shinto (thematic category)

jinrin. See Human Relations (lexical category)

jirenga (background links), 211 n. 56. *See also ji* and *ji/mon*

jo: defined, 92–95, 211 n. 45; in Komatsubara *dokugin*, 123–124. *See also jo-ha-kyū*

jo-ha-kyū: defined, 92–95, 100, 123, 211 n. 45; in Komatsubara *dokugin*, 122–124, 142–143, 161–162

Jōha. *See Satomura Jōha*

jōku (strong verses), 96, 211 n. 566. *See also mon* and *ji/mon*

Joren, Monk, 131

jouissance, 76

jukkai. See Lamentation (thematic category)

Juntoku, Emperor (1197–1242): and repetition, 29, 30. *See also Yakumo mishō*

Kachō yosei (In a setting of flowers and birds, 1472): and allusion to *Genji monogatari*, 150. *See also Ichijō Kanera*

kadai (conventional *waka* topics), 63

kaikyū. See Reminiscence (thematic subcategory)

kakekotoba (pivot word), 70

Kakinomoto Hitomaro (fl. ca. 680–700): *uta* by, 24

Kakitsu Disturbance of 1441, 111

kakushidai (hidden topics): compared to *fushimono*, 11, 117

Kamakura period, 107, 110; and development of *renga* as genre, 11–13; and thematic categories, 15; and development of *yoriai*, 24–25, 151; and development of rules, 30; and faith sects, 144

Kaneko Kinjirō: 106, 185, 189 n. 1; and *kochū*, 216 n. 15

Kanera. *See Ichijō Kanera*

Kanshō ninen kugatsu nijūsannichi nanihito dokugin hyakuin (Solo sequence composed on the 23rd day of the 9th lunar month of the 2nd year of the Kanshō era, 1461): *tsukeku* from, 103–104

Kaoru, 155–156. *See also Genji monogatari*

Katahashi (Fragments, 1476?): on use of allusion, 89; on *jo-ha-kyū*, 93, 211 n. 45. *See also Senjun*

Kawabata Yasunari, 179

kedamono. See Beasts (lexical subcategory)

Keene, Donald: and Sōgi's personality, 109

Keiboku: *renga* by, 17

Keibutsushō (Images of the seasons), 63

keiko, 75

Kenkō. *See Yoshida no Kenkō* and *Tsurezuregusa*

Kensai (1452–1510), 36, 100; *renga* by, 16, 17, 88, 97; and *jo-ha-kyū*, 93–94, 142; and plans for imperial anthology of *renga*, 211 n. 12; and authorship of verses in *Kyōchūshō*, 212 n. 59. *See also Baikunshō* and *Wakakusayama*

ki. See Trees (lexical subcategory)

Kidō Saizō, 183; and Shōhaku's rulebook, 36; and constitution of *Shinsen tsukubashū*, 111, 213

Kii Province, 1

ki moji (words ending in *ki*), 69, 207–208 n. 271

Ki no Tsurayuki (884–946), 139, 151; *uta* by, 118

Kirihioke (The paulownia brazier): on *ji/mon*, 211 n. 55.

Masaharu. *See* Yukawa Masaharu

masks and personas: defined, 100–103; in Komatsubara *dokugin,* 130, 140, 142, 146, 158; departures from, 172–173.

matsu koi. See Pining Love (thematic subcategory)

Meiō hachinen Sōgi dokugin nanihito hyakuin (Solo sequence of 1499): *tsukeku* from, 63

Minamoto no Shitagō (911–983), 55; and early lexicography, 20

Minamoto no Toshiyori (d. 1129): description of *renga* by, 9; *uta* by, 160

Minase sangin hyakuin (Three poets at Minase, 1488), 2; *renga* from, 90; as example of conventional perfection, 174

Miner, Earl, 13, 90, 95, 211 n. 50, 213; and practice of *renga,* 3, 13, 213 n. 9; and subdivision of thematic categories, 190 n. 11

Ming Dynasty, 107

Mino senku (One thousand verses at Mino, 1472), 100; *tsukeku* from, 81, 97

Miscellaneous (zō; thematic category): in *waka* anthologies, 14–15; in *renga* anthologies, 14–156; relevant vocabulary lists, 49, 63, 64, 65, 68; and categorization, 120, 123, 142, 143, 161; and subdivision of thematic categories, 190 n. 11

Miyoshi Chōkei (1522–1564), 112

mon (Design): defined, 95–100, 211 n. 55; in Komatsubara *dokugin,* 123, 124, 129, 132, 142, 145, 147–148. For other examples in Komatsubara *dokugin,* see translation (115–165) and chart on 166–170. *See also ji/mon, jōku, sakotsu,* and *shūitsu*

Mongol invasions, 13

mono no na (nouns, lit. "names of things"), 193

Moon (tsuki; lexical/thematic category): and rules of intermission and repetition, 30, 215 n. 6; and rules of intermission, 60; and categorization, 78; and *ji/mon,* 95–100, 127–128, 132, 157; as symbol of *Autumn,* 119, 159, 162, 215 n. 6; as symbol of poetic beauty, 128; and reflexive interpretation, 175. For examples in Komatsubara *dokugin,* see translation (115–165) and chart on 166–170.

Mototoshi. *See* Fujiwara no Mototoshi

Mototoshi shō, 201 n. 136

Mountains (sanrui; lexical category): and *Renjugappekishū,* 19; and categorization, 20, 120; and rules of intermission, 53, 62; relevant vocabulary lists, 62, 69, 70, 71; and rules of seriation, 70; and Essential and Attributive categories, 71. For examples in Komatsubara *dokugin,* see translation (115–165) and chart on 166–170.

Mugonshō (Silent notes, 1598), 38, 183, 192–211 passim; and categorization, 79, 131, 147, 152, 195–196 n. 32, 199 n. 94, 201 n. 135, 205 n. 199; and repetition, 195 n. 26; and intermission, 199 ns. 92 & 104. For references in reading of Komatsubara *dokugin,* see translation (115–165).

mujō. See Transience (thematic subcategory)

mumon, 145. *See also ji/mon*

Murakami, Emperor (r. 946–967), *renga* by, 9

Murasaki Shikibu, 155

Muromachi period, 74, 102, 112, 141, 149, 150, 179; and development of *renga* as genre, 3, 4, 9, 10, 11, 107–108, 110; and thematic categories, 14–15; and *yoriai,* 25; and aesthetic ideals of *renga,* 13, 28–29; and "kinetic" values, 28–29; and development of rules, 29–31, 34, 38, 75, 172; and *San t'i shi,* 86–87; and allusion, 86, 139, 155; and *haikai,* 89–90, 91–92; and orthodoxy, 91; and *ji/mon,* 95–96, 145; and neoclassicism, 107–108; and didactic function of *renga,* 213 n. 9

mushi. See Insects (lexical subcategory)

mythology, Japanese, 150

Nabokov, Vladimir, 177

nadokoro. See Famous Places (lexical category)

Nagabumi (Long letter, 1490): on clashing, 82; on *jo,* 211 n. 45

Nagayasu: *renga* by, 17

Nakanokimi, 156. *See also Genji monogatari*

natsu. See Summer (thematic category)

neo-classicism: and development of *renga* as genre, 4, 13; and allusion, 6, 85–89, 139, 150, 155; and Sōgi, 108–111; and fifteenth-century poetics, 108–111, 155.

also Lamentation (thematic category)

remote recurrence. *See tōrinne*

Renaissance literature, 100

renga (linked verse): and court *waka* traditions, 3–5, 9–27 passim, 100–104, 108, 110, 130, 132–134, 146, 148, 150, 151, 158, 174; defined, 3–6, 145; and linking, 4–5, 13–14, 23–27, 29–30, 178; and *yoriai*, 4–5, 23–27; and "kinetic" values, 4, 28, 92–100; and neoclassicism, 4, 110–112; as a modernistic art form, 7, 29, 216 n. 13; early forms of, 9–13; and medieval ideals of change and disunity, 9–13, 13–14; and development of *hyakuin*, 10–14; and *fushimono*, 11–12; rules of, 27–72 passim; and Nō drama, 30; and Zen landscape gardens, 28, 30; and *haikai*, 89–92, 125, 145, 153; didactic function of poetry, 105, 111. *See also hyakuin*

renga hyakuin. See hyakuin

Renga kaiseki nijū-go kin (Twenty-five rules for conduct in the *za*, 1489), 209. *See also* Sōgi

renga kaishi (sheet): defined, 39; and Shōhaku's rulebook of 1501, 41–72 passim

Rengaki (A *renga* record): and text of Komatsubara *dokugin*, 185

Renga kyōkun (A *renga* primer, date uncertain): and *jo-ha-kyū*, 211 n. 48. *See also* Satomura Jōha

Renga sahō (How to compose linked verse, 1489), 129. *See also* Sōchō

rengashi (master of linked verse), 73, 75; Sōgi as, 1, 109–110, 112–113; illustration of, 74; as mask, 140, 172

Renga shinshiki: Hasedera text of, 32; and *Ōan shinshiki*, 192 n. 2; and development of rules, 192 n. 4. *See also* Nijō Yoshimoto

Renga shinshiki tsuika narabi ni Shinshiki kon-an tō (The new rules of linked verse, with Kanera's new ideas on the new rules, and additional comments by Shōhaku, 1501); and categories of composition, 14–15; composition of, 36–38; format of, 38–40; complete translation, 41–72; for references in Komatsubara *dokugin*, see translation (115–165) and chart on 166–170.

Renga shogakushō (Notes for *renga* begin-

ners, 1456): on problems of categorization, 138. *See also* Ichijō Kanera

Renga shogakushō (Notes for beginners in linked verse, 1569?): on definition of *nigeuta* (escape poem), 193–194 n. 5

Renga yoriai (A selection of *renga* associations), 25

Renjugappekishū (Strings of linked jewels, 1476?): and Ichijō Kanera, 5, 35, 191 n. 15; and other *renga* handbooks, 18, 190–191 n. 14; and thematic categories, 18–19, 22, 79, 129, 134; and lexical categories, 19–20, 77, 120, 149; and classical lexicography, 19–20, 191 n. 15; and *hon'i*, 22; and *yoriai*, 25–26, 135; and competence of classical readers, 77; and categorization, 79, 80–81, 120, 129, 134. For references in reading of Komatsubara *dokugin*, see translation (115–165).

Renri hishō (Treasured notes on the principles of linked verse, 1349), 183: on origins of *renga*, 9; on problems of categorization, 138; on use of *fushimono*, 190 n. 8; and development of rules, 192–194. *See also* Nijō Yoshimoto

Renshōshū (Collection of sample associations, date uncertain): and *yoriai*, 24–25; as foundation for allusion, 151

ren'yōkei ("the conjunctive"), 42, 193 n. 2

repetition: and development of rules, 5, 12; defined, 31; and *Ōan shinshiki*, 34; and Shōhaku's rulebook of 1501, 37; in Shōhaku's rulebook of 1501, 43–52 passim; and categorization, 77–79; and *tōrinne*, 156. For examples in Komatsubara *dokugin*, see translation (115–165) and chart on 166–170. *See also rinne*

rinne (recurrence): defined, 38–39; in Shōhaku's rulebook of 1501, 41–42. *See also* repetition

Rising Things (*sobikimono*; lexical category): and Renjagappekishū, 19; and categorization, 20, 78–81, 177; and rules of intermission, 58; relevant vocabulary lists, 58. For examples in Komatsubara *dokugin*, see translation (115–165) and chart on 166–170.

Robes (*ishō*; lexical subcategory)

Rulebook of 1501. *See Renga shinshiki tsuika narabi ni Shinshiki kon-an tō*

rules of *renga:* historical evolution of, 3–

rules of *renga (continued)*
6 passim, 10–31 passim, 33–40 passim;
and competence of classical readers, 5–
6, 27–31, 75–104 passim; Emperor
Juntoku, 29–30; and Nijō Yoshimoto,
33–40; and Ichijō Kanera, 35–40; and
Shōhaku, 36–40; and Shōhaku's rulebook of 1501, 41–72 passim; and operations of classical reading, 76–104
passim; in Komatsubara *dokugin,* 117–
118, 120–121, 122, 124, 128, 130–131,
134, 139, 142, 152, 159, 161, 163–164,
165, 166–170 (chart). *See also Renga
shinshiki tsuika narabi ni Shinshiki kon-
an tō* and *Shinshiki kon-an,* 172
Ryōa (mid-fourteenth century): *renga* by,
143–144

saibara (court folk songs): and allusion, 139
Saigyō (1118–1190): and topic of travel, 146;
uta by, 157
Saikaku. *See* Ihara Saikaku
sakotsu (well-built verses): as synonym for
mon: 211 n. 56. *See also mon* and *ji/
mon*
sakushu (author), 102. *See also* masks and
personas
Sanekuni: *uta* by, 131
Sanetaka. *See* Sanjōnishi Sanetaka
sanji gana (three-syllable words), 58, 201
n. 129
Sanjōnishi Sanetaka (1455–1537): and Sōgi,
91, 92, 112, 113; and *fushimono* collection, 117
sanrui. See Mountains (lexical category)
Santaishi. See San t'i shi
San t'i shi (Poems in three styles): poem
from, 86, 138–139; and *renga* poets, 87,
139
Sarashina, 150
Sasamegoto (Whisperings, 1463): *renga* by
Ryōa from, 144. *See also* Shinkei
sato dairi ("town palace"), 107
Satomura Jōha (1524–1602), 38; and *hon'i,*
23, 159; and *dōi no renga,* 82, 159
seas (lexical subcategory), 141, 149. *See also
Waters* (lexical category)
Sei Shōnagon, 162. *See also Makura no sōshi*
semantic categories, 20
semic code. *See* Barthes, Roland

Senjun (1411–1476), 110, 172; *renga* by, 81,
87, 132; and allusion as stylistic technique, 89; and *jo-ha-kyū,* 93–94, 211 n.
45; and composition of *dokugin,* 101;
and *yoriai,* 191
seri (the logic of the world), 111
seriation: and development of rules, 5, 12;
defined, 30–31; and *Ōan shinshiki,* 34;
and Shōhaku's rulebook of 1501, 37; in
Shōhaku's rulebook of 1501, 70; and
categorization, 77–79; and *tōrinne,* 156
Settsu province, 36
Shakespeare, 88
shakkyō. See Buddhism (thematic category)
sheet. *See renga kaishi*
Shichijū-ichiban shokunin uta-awase (Seventy-round poetry contest of the various
professions), 209 n. 1; illustration of
renga master in, 73–74
Shiga, 148–149
Shigeno no Naishi: *renga* by, 10
Shimazu Tadao: and subdivision of thematic categories, 190 n. 11; on *kochū,*
216
Shining Things (hikarimono; lexical category): and *Renjugappekishū,* 19; relevant vocabulary lists, 58; and rules of
intermission, 58. For examples in
Komatsubara *dokugin,* see translation
(115–165) and chart on 166–170.
Shinkei (1406–1475), 99, 110, 128, 155, 172;
and *ji/mon,* 96, 99; and composition of
dokugin, 101, 110; *renga* by, 127, 132;
and emphasis on darker thematic
topics, 174. *See also Hitorigoto, Sasamegoto,* and *Shiyōshō*
Shinkokin generation: and development of
renga aesthetic, 11–12; and early rulebooks, 33
Shin kokinshū (New collection of ancient
and modern times, 1206): and thematic
categories, 15; *uta* from, 87, 88, 135,
137, 157
Shining Prince. *See Genji,* Prince
Shinsen tsukubashū (New Tsukuba collection, 1495): and Yukawa Masaharu, 1;
and thematic categories, 14; *renga* from,
86, 87, 88; and Sōgi, 86, 112; special
character of, 110–111
Shinshiki kon-an (New ideas on the new
rules, 1452): and Ichijō Kanera, 35–

40, 192 n. 6; and development of rules, 35–36, 39–40, 81; and Shōhaku's rulebook, 36–40, 41–72 passim. *See also* Ichijō Kanera, *Renga shinshiki tsuika narabi ni Shinshiki kon-an tō*, and Shōhaku

Shinto (jingi; thematic category): in *waka* anthologies, 14–15; in *renga* anthologies, 14–15; relevant vocabulary lists, 53, 64, 65, 67–68; and rules of intermission, 59; and categorization, 163–164. For examples in Komatsubara *dokugin*, see translation (115–165) and chart on 166–170.

Shirakawa kikō (Journey to Shirakawa, 1468), 146, 215. *See also* Sōgi

Shitakusa (Undergrowth, 1493), 112; *renga* from, 123; and *kochū*, 209

Shiyō shō (Notes on my own use of the rules, 1471), 206 n. 240

Shōei (fl. ca. 1470), 82, 100; *renga* by, 81, 99; and authorship of verses in *Kyōchūshō*, 212 n. 59

Shogakushō (Notes for beginners): on categorization, 21; and *hokku* of Komatsubara *dokugin*, 118; and *Shogaku yōshashō*, 191 n. 19

Shogaku yōshashō (Directions for beginners). *See Shogakushō*

Shōhaku (1443–1527): and rulebook of 1501, 15, 36–40, 41–72 passim, 76, 77–81, 100, 120, 156, 161, 163, 183, 189, 193–209 passim; and allusion, 42–43, 193–194 ns. 5–9; and rules of repetition, 42–52 passim; and categorization, 43–70 passim, 76–77, 77–81, 120, 163, 209 n. 15; and rules of intermission, 52–70 passim; and rules of seriation, 70; and *taiyū*, 71–72, 194 n. 11, 201 n. 144, 208 n. 288; and *hon'i*, 77; *renga* by, 78, 90; and distancing, 81; and *fushimono* collection, 117; and *rinne/tōrinne*, 41–42, 156; and blossom verses, 211 n. 49; and authorship of verses in *Kyōchūshō*, 212 n. 59. *See also Renga shinshiki tsuika narabi ni Shinshiki kon-an tō*

Shōhaku's rulebook. *See Renga shinshiki tsuika narabi ni Shinshiki kon-an tō*

shōka: 42, 194 n. 8.

Shōkokuji, 110

Shoku gosenshū (Later collection con-

tinued, 1251): and allusion, 42, 85, 139; *uta* from, 126

shōrui. *See Living Things* (lexical subcategory)

Shōtetsu (1381–1459), 139; and *nadokoro*, 148; and study of *Genji monogatari*, 155

Shōtetsu monogatari (Tales of shōtetsu, 1450?): on *nadokoro*, 148

Shūchūshō, 55

shuhitsu (referee): duties of, 122

shūitsu (excellent verses): as synonym for *mon*, 211 n. 56. *See also mon* and *ji/mon*

Shun'e (fl. ca. 1160–1180): *uta* by, 87

Shunmusō chū (A commentary on Shōhaku's *Spring dream*): *tsukeku* from, 78

Side (*omote* or *ura*): defined, 39; in Shōhaku's rulebook, 46, 57

sobikimono. Rising Things (lexical category)

Soboku (d. 1545): and development of rules, 38–39; and *rinne*, 39; critical work by, 39; *renga* by, 77, 82–83; and distancing, 83, 129, 177, 129; and allusion, 86, 151; and *jo-ha-kyū*, 93–96, 211 n. 45; and *ji/mon*, 95–100, 123, 212 n. 59; and composition of *Design* verses, 95–100, 129, 147; and *Kyōchūshō*, 96–100, 212 n. 59; and composition of *Ground* verses, 100, 123, 145; and Komatsubara *dokugin*, 113, 115, 125, 129, 138, 175, 177, 185, 189; and duties of *shuhitsu*, 122; and *hon'i* of *Love* category, 138; and orthodoxy, 178–179; and authorship of verses in *Kyōchūshō*, 212 n. 59. *See also Kyōchūshō* and *Tōfū renga hiji*

Sōchō (1448–1532): *renga* by, 17, 27, 83, 90, 96; and Shōhaku's rulebook of 1501, 36; and distancing, 82–83; and *ji/mon*, 96; and categorization, 79, 129; and *jo-ha-kyū*, 211 n. 45; and authorship of verses in *Kyōchūshō*, 212 n. 59. *See also Nagabumi, Renga sahō*, and *Renga kawa*

Sōchō kawa (Sōchō's talks on poetry, 1495): on categorization, 79, 129

Sōgi (1421–1502): and court classics, 1; and Komatsubara *dogugin*, 1, 2, 3, 6, 26, 27, 38, 101, 103, 104, 105, 112–113, 123, 155–165 passim, 173; biographical information on, 1, 2, 31, 104–105,

Yukawa Masaharu: in *renga* circles, 1–2, 110, 113; as patron of *Sōgi*, 1–2, 113, 118, 140, 151, 189 n. 1; and Komatsubara *dokugin*, 1–2, 105, 140, 151; military defeat of, 106–107, 113. *See also* Yukawa clan

Yuyama sangin hyakuin (Three poets at Yuyama), 2, 173, 185; and *hon'i*, 191 n. 18; *renga* from, 27, 96, 172

za (linking session), 86, 101, 172; and need for rules, 30, 33; behavior in, 73; and *renga* as performance, 76, 100

Zeami (1363–1444), 139

Zen, 28: and Sōgi, 87, 109–110, 144, 163

Zen landscape paintings, 28

Zen landscape gardens, 30

zō. See Miscellaneous (thematic category)

Harvard East Asian Monographs

69. Eric Widmer, *The Russian Ecclesiastical Mission in Peking during the Eighteenth Century*

70. Charlton M. Lewis, *Prologue to the Chinese Revolution: The Transformation of Ideas and Institutions in Hunan Province, 1891–1907*

71. Preston Torbert, *The Ch'ing Imperial Household Department: A Study of its Organization and Principal Functions, 1662–1796*

72. Paul A. Cohen and John E. Schrecker, eds., *Reform in Nineteenth-Century China*

73. Jon Sigurdson, *Rural Industrialization in China*

74. Kang Chao, *The Development of Cotton Textile Production in China*

75. Valentin Rabe, *The Home Base of American China Missions, 1880–1920*

76. Sarasin Viraphol, *Tribute and Profit: Sino-Siamese Trade, 1652–1853*

77. Ch'i-ch'ing Hsiao, *The Military Establishment of the Yuan Dynasty*

78. Meishi Tsai, *Contemporary Chinese Novels and Short Stories, 1949–1974: An Annotated Bibliography*

79. Wellington K. K. Chan, *Merchants, Mandarins, and Modern Enterprise in Late Ch'ing China*

80. Endymion Wilkinson, *Landlord and Labor in Late Imperial China: Case Studies from Shandong by Jing Su and Luo Lun*

81. Barry Keenan, *The Dewey Experiment in China: Educational Reform and Political Power in the Early Republic*

82. George A. Hayden, *Crime and Punishment in Medieval Chinese Drama: Three Judge Pao Plays*

83. Sang-Chul Suh, *Growth and Structural Changes in the Korean Economy, 1910–1940*

84. J. W. Dower, *Empire and Aftermath: Yoshida Shigeru and the Japanese Experience, 1878–1954*

85. Martin Collcutt, *Five Mountains: The Rinzai Zen Monastic Institution in Medieval Japan*

STUDIES IN THE MODERNIZATION OF THE REPUBLIC OF KOREA: 1945–1975

86. Kwang Suk Kim and Michael Roemer, *Growth and Structural Transformation*

87. Anne O. Krueger, *The Developmental Role of the Foreign Sector and Aid*

88. Edwin S. Mills and Byung-Nak Song, *Urbanization and Urban Problems*

89. Sung Hwan Ban, Pal Yong Moon, and Dwight H. Perkins, *Rural Development*

110. Benjamin A. Elman, *From Philosophy to Philology: Intellectual and Social Aspects of Change in Late Imperial China*

111. Jane Kate Leonard, *Wei Yuan and China's Rediscovery of the Maritime World*

112. Luke S. K. Kwong, *A Mosaic of the Hundred Days: Personalities, Politics, and Ideas of 1898*

113. John E. Wills, Jr., *Embassies and Illusions: Dutch and Portuguese Envoys to K'ang-hsi, 1666–1687*

114. Joshua A. Fogel, *Politics and Sinology: The Case of Naitō Konan (1866–1934)*

115. Jeffrey C. Kinkley, ed., *After Mao: Chinese Literature and Society, 1978–1981*

116. C. Andrew Gerstle, *Circles of Fantasy: Convention in the Plays of Chikamatsu*

117. Andrew Gordon, *The Evolution of Labor Relations in Japan: Heavy Industry, 1853–1955*

118. Daniel K. Gardner, *Chu Hsi and the Ta Hsueh: Neo-Confucian Reflection on the Confucian Canon*

119. Christine Guth Kanda, *Shinzō: Hachiman Imagery and its Development*

120. Robert Borgen, *Sugawara no Michizane and the Early Heian Court*

121. Chang-tai Hung, *Going to the People: Chinese Intellectuals and Folk Literature, 1918–1937*

122. Michael A. Cusumano, *The Japanese Automobile Industry: Technology and Management at Nissan and Toyota*

124. Steven D. Carter, *The Road to Komatsubara: A Classical Reading of the Renga Hyakuin*

125. Katherine F. Bruner, John K. Fairbank, and Richard T. Smith, *Entering China's Service: Robert Hart's Journals, 1854–1863*

126. Bob Tadashi Wakabayashi, *Anti-Foreignism and Western Learning in Early Modern Japan: The New Theses of 1825*

127. Atsuko Hirai, *Individualism and Socialism: The Life and Thought of Kawai Eijirō (1891–1944)*

128. Ellen Widmer, *The Margins of Utopia: Shui-hu hou-chuan and the Literature of Ming Loyalism*

129. R. Kent Guy, *The Emperor's Four Treasuries: Scholars and the State in the Late Ch'ien-lung Era*

130. Peter C. Perdue, *Exhausting the Earth: State and Peasant in Hunan, 1500–1850*